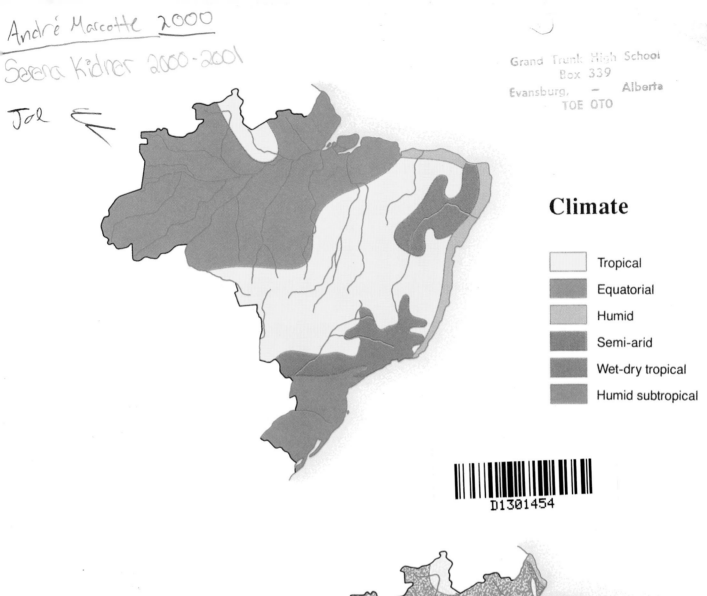

Climate

- Tropical
- Equatorial
- Humid
- Semi-arid
- Wet-dry tropical
- Humid subtropical

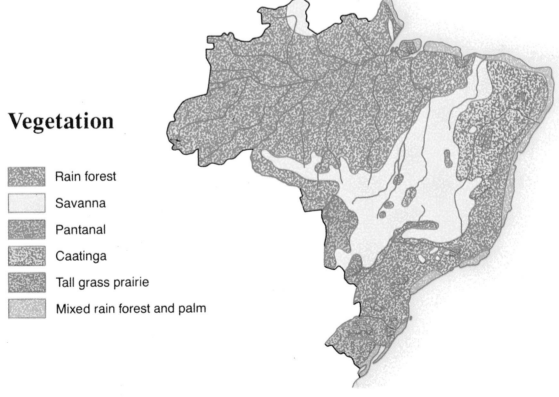

Vegetation

- Rain forest
- Savanna
- Pantanal
- Caatinga
- Tall grass prairie
- Mixed rain forest and palm

Brazil

Trudie BonBernard

Arnold Publishing Ltd

Arnold Publishing Ltd.
11016 - 127 Street NW
Edmonton, Alberta, Canada T5M 0T2
Phone (403) 454-7477 • Fax (403) 454-7463
1-800-563-2665

Author: Trudie BonBernard

Canadian Cataloguing in Publication Data
BonBernard, Trudie.
    Brazil

ISBN 0-919913-34-2

1. Brazil–Juvenile literature. I. Title.
F2508.5.B64 1989 981 C89-091516-4

Arnold Publishing gratefully acknowledges the support of the Alberta Foundation for the Literary Arts and Alberta Culture for the research, preparation and design of this book.

Brazil Project Team

Project Director	Phyllis Arnold
Project Manager	Margaret Negenman
Educational Editor	Phyllis Arnold
Copy Editors	Nancy Marcotte, Elaine Chalus, Barbara Demers
Glossary	Carrie Shemanko
Design	Phyllis Arnold, Trudie BonBernard
Photographers	Glen BonBernard, Herbert Knup, Siegfried Mühlhäusser
Illustrators	Larisa Sembaliuk-Cheladyn, Tom Wilcox
Computer Graphics	Bruce Campbell, Margaret Negenman
Cartography	Wendy Johnson, Bruce Campbell
Typesetting and Layout	Margaret Negenman, Bruce Campbell
Case Study Layout	Elaine Chalus
Proof Readers	Carole Howrish, Barbara Demers, Carrie Shemanko, Don Jones, Margaret Barry
Manufacturers	Gabriel Communications Inc., Scangraphics Ltd., Color Graphics Edmonton Ltd., Quality Color Press Inc. Printed in Canada; Bound in U.S.A.

Special Consultants

Latin American Consultants
Professor J. Garcia
Latin American Studies Program
Simon Fraser University
Burnaby, British Columbia

Herbert Knup
Latin American Institute
University of New Mexico
Albuquerque, New Mexico

Educational Consultant
Fern Schmidt
Curriculum Consultant
Edmonton Public School Board
Edmonton, Alberta

Student Consultants
Heather Arnold
Terri Howrish
Ryan Howrish
Sean Carr
Charlene Cameron

Additional Consultants

Ray Kennedy
Program Coordinator
Center of Brazilian Studies
Johns Hopkins University

Randy Hayes and Dev Weiss
Rainforest Action Network
San Francisco, California

Linda Rabben
Brazil Network
Washington, D.C.

Peggy Hallward
PROBE International
Toronto, Ontario

Anne Blain
Resource Center for NonViolence
Santa Cruz, California

John Walsh
Washington Office on Latin America
Washington, D.C.

Kevin Vang
National Wildlife Federation
Washington, D.C.

Tony Burley
Coordinator of Instruction for
Social Studies
Red Deer Public School Dist. #104
Red Deer, Alberta

Jim Latimer
Social Studies Consultant
Calgary Public School Board
Calgary, Alberta

Tom Landsman
Educational Consultant
Spirit River, Alberta

Acknowledgments

I would like to acknowledge the efforts of the great many people who helped produce this textbook. Thanks to Ray Kennedy (The Johns Hopkins University), Randy Hayes and Dev Weiss (Rainforest Action Network), Linda Rabben (Brazil Network), Peggy Hallward (PROBE International), Anne Blain (Resource Center for NonViolence), John Walsh (Washington Office on Latin America), and Kevin Vang (National Wildlife Federation). They were always there to offer helpful advice and answer queries.

My grateful appreciation to John Tolman and Herbert Knup of the University of New Mexico, for the use of their wonderful Brazil photographs. Many thanks to Professor J. Garcia of Simon Fraser University, for his thoughtful comments and additions to the text. His knowledge of Brazil provided me with invaluable details. Thanks are also extended to Canadian Ambassador John Bell in Brasília for his warm hospitality—and terrific coffee!

Special thanks must certainly go to the production team at Arnold Publishing. Their outstanding and creative efforts somehow transformed rough drafts into a finished text.

As always, my special thanks go to Phyllis Arnold for guiding this project to completion. Her keen awareness of how to enrich student learning substantially contributed to the form and content of this text. Her unwavering support and encouragement over the past two years has been greatly appreciated.

Finally, thanks must go to my very understanding husband, Glen, for his good humor and patience in accepting *Brazil* as a major part of our life for the past year.

Trudie BonBernard
September, 1989

Table of Contents

PART III: SETTLEMENT PATTERNS 1890—1990

To the Student

Focus of Text

This text focuses on the interaction between physical and human geography in Brazil. It asks you to examine the ways that physical geography has influenced settlement patterns. It also asks you to look at how human settlement has altered the physical environment of Brazil.

This book is written with your participation in mind. Early in the text you are presented with a decision making activity on this important issue: **To what extent do you think Brazil considers its physical environment as it develops its natural resources?** These activities will make you aware of the positive and negative consequences of development. At the end of the textbook you will be asked to decide whether or not you think the resources of Brazil should be developed.

Each chapter starts and ends with a problem solving activity that focuses on the interaction between physical and human geography. You are encouraged to carry out the different problem solving strategies as you go through the text. Decision making logos and problem solving logos appear throughout the book to alert you to these activities.

Vocabulary

As you read through the textbook, you will see words in **bold** print. Each of these words is explained for you at the bottom of the page where it appears. Words are in **bold** print for two reasons. Sometimes they give you the pronunciations for unfamiliar Portuguese words. Most of the time they give you definitions for new words or expressions. These words also appear in the glossary at the end of the text.

You will notice that some words appear in SMALL CAPS. This has been done to help you learn new Social Studies vocabulary. Whenever you see words in SMALL CAPS, you are being introduced to a new Social Studies term. To make things even easier, these terms are defined for you. The definition is in the same sentence or paragraph where the SMALL CAPS first appear. In case you forget a term, they are also listed in the glossary.

Social Studies terms and important ideas are easy to recognize. They can be found on special notebook pad pages so they can be seen easily. They will provide you with background Social Studies information that you will need to understand the pages that follow.

* Further Explanation

Asterisks (*) are used to identify areas that need further explanation or additional information. The explanation is given at the bottom of the page.

Interviews/Points-of-View Statements

This book contains many interviews with Brazilians and point-of-view statements by Brazilians. This is an important part of the textbook. Not all Brazilians think alike. Different groups have different points-of-view. In order to complete the main decision making activity, you must be familiar with these differences. You must be aware that the people being interviewed are fictional. However, their comments and viewpoints are real. They present views expressed by real Brazilians.

The native Brazilians lived as **nomadic** tribes.

Nomadic—moving from place to place

The exact location of a place is called ABSOLUTE LOCATION.

Population Terms

Population is the total number of people in a country, region, city, or specific area. The population of a country does not stay the same over periods of time. Populations can increase or decrease. Populations can change slowly or rapidly. There are several factors that influence whether a country's population will increase, decrease, or stay the same. But first it is important to define some terms used to describe populati

1. Birth Rate

Birth rate is the number of babies born for every thousand people in a country.

4. Life Expectancy

Life expectancy is the a most people in a country c expectancy rates are often and women. Life expectan one part of a country to an

By the beginning of 1990, Brazil's population was estimated to be 153 million.*

---

*The last census was taken in 1980.

Works at a radio station in Brasília

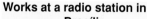

My husband and I live in **Taguantinga**, one of Brasília's SEVEN SATELLITE CITIES. Satellite cities are located far outside Brasília. They are cities for workers. We live in Taguantinga because we

Narratives

Narratives are fictional stories that give you a view of life in Brazil. They can be identified by the opening dropped cap letter, the term *(Factual Narrative)*, and a green background page. Narratives also reinforce the information presented in text sections.

Statistics Used in Text

This book uses many statistics. The statistics come from a variety of North American and Brazilian sources. The most current figures have been used. In some cases, estimates have been used. Statistics can vary between sources. The statistics used in this text may occasionally be different than those found in school library reference books.

Maps

The maps on the inside covers of the textbook are there to help you. Please refer to these pages whenever you need help locating a place in Brazil.

Photographs, Illustrations and Graphics

Visuals are included in the textbook to reinforce your learning. Although they are attractive, they are not decorations. The visuals have been carefully chosen to help you understand the text. By flipping through the book and glancing at the visuals, you can see the main topics of the textbook. When you are studying, use the visuals to give you more information on specific topics.

Case Studies

Case studies are presented at the end of Chapters 4, 5, and 7. They are optional study units that examine specific human settlement inquiries. Case studies can be easily recognized. You will find them on pages with light yellow file folders. In the case studies you will read factual narratives about what Brazilians think and feel about the issues affecting them.

Study Aids

Each chapter has introductory paragraphs and objectives that you can use as guidelines. These objectives are listed in question form on each chapter title page. Try to read them before starting each chapter. They will help you to pick out the important points in the chapters.

To make studying easier, each chapter ends on a blue page with a detailed chapter summary. The summary is followed by chapter review questions. Two types of questions are included with each chapter summary: For Your Notebook and Exploring Further. For Your Notebook questions are usually answered in the textbook. The questions in Exploring Further usually ask you to be creative, do research, or stretch your thinking skills. These review questions can be used as a study guide. You can also use them as self-tests to check your understanding of the main ideas of the chapter.

An effort has been made to make note-taking easier for you. A variety of charts have been included to help you organize your information.

The text is organized to allow you to find information quickly. Introductory paragraphs for topics are placed across the tops of pages in a column 13 cm wide. Most paragraphs contain a main idea in the opening sentence. The following sentences contain the supporting details. Major titles are in large, bold type. Sub-headings are in smaller, bold type.

(Factual Narrative)

A Winter Day in São Paulo

The cold wind blew down the street. It rattled the folding tables set up along the sidewalk. Luckily Everton's table was loaded with heavy gas stove parts, light bulbs, electric cords, and sockets. His table shook briefly in the wind. Many of the tables had to be held in place by the vendors to keep them from toppling onto the sidewalks.

Everton pulled his scarf tighter around his neck. He tugged his wool cap down farther on his head and blew on his hands as he rubbed them together for a little extra warmth. His light

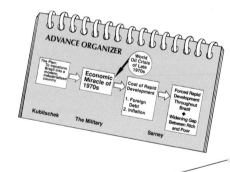

CASE STUDY: Endangered Pantanal

The wildlife of the Pantanal has been seriously affected by recent developments in the Center West. Development of logging, mining, cattle ranching, farming, and industries has produced some devastating results. Many Brazilian ecologists are worried that human activities will eventually destroy the wildlife of the Pantanal.

Large areas of natural vegetation in the Center West region have been cleared for pasture, farmlands, and logging. Since building Brasília and constructing the BR-364 Highway across the interior, the Center West has

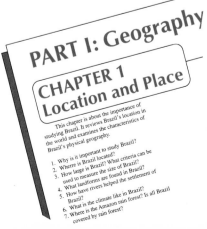

ADVANCE ORGANIZER

PART I: Geography

CHAPTER 1
Location and Place

This chapter is about the importance of studying Brazil. It reviews Brazil's location in the world and examines the characteristics of Brazil's physical geography.

1. Why is it important to study Brazil?
2. Where is Brazil located?
3. How large is Brazil? What criteria can be used to measure the size of Brazil?
4. What landforms are found in Brazil?
5. How have rivers helped the settlement of Brazil?
6. What is the climate like in Brazil?
7. Where is the Amazon rain forest? Is all Brazil covered by rain forest?

Portuguese/English Dictionary

Common terms and phrases

good morning	bom dia	(bone dee–uh)
good afternoon	boa tarde	(boh–ah tar–day)
good evening	boa noite	(boh–a noy–te)
all right	muito bem	(moo–ee–too bayng)
very good	muito bem	(moo–ee–too bayng)
please	por favor	(poor fa–voir)
thank you	obrigado (male)	(og–bree–gah–doo)
thank you	obrigada (female)	(og–bree–gah–da)
Many thanks!	Muito obrigado/obrigada	
How are you?	Como está?	(comb–oo ess–taw)
Very well, thank you	Muito bem, obrigado	(mwee–too bain)
My name is ...	Chamo–me	(sher–moo me)
goodbye	adeus	(a–day–oos)
See you later	Até logo	(ah–tay low–go)
today	hoje	(oh–jee)
tomorrow	amanha	(ah–mahn–ah)
yesterday	ontem	(on–tain)
this week	esta semana	(es–ta se–mah–na)
don't forget	nao de esqueca	(nah–oong se is–kay–sa)
What do you call this?	Como chama isto?	(kao–moo sher–moo eesht–oh)

Numbers

one	um	(oong)
two	dois	(doys)
three	tres	(trays)
four	quatro	(kway–troo)
five	cinco	(seeng–koo)
six	seis	(say–ess)
seven	sete	(se–te)
eight	oito	(oy–too)
nine	nove	(noh–ve)
ten	dez	(dayz)

Days of the Week

domingo	Sunday
segunda–feira	Monday
terça–feira	Tuesday
quarta–feira	Wednesday
quinta–feira	Thursday
sexta–feira	Friday
sábado	Saturday

Lanchonette Brasil

Bebidas / Drinks

Bebidas	Drinks
aqua	water
batido	milkshake
café	coffee
cafezina	strong black coffee
chá	tea
gasosa	North America pop
leite	milk
leite com chocolate	chocolate milk

Fruta / Fruit

Fruta	Fruit
laranja	orange
maca	apple
banana	banana
morango	strawberry
abacaxi	pineapple
coco	coconut
framboesa	raspberry
limao	lemon
melao	honeydew melon
melancia	watermelon
pera	pear
uva	grape

From the Author:

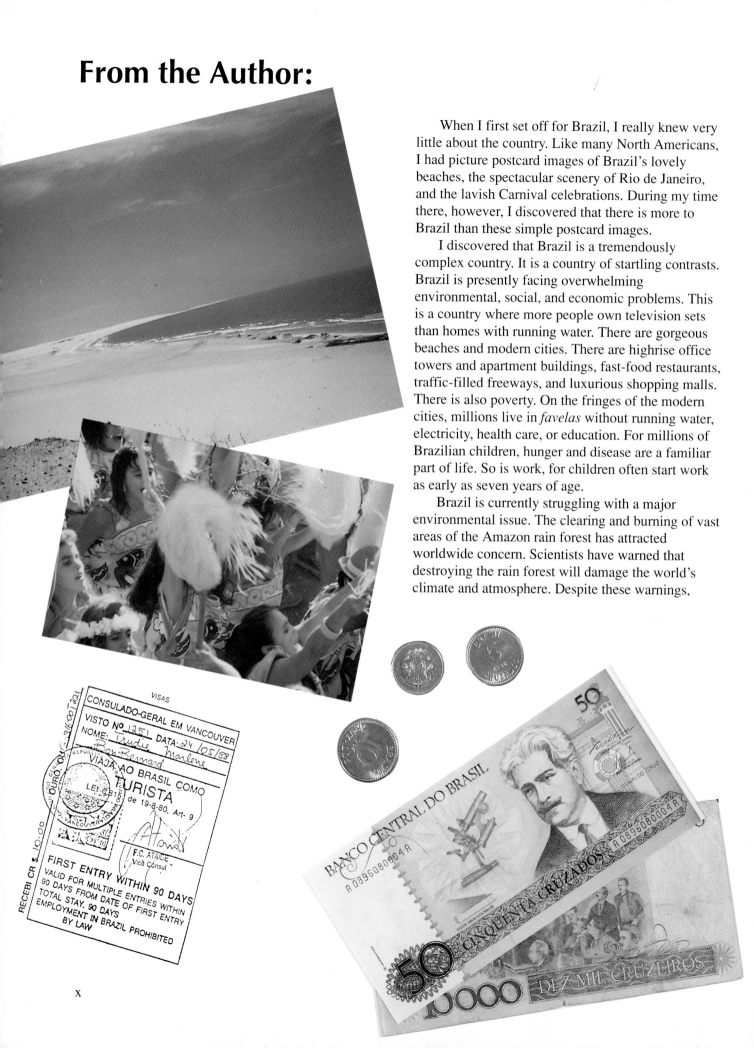

When I first set off for Brazil, I really knew very little about the country. Like many North Americans, I had picture postcard images of Brazil's lovely beaches, the spectacular scenery of Rio de Janeiro, and the lavish Carnival celebrations. During my time there, however, I discovered that there is more to Brazil than these simple postcard images.

I discovered that Brazil is a tremendously complex country. It is a country of startling contrasts. Brazil is presently facing overwhelming environmental, social, and economic problems. This is a country where more people own television sets than homes with running water. There are gorgeous beaches and modern cities. There are highrise office towers and apartment buildings, fast-food restaurants, traffic-filled freeways, and luxurious shopping malls. There is also poverty. On the fringes of the modern cities, millions live in *favelas* without running water, electricity, health care, or education. For millions of Brazilian children, hunger and disease are a familiar part of life. So is work, for children often start work as early as seven years of age.

Brazil is currently struggling with a major environmental issue. The clearing and burning of vast areas of the Amazon rain forest has attracted worldwide concern. Scientists have warned that destroying the rain forest will damage the world's climate and atmosphere. Despite these warnings, millions of hectares of rain forest continue to be cleared to make way for highways, mines, hydro-electric dams, cattle ranches, and farms. After only a week of touring the devastated areas of burned rain forest, it would be easy for a North American to say "Stop cutting the rain forest!" However, there are many reasons why Brazilians feel they must clear the rain forest. Even among Brazilians, there are widely opposing views on the issue of using or preserving the rain forest.

There are no easy answers to Brazil's problems. Many of Brazil's economic problems, and even the reasons for clearing the rain forest, are linked to the billions of dollars that the Brazilian government owes to banks across the world. In the last few years, many events in Brazil have been influenced by government efforts to meet the repayment demands of foreign banks—many of them American and Canadian. Hydro-electric projects, highways, and mines that have contributed to the devastation in the rain forest have also been financed by North American banks. In many ways, what happens in Brazil is influenced by decisions made right here in North America.

In this textbook I have tried to explain the many issues which Brazilians are struggling to resolve. I hope that through this text you will acquire a better understanding of the problems facing Brazil and a greater appreciation for the Brazilian point-of-view. There are many parallels between what is happening in Brazil and in North America. I hope that by exploring Brazil you will gain a better understanding of your own country.

Trudie BonBernard
September, 1989

PART I: Geography

CHAPTER 1
Location and Place

This chapter is about the importance of studying Brazil. It reviews Brazil's location in the world and examines the characteristics of Brazil's physical geography.

1. Why is it important to study Brazil?
2. Where is Brazil located?
3. How large is Brazil? What criteria can be used to measure the size of Brazil?
4. What landforms are found in Brazil?
5. How have rivers helped the settlement of Brazil?
6. What is the climate like in Brazil?
7. Where is the Amazon rain forest? Is all Brazil covered by rain forest?

? Problem Solving

Throughout this text, you will be presented with several problem solving questions. Problem solving is a strategy of using a variety of skills to answer a question or solve a problem.

Getting Started

1. Explore possible answers to the question:

What are the Physical Features of Brazil?

2. Develop a hypothesis by skimming through the first chapter. Look at the photographs and charts. Look at the headings in dark type. Draw a retrieval chart* in your notebook. Fill in what you remember are physical features of Brazil based on your quick skim through the chapter.

3. Use the retrieval chart to gather and organize information as you read through the chapter. You may need to revise some parts of your original hypothesis.

4. At the end of the chapter you will be asked to make a concluding statement about the physical features of Brazil. This will be based on the information that you have gathered.

Problem Solving Strategy

1. Define a question or problem.
2. Develop questions or hypotheses to guide research.
3. Gather, organize, and interpret information.
4. Develop a conclusion or solution. A conclusion is a statement of knowledge developed as an answer to a question or problem about a specific situation.

Retrieval Chart

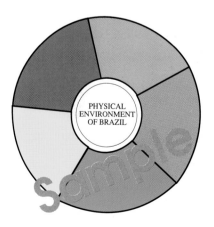

PHYSICAL ENVIRONMENT OF BRAZIL

*Retrieval Chart available as a black-line master in the Teacher Resource Package.

WHY STUDY BRAZIL?

There are many reasons for North American interest in Brazil. For instance, Brazil has one of the world's fastest growing populations, and over half the people of South America live in Brazil. Brazil is also one of the largest countries in the world. It occupies nearly half of the South American continent. Brazil is a rapidly growing economic leader in South America. Not only is Brazil South America's leading producer of manufactured goods, it is also one of the world's top exporters of agricultural products. With its vast mineral, land, and hydro-electric resources, Brazil has the potential to become a major industrialized country.

A Great Deal in Common

In many ways Brazilians and North Americans have a great deal in common. Canada, the United States, and Brazil are all large countries that occupy important positions on their continents. Each country has distinctly different geographic regions and settlement patterns. Each country has vast natural resources that it wants to develop. The conflict between developing natural resources and protecting the natural environment is of concern to all three countries. Each country is attempting to deal with Indian claims to large land areas. North Americans and Brazilians even share a similar settlement pattern. In both cases, early European settlements began along the Atlantic coast. It took several hundred years for settlement to gradually move into the vast, unexplored interior.

A Special Relationship

North America and Brazil share a relationship that goes back many years. Many Canadian and American mining, hydro-electric, and manufacturing companies have operated in Brazil for a number of years. Some companies were in Brazil during the early 1800s. For example, Canadian-owned Brascan provided the first electrical and telephone service in Rio de Janeiro and São Paulo. In recent years, political and business contacts with Brazil have increased substantially.

Investments in Brazil

Canadian and American banks are very active in Brazil. They have invested millions of dollars. These banks have also provided billions of dollars in loans to the Brazilian government. This money has financed the construction of highways, hydro-electric dams and mines. It has also allowed the government to sponsor other projects which develop the country's natural resources.

Trade

Brazil is one of North America's important trading partners. In the last ten years, trade between Brazil and North America has increased substantially. Brazil is a major buyer of North American coal, sulphur, and potash. Brazil imports wheat, newsprint, and telecommunication equipment. North Americans import orange juice, tin, electrical appliances, shoes, and clothing items from Brazil. "Made in Brazil" labels are fast becoming common in shoe and clothing stores throughout North America.

The Destruction of the Rain Forest

In the last decade, millions of hectares of rain forest have been cleared and burned. This land is being used for farmland, cattle ranches, logging operations, mines, highways, and hydro-electric dams. North American scientists and environmentalists are very concerned about the rapid destruction of the Amazon rain forest. They fear the effect that burning the rain forest might have on the world's climate and atmosphere. Many scientists and environmental groups are trying to persuade the Brazilian government to save the Amazon rain forest before it disappears completely.

A study of the destruction of the Amazon rain forest highlights similar North American problems. North Americans are also trying to balance developing natural resources with preserving the natural environment. Environmental groups in North America are also active. They are trying to persuade North American governments to save our forests from destruction.

A Growing Interdependence

North Americans do not live in isolation. We import raw materials and manufactured goods from other countries. We depend on selling our food and manufactured goods to other countries. Our daily lives are increasingly affected by events in distant countries. For example, an unusually cold winter in South America can increase our prices for coffee and chocolate bars. We also cannot isolate our environment from the effects of events in other countries. Clearing the Amazon rain forest may produce summer droughts in North America. Industrial pollution in one part of the world can produce acid rain in another. One country's over-fishing in the Atlantic can reduce North American salmon catches. By studying Brazil, North Americans can develop a greater understanding of other places and other peoples. This can lead to a greater understanding of the interdependence of the world.

BRAZIL: LOCATION

An important aspect of geography is the position or location of a place on the earth's surface. This includes both absolute and relative location.

Absolute Location

The exact location of a place is called ABSOLUTE LOCATION. To find the exact location of any place on the surface of the earth, maps and globes use a grid system. The grid is made up of two sets of imaginary lines.

The horizontal lines of the grid are called PARALLELS OF LATITUDE. Lines of latitude are numbered in degrees north and south of the Equator, which is numbered 0°.

The vertical lines on the grid are known as MERIDIANS OF LONGITUDE. Longitude is measured in degrees east and west of the Prime Meridian, which is numbered 0°.

Every place on earth can be located by identifying which lines of latitude and longitude cross through it. Brazil is located in the northeastern part of the South American continent between 5° N latitude and 33°S latitude. It extends from 35°W longitude to 74°W longitude.

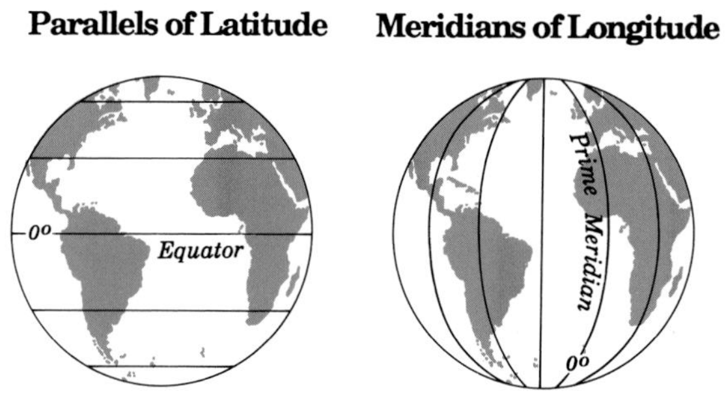

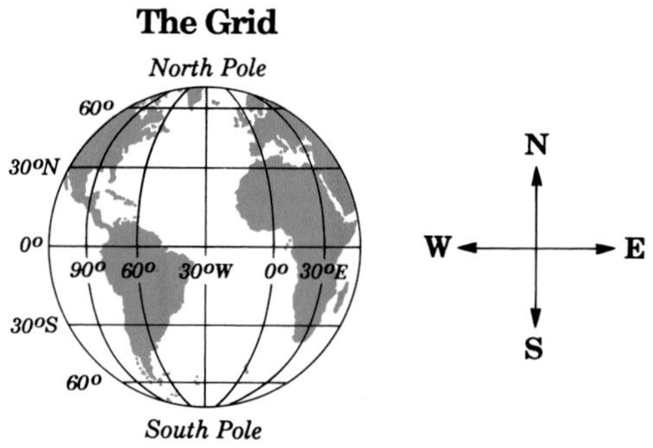

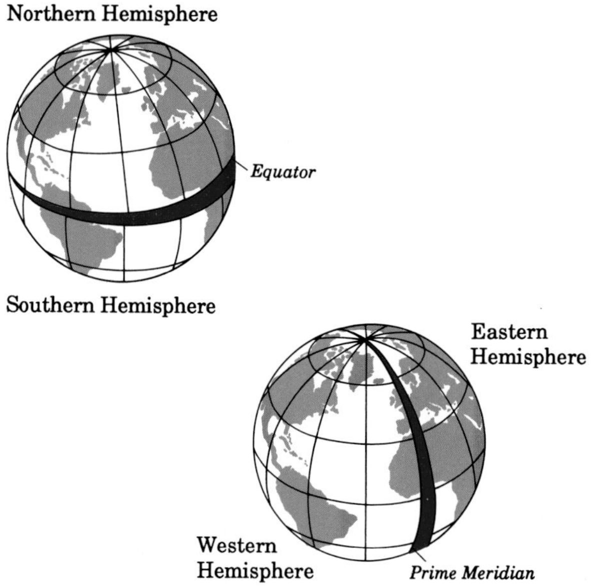

Parallels of Latitude

Meridians of Longitude

The Grid

The Hemispheres

The EQUATOR is the imaginary line of latitude that divides the earth into two halves. The part of the earth's surface above the Equator is called the NORTHERN HEMISPHERE. The part of the earth's surface below the Equator is called the SOUTHERN HEMISPHERE.

The PRIME MERIDIAN is an imaginary line that divides the earth into two halves called the Western Hemisphere and the Eastern Hemisphere. All of Brazil is located in the Western Hemisphere.

Nearly 93% of Brazil lies below the Equator, in the Southern Hemisphere. In the Southern Hemisphere the seasons are opposite to those in the Northern Hemisphere. During July and August, when it is summer in the Northern Hemisphere, it is winter in the Southern Hemisphere.

Northern Hemisphere

Equator

Southern Hemisphere

Eastern Hemisphere

Western Hemisphere

Prime Meridian

Relative Location

RELATIVE LOCATION describes where a place is in relation to other places in the world. Relative location identifies the distances between countries. It designates the borders that separate one country from another. Relative location identifies how one place may be connected to other places in the world by similar language, religion, **natural resources**, form of government, or trade. Relative location also identifies how one place can be influenced by events in other, often very distant, places.

Brazil has many close connections with the other countries in South America. Brazil shares borders with all the countries of South America except Chile and Ecuador.

South America is part of Latin America. Latin America includes Mexico, all the countries of **Central America** and South America,

and the **Caribbean**. This part of the world is called Latin America because it was largely settled by Latin peoples. Latins are people from the European countries of Spain, Portugal, France, and Italy. They speak languages that developed from an old language called Latin. Today Spanish, Portuguese*, and French are the three main languages spoken in Latin America**.

The countries of Latin America are shaded gray on the map below. See also the map on the inside cover of this book.

Brazil is not located directly south of North America. It is southeast of Canada and the United States, only 1 900 kilometres from Africa. Brazil is closer to Africa than any of the other countries in North or South America.

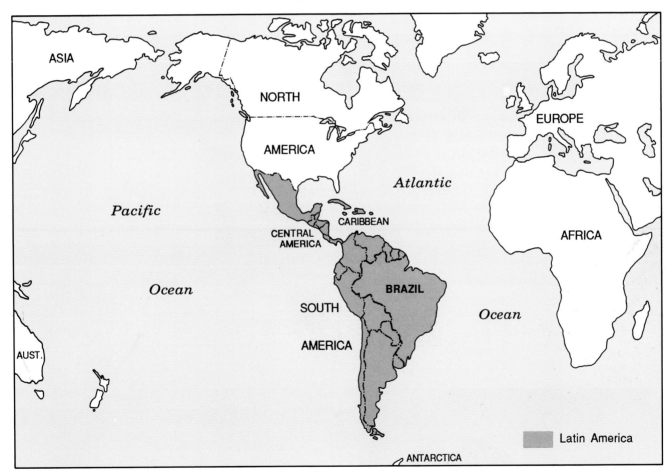

Natural resources—materials from nature such as natural gas, water, trees, and furs from animals
Central America—Belize, Costa Rica, El Salvador, Guatemala, Honduras, Nicaragua, Panama
Caribbean—Cuba, Haiti, Dominican Republic, Puerto Rico, Trinidad and Tobago, and the Lesser Antilles nations

*Brazil is the only country in Latin America to use Portuguese.
**These are not the only languages used in Latin America. English and Dutch are spoken in a few countries and millions of Indians in Latin America speak Indian languages.

7

Connections with the World

Brazil has many connections with the rest of the world. Brazil is a major trading partner with Canada, the United States, and many countries in Europe, Africa, and Asia. North Americans wear Brazilian-made shoes and shirts. They drink Brazilian orange juice for breakfast. Chinese businesses use Brazilian-made computers. Armies in the Middle East, Africa, and Latin America use Brazilian-made guns.

Many Canadian, American, Japanese, and European companies operate industries in Brazil.

People in Brazil dress like people in North America. They enjoy similar foods, music, television, and sports. People in Brazil wear North American-style clothes and listen to American and European rock music. They eat at fast-food restaurants and drink Coca-Cola or Pepsi. Brazilian supermarkets are filled with products familiar to any North American or European shopper. Well-off Brazilians own microwave ovens and VCRs. North American movies are very popular in Brazil. Religion and language are a link between Brazilians and other people in the world. Nearly 94% of Brazilians belong to the Roman Catholic Church. Over half the Roman Catholic priests in Brazil come from other countries. Many Protestant churches from Europe and North America operate missions and churches in Brazil. Brazil also maintains close contacts with Portugal and other Portuguese-speaking communities in the world.

Brazil's government maintains contact with the governments of countries throughout the world. Brazil invests millions of dollars in projects to develop highways, hydro-electric dams, and industries in several South American and African countries. Canadian, American, Japanese, and European banks and businesses have invested billions of dollars in Brazilian industries. They have helped finance the construction of highways, hydro-electric dams, mines, and railways.

BRAZIL: SIZE

The size of a country may be illustrated using a variety of criteria.

1. Comparing the Area of Brazil with the Continents and Other Countries in the World

Geographers use estimated land area to compare the sizes of countries. Land area is measured in square kilometres. With a land area of 8 511 965 km^2, Brazil is the fifth largest country in the world.

Continents	Sq. Kilometres
Asia	44 000 000
Africa	29 000 000
North America	24 320 000
South America	17 600 000
Antarctica	14 240 000
Europe	9 700 000
Australia	7 690 000
Brazil *	**8 511 965**

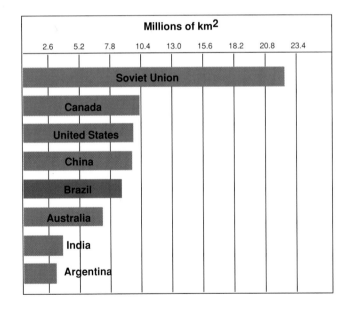

Country	Sq. Kilometres
1. Soviet Union (USSR)	22 402 200
2. Canada	9 976 137
3. United States	9 363 124
4. China	9 327 600
5. Brazil	8 511 965
6. Australia	7 690 000
7. India	3 287 590
8. Argentina	2 780 092

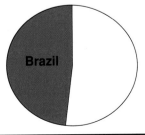

Brazil is the largest country in South America. It covers nearly half the land area of the continent of South America.

---

* Remember that Brazil is a country. The other land areas listed on this chart are continents.

8

2. Using Latitude to Illustrate the Size of Brazil

Lines of latitude can be used to indicate the size of a country. The number of degrees of latitude a country stretches from north to south is called the range of latitude. As may be seen on the map to the right, Brazil extends from 5°N latitude to 33°S latitude. This means that Brazil extends over 38° of latitude.

The distance between each degree of latitude is 111 kilometres. Using the range of latitude, the distance a country stretches from north to south can be calculated. Figure out the distance in kilometres from the north to the south of Brazil. Compare it with that of Canada and/or the United States.

3. Using Time Zones to Illustrate the Size of Brazil

The number of time zones a country has can be an indication of its size. The earth has 24 time zones. Each time zone is 15 degrees of longitude wide. Large countries that stretch across many degrees of longitude will have several time zones. The Soviet Union, the largest country in the world, has eleven time zones. Canada has six* time zones and the continental United States has four. Brazil also has four time zones, as is seen in the diagram to the right.

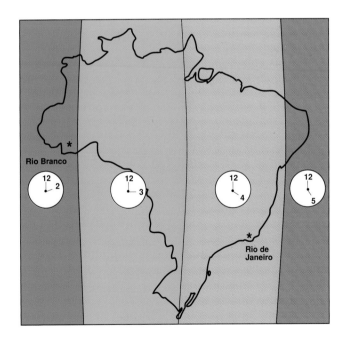

---

* Canada actually has 5 ¹/₂ time zones. Newfoundland is only
30 minutes earlier than the Maritimes, Canada, not a full hour.

4. Using Borders and Coastlines to Illustrate the Size of Brazil

The length of a country's coastlines and borders can also give an indication of size. Brazil's Atlantic coastline extends for 5 864 kilometres. This is one of the longest coastlines in the world. Brazil has a 12 000-kilometre interior border with ten South American countries.

Brazil's Neighbors

Uruguay	Colombia
Argentina	Venezuela
Paraguay	Guyana
Bolivia	Surinam
Peru	French Guiana

For Your Notebook

Exercise 1:

Write the following sentences in your notebooks, completing each as you go. Use an atlas and/or the maps on the inside of the front cover of this book. Also use the maps on pages 6 to 9 as references.

1. Brazil is located in the _____ Hemisphere and the _____ Hemisphere. A small portion of northern Brazil is located in the _____ Hemisphere.
2. Brazil is located in the northeastern part of the _____ continent.
3. Brazil borders all the countries in South America except _____ and _____.
4. The two important lines of latitude that cross through Brazil are the_____ and the _____.
5. Brazil borders on the _____Ocean.
6. The Brazilian city of _____ is located on the Tropic of Capricorn.
7. The Brazilian city of _____ is located on the Equator.
8. Brazil extends from _____ north latitude to _____ south latitude.
9. Brazil extends _____ kilometres from north to south and _____ kilometres from east to west.
10. Brazil ranks as the _____largest country in the world.

Exercise 2:

1. On an outline map of Brazil, label the following: Atlantic Ocean, Rio de Janeiro, São Paulo, Salvador, Brasília, Manaus, Rio Branco, Porto Velho, Belém.
2. On the outline map of Brazil, draw in the Equator and the Tropic of Capricorn.
3. Using the information presented in this section, write two sentences describing Brazil's location in the world.
4. Describe the size of Brazil compared to other countries in the world.
5. Compare the size of Brazil to your own country.
6. Make a chart or graph illustrating Brazil's size compared to the size of Canada and the United States.
7. Silvia lives in Rio de Janeiro. She wants to telephone her father, who works at a mine site outside Rio Branco. Her father doesn't get back to his apartment until after 8 p.m. Use the time zone chart to calculate what time it needs to be in Rio de Janeiro for Silvia to call her father in Rio Branco.
8. Using your knowledge about Brazil's location, what might you predict about the climate in Brazil?
9. What advantages might there be for a country to have a vast land area? What disadvantages might there be with a large land area?
10. Why do you think Brazil is the only country in Latin America to use Portuguese?

BRAZIL: PLACE

All places on earth have features that distinguish them from other places on earth. Geographers divide these features into physical and human features. Physical features include landforms, bodies of water, climate, natural vegetation, and soils. Human features include population size, population density and distribution, ethnic groups, language, religion, land use, settlement patterns, and social, political, and economic activities. The physical features of Brazil will be discussed in this chapter.

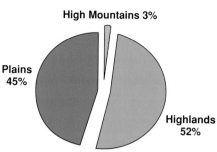

High Mountains 3%

Plains 45%

Highlands 52%

PHYSICAL FEATURES*

(Environment)

Topography of Brazil

TOPOGRAPHY is also called landforms or landscape. Topography includes the surface features of the land such as mountains, hills, plateaus, and valleys. Topographical features may be divided into highlands (mountains, hills, plateaus) and lowlands (plains). PLATEAUS are high, level land.

Lowlands

Nearly 45% of Brazil is low, flat land called PLAINS. These plains are less than 200 metres above sea level. The Amazon Lowlands and the coastal plain, shown on the map on page 13, are the two major plains in Brazil.

A large part of Brazil is low mountains, hills, and plateaus called highlands.

Highlands

Brazil has few high mountains. Low mountains, hills, and plateaus 200 to 900 metres above sea level occupy about 52% of Brazil. In Brazil these areas of low mountains, hills, and plateaus are referred to as highlands on topographical maps. The Brazilian Highlands occupy a large area of southeastern Brazil.

There are no mountains in Brazil as high as the Rocky Mountains** in North America or the Andes in South America. High mountains over 900 metres occupy only about 3% of Brazil. The Serra do Mar, Serra da Mantiqueira, and Serra do Espinhaco along Brazil's eastern coast and the Serra Imeri in the Guiana Highlands are the only high mountain ranges in Brazil.

Much of Brazil is low, flat land called plains.

---

* Physical features are also referred to as the physical environment and natural environment.

**Mt. Robson, British Columbia is 3 954 metres. Mt. McKinley, Alaska is 6 194 metres. Mt. Aconcagua with 7 021 metres is the highest peak in the Andes.

11

GUIANA
HIGHLANDS

RIO DE JANEIRO

Brazilian Highlands

Guiana Highlands

Amazon Lowlands

The Pantanal

This profile of Brazil from Rio de Janeiro to Boa Vista
gives an impression of how the topography changes
from west to east.
This diagram is greatly compressed horizontally.

Coastal Plain

12

Major Topographical Areas

Amazon Lowlands

- largest lowland (plains) in Brazil—40% of Brazil's land area
- Amazon river system flowing across Amazon Lowlands
- new roads into Amazon Lowlands opening area for farming, cattle ranching, mining
- most of lowland covered by rain forest
- clearing of rain forest causing world concern
- few people living in Amazon Lowlands

Guiana Highlands

- contain Brazil's highest mountain, Pico da Neblina (3 014 m)
- very few people
- new road opening area for mining (gold, diamonds)
- recent gold rush

The Pantanal

- lowlands only 150 m above sea level
- land flooded for half the year
- vast wildlife area—nesting ground for thousands of birds and ducks
- very undeveloped—only one road into area
- land used for cattle ranching during the dry season

Brazilian Highlands

- often called Central Highlands
- region of low mountains, high plateaus, hills
- steepest mountains along eastern coast
- covers most of southeastern Brazil—nearly 45% of Brazil's land area
- difficult to build roads, highways through Brazilian Highlands
- land used for lumbering, farming, mining, cattle ranching

Coastal Plain

- narrow strip of low, flat land along the eastern coast
- 40% of Brazil's population living on coastal plain
- Brazil's major cities located along coastal plain
- first area settled by Portuguese
- land used for agriculture

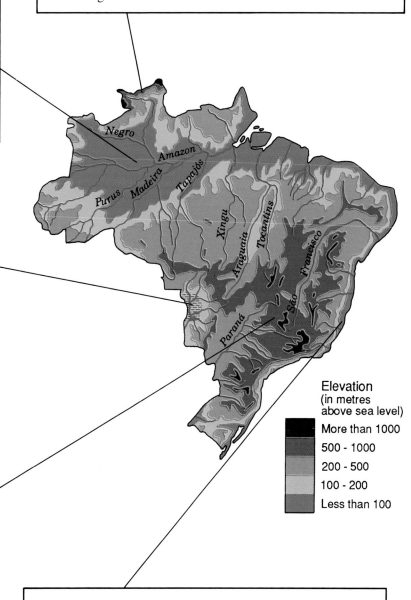

Elevation
(in metres
above sea level)

More than 1000
500 - 1000
200 - 500
100 - 200
Less than 100

Rivers

Brazil has some of the largest river systems in the world. The Amazon, Rio São Francisco, and the Paraná-Paraguay-Uruguay river systems flow over an extremely large area of land and carry an enormous amount of water. The Amazon river system alone carries 20% of the world's fresh water. This is more water than the combined totals of the next three largest rivers in the world.

The Importance of Rivers

1. Transportation

The rivers have influenced the settlement of Brazil's interior. In some areas, rivers provided the only means of transportation. For many years the Amazon river system provided the only transportation through the Amazon Lowlands. Roads into this area were not built until the 1960s. Early settlements in the Amazon area were always along rivers.

Not all of Brazil's rivers provided such good access to the interior. Many of the rivers form rapids and waterfalls as they drop from the highlands to the coastal plain. These rivers have unnavigable stretches. This made movement to the inland areas difficult. Early plantations, cattle ranches, and towns were often along the sections of rivers that provided good navigation. Another problem is that many rivers in Brazil flow inland away from the coast. These rivers did not provide any means of transportation from the early coastal settlements to the **interior**. The lack of navigable rivers to the interior was one reason the early settlers stayed along the coast. This slowed the settlement of the interior.

2. Hydro-Electric Power

Today the rivers of the Amazon system are still important transportation routes. Most of the rivers in Brazil are even more important as sites for hydro-electric dams. Electricity is needed to light homes and cities, and to power factories and industries.

It is estimated that Brazil has one of the world's largest hydro-electric potentials. Unfortunately many of the rivers most suitable for hydro-electric dams are located far from the large cities and industries that require large amounts of electric power. These cities are along the eastern coast. Over half the rivers suitable for dams are in remote locations in the Amazon area. Until recently these sites were considered too remote for development. In recent years, however, better transmission systems have been developed. Now power can be carried cheaply over long distances. This has made it possible to develop these remote sites.

These dams have provided huge amounts of electricity. They have also created problems. They have flooded large areas of the Amazon rain forest and destroyed many Indian settlements. The Brazilian government has been forced to borrow millions of dollars from world banks to pay for the projects. Many people are concerned about the effect of these dams on the physical environment and the natives of Brazil.

World environmental and nature protection groups are joining with Brazilian Indians to protest the building of new hydro-electric dams in the Amazon. They know the hydro-electric dams have many benefits for Brazil. However, there is a great deal of concern about the negative effect on the people and the natural environment of Brazil. These effects will be examined in the Amazon chapter. Itaipú Dam, shown to the left, is one of the largest hydro-electric power dams in the world.

Interior—land some distance from the coast

Major River Drainage Basins

There are several major drainage basins in Brazil. A drainage basin is an area of land drained by a river system. A river system is made up of all the rivers that flow into one major river. The rivers that flow into the larger river are called TRIBUTARIES.

The Amazon

The Amazon is one of the largest river systems in the world. From its source in the Andes Mountains of Peru, the Amazon travels across South America for 6 400 kilometres. Large ocean freighters are able to travel 1 700 kilometres inland to Manaus. Smaller ships can travel farther up the Amazon to Iquitos in Peru. Iquitos is nearly 3 600 kilometres inland from the Atlantic Ocean. The Brazilian government has already built several massive hydro-electric dams on Amazon rivers. At least a dozen more dam projects are planned. World-wide concern has been expressed about the effect of these dams on the natural environment of the Amazon.

Coastal

The rivers forming this drainage basin flow short distances from the Brazilian Highlands to the Atlantic Ocean. The valleys of these rivers were sites of some of the earliest coffee and cocoa plantations in Brazil. Navigation on these rivers is often interrupted by rapids and waterfalls. These occur where rivers drop from the highlands onto the coastal plain.

Northeast

The rivers in the northeast drainage basin flow short distances from the interior to the Atlantic Ocean. These rivers provide irrigation water for the cultivation of rice and other crops in the drier areas of the northeast.

Rio São Francisco

The Rio São Francisco is 2 900 kilometres long. It is the largest river totally within Brazil. It flows northward from the mountains in the Brazilian Highlands in a gentle curve to the Atlantic Ocean. There are steep waterfalls and rapids along the Rio São Francisco as it drops from the highlands to the coastal plain. They make some long stretches of the river unnavigable. Nearly 1 200 kilometres of the river as it flows through the interior are navigable. It provided the early settlers in Brazil with a means of transportation amongst the interior plantations and cattle ranches. Today, there are many hydro-electric dams on the river. They provide electricity for the large cities along the northeast coast.

Paraná-Paraguay-Uruguay River System

These three rivers flow into the Rio de la Plata river system. Together they form the second largest river system in South America. These vast rivers flow south away from the Brazilian Highlands. Eventually they empty into the Atlantic Ocean below Brazil's southern border. Navigation on these rivers is limited in places. As the rivers flow south they drop sharply from the plateaus, forming many rapids and waterfalls. These waterfalls limit navigation on the rivers. However, they make ideal sites for hydro-electric dams. Itaipú, one of the world's largest hydro-electric project, has already been built on the Paraná. Many more dams are planned for the rivers in this system.

Paddle to the Amazon

(Factual Narrative)

On June 1, 1980, three Canadians put their canoe into the waters of the Red River near Winnipeg. This began an extraordinary canoe adventure. Don Starkell and his two teenage sons, Dana and Jeff, began the challenge of paddling from Canada to the Amazon River. Nearly two years and millions of paddle strokes later, Don and Dana reached the Amazon. The map on the right shows the route they took to reach the Amazon.

The following excerpts are from the diary Don Starkell kept. These pages were written on their journey along the Rio Negro and Amazon rivers.*

MARCH 14: on the Rio Negro

What surprised us most during our first few days on this wild stretch of the Rio Negro is the number of houses along the banks. Every mile or so the jungle will open, and a little thatched dwelling will reveal itself. At first there'll be no sign of life, but as we pass a family will generally materialize along shore, straining their eyes to see us. Occasionally, they'll jump into their rickety dugouts and paddle out to get a better look.

Last night at Madia we camped with an Indian family at one of these clearings—what an industrious bunch they were. The grand-father was making paddles when we got there; he carves one enormous paddle about 8 inches thick, then delicately splits it into three or four thin paddles. We hadn't been there long when a couple of family members arrived in a dugout, carrying two big pots of white liquid. I mistook the stuff for milk until they told me they'd been gathering sap from the hundreds of nearby rubber trees. They took me into the bush to show me how they cut deep Vs into the tree trunks, then ram in spouts just beneath the Vs. Some of the trees were gouged with long vertical nests of Vs, with a deep groove down the center, presumably to facilitate the flow of sap. The spouts drip into little cups made of palm leaves. The harvesters prepare this liquid latex by pouring it on a stick which they rotate over a fire. As the latex grows **viscous**, more is added, until a big spool of crude rubber forms. The spools are sold to river traders.

Our friends also produced manioc, which has become a staple of our diet during the past couple of weeks. It's made from the cassava plant, which is peeled, boiled, and ground up, then run through woven wicker strainers to allow undesirable acids to drain out. The moist grindings are then spread on metal sheets and roasted above a fire to produce manioc. I asked about a pot of fluid that was sitting near the house and was told it was cassava juice being made into tapioca. All my life I've eaten tapioca and have never had a clue what it was or where it came from. As the cassava juice evaporates in the sun, it crystallizes into hard little nuggets. Tapioca!

Just before sunset, I walked out through the fruit trees and garden and discovered the family graveyard in the jungle. I counted more than 50 unpainted wooden crosses, almost all of them rotting. The tragedy was that 30 or more of the graves were those of young children—tiny little plots three or four feet long. It was a sad reminder that fever and catastrophe and poor diet still claim many in these outlying regions of the planet. The people here work hard and have little. We've passed dozens of homes like this one, and undoubtedly each has its own little cemetery full of bones of children.

* Don Starkell, *Paddle to the Amazon,* edited by Charles Wilkins (Toronto: McClelland and Stewart, 1987). Reprinted with permission.
Viscous—thick like syrup or glue

16

At about 7 o'clock we joined the family for their daily river bath. We all waded in together and scrubbed away the dirt and heat of the day. I felt better for the cleansing, but couldn't get my mind off those little graves out behind the house.

MARCH 16: Sao Gabriel, at the Uaupes Rapids, on the Rio Negro

We've been counting down degrees of latitude for nearly two years now, and yesterday morning, just after sunrise, our count reached zero. As we passed the south end of Ilha Guia, we put our paddles down so that we could savor the moment. On the glassy calm water, we drifted across the equator into the southern hemisphere.

MARCH 30: near Airão, on the Rio Negro

I imagined that as we got closer to Manaus, the river population would increase. But for the past 100 miles we've hardly seen a single dwelling. With houses denied us as stopping spots, and with our sand bars and rocks now submerged, we've had no choice for the past couple of nights but to make our beds on the floor of the jungle. Today, like yesterday, we were driven off the water during the late afternoon by the torrential rains of the season. We could hear the deluge coming from a mile or more away—first as a distant hiss, then a percussive, snare-drum clatter as it moved onto the heavy canopy of foliage where we'd taken shelter. At the first distant sounds, the howler monkeys set up an intense whine and roar, which increased as the rain got closer.

It rained for an hour, and the thick leaves were an efficient umbrella. But when the rain stopped, the water that had collected in the nooks and crooks of the foliage began falling in cup-sized dollops from 100 feet up. Every so often, a little water-bomb would crash onto our heads or shoulders.

At dusk, we crawled beneath our tarp. But it wasn't long before I had to roll it back because of the stifling humidity. As the darkness deepened, our little jungle enclave came alive with the sounds of nocturnal birds and animals—mostly just peeps and rustlings but the occasional squawk or cry in the distance. Flecks of light from hundreds of fluorescent insects shone on the ground around us.

MARCH 31: Manaus

About 20 miles northwest of Manaus the Rio Negro becomes one great open freeway as it bears down on the Amazon. In places, it is up to seven miles wide. Manaus is not on the Amazon, where it's sometimes said to be in tourist literature, but on the north shore of the Rio Negro about 10 miles from the Amazon. It's a city of about a million people, and as we approached it yesterday morning boat and jet traffic picked up. Our first glimpse of the skyline set our hearts pounding, and we figured we were only two hours away. In fact, it took five hours of paddling to bring us in.

APRIL 4: at the meeting of the Rio Negro and Amazon Rivers

The confluence of the Rio Negro and Amazon—the Meeting of the Waters it's called—is a great marbled swirl of black and brown water, black from the Rio Negro, brownish-yellow from the Amazon. At about 9:30 yesterday we crossed that swirl and entered the mythic river that will take us to the end of our journey.

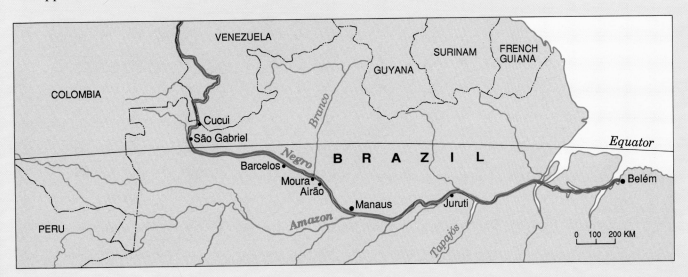

17

Curiously enough, one of the first thoughts I had as we paddled out into the current was that the great river wasn't as big as I'd expected it to be. Not that I was disappointed—in fact, I was extremely excited; the river is huge. The warp in my expectations lay in the incredible fantasies I'd built around the Amazon over the years; no mere earthly flow of water could match them.

The facts about the Amazon are staggering: it is 4 000 miles long and has a flow about 11 times as great as that of the Mississippi. One day's discharge into the sea is said to be the equivalent of a nine-year supply of fresh water for New York City. The river supports over 2 000 species of fish, and the plants and trees along its banks supply half the world's oxygen. It is the largest river on the planet.

APRIL 9: Sao Agostinho, on the north shore of the Amazon

One thing that has impressed us about the Amazon is the density of population along its banks; every day we see dozens of homes and ranches. Compared to the Rio Negro or the Orinoco, there's relatively little jungle or animal life. Certainly little romance. I imagine things are different on the isolated upper river, but on these stretches we see far more trade boats than *toninas* (river dolphins), far more cattle than crocodiles.

The river is so big in parts that the locals refer to its shores as *costas* or coasts. The other day, I thought I was seeing its entire width and that the far bank was about 3 miles away. It turned out I was looking at an island some 26 miles long and 11 miles wide. The far shore was 15 miles off!

For Your Notebook

1. The Amazon River carries more water than any other river in the world. Where might all this water come from? Locating the source of the Amazon River on a map may be helpful.

Exploring Further

1. Carry out library research to compare the importance of the rivers in Brazil to the importance of rivers in Canada or the United States.

18

ADVANCE ORGANIZER

Several factors affect land use in Brazil. These factors will be examined in detail on pages 20 to 36.

1. Climate
2. Natural Vegetation
3. Soil

Climate

CLIMATE describes the typical weather conditions of an area over a long period of time. Two important characteristics of climate are air temperature and precipitation. PRECIPITATION is moisture that falls to the ground as rain, snow, or hail.

The climate of a place depends largely on distance from the Equator. Altitude, wind patterns, mountain ranges and closeness to a warm or cold ocean also influence climate. Distance from the Equator, however, is usually the major factor that determines the climate of a place.

Climate is usually the most important factor influencing what vegetation will grow in a region. Climate also influences the soil conditions of a region. Climates that are favorable for agriculture assist human settlement. Climates that are unfavorable for agriculture make human settlement more difficult.

Most of Brazil has a tropical climate: hot and wet.

Natural Vegetation

NATURAL VEGETATION is the mixture of trees, shrubs, and grasses that grow without interference from humans. Natural vegetation is determined by climate, soil types, and topography.

Natural vegetation is a factor that influences where people settle. It also influences what use they make of the land. Natural vegetation may be sources of food, fuel, clothing, shelter, and many other essentials. Some varieties of natural vegetation may be harvested and sold. Natural vegetation usually provides a good indication of an area's potential for agriculture.

Soil

SOIL is a natural surface layer of the land that is capable of supporting plants. The soil layer holds water and contains **nutrients** plants need to grow. The ability of the soil to store water and the amount of nutrients in the soil determine how capable the soil is of supporting plant life. This capability of supporting plant life is called SOIL FERTILITY. Soils with high fertility are able to grow many plants for long periods of time. Soils with low fertility are able to support only a limited amount of plants for short periods of time.

The capability of soils for growing agricultural crops often determines which areas of the country will be settled. Soils often determine where people will live.

Nutrients—food for plants or animals; minerals in the soil that provide food and nourishment for plants

REGIONS OF BRAZIL

Geographers use regions to describe, explain, and analyze the physical environment. In 1944 the National Geographic Council of Brazil divided Brazil into five regions: the North, the Northeast, Center West, the Southeast, and the South. Climate, soil, and natural vegetation characteristics were three of the features used to define the five regions. Because they vary from one region to another, the climate, soil, and natural vegetation of Brazil will be more easily understood if we discuss one region at a time.

Northeast

The North

Center West

Southeast

The South

20

The North—In the Rain Forest

We had been chugging slowly up the river for three hours when the storm struck. Orlando pointed out the reddening sky and warned us of the coming rain. He quickly pulled the motorboat over to the riverbank. We would wait out the rainstorm under the protective canopy of trees. In a few minutes the sky darkened to a lead gray. The temperature dropped several degrees. A cold wind swooped up the river in front of the rainstorm. A blast of wind whipped the smooth dark surface of the river into frothy whitecaps. Sheets of lightning whitened the sky. Thunder rumbled up the river.

At first only a few drops pelted the river, dimpling the dark surface. Then the full force of the rain hit. The skies opened to a torrent of rain. It beat down on the river and forest in great sheets of water. The river was hidden by a solid gray wall of rain. We were under the partial protection of the trees along the riverbank. Still the rain drummed down on the tin roof of the boat. It had such force that it drowned out the chugging motor.

As fast as it came, the storm passed. The hot sun cut through the clouds, returning the forest to a thousand shades of green. Swirling clouds of steam rose from the river as the hot sunshine returned. Orlando explained that even in the dry season the Amazon can get these sudden rainstorms. They usually last less than an hour but during the rainy season the rain can beat down steadily for days at a time. I was glad this was the dry season. This short Amazon rainstorm had been frightening enough.

While Orlando worked bailing the rainwater that had flooded the bottom of the boat, brilliant yellow butterflies the size of my hand danced around us. The forest was so shadowy I could barely see more than a few metres into the depths. Two days before, my father and I had passed over this endless green sea of rain forest. We were flying from Manaus to Codajás. This morning we'd left Codajás for the six-hour trip up the Purus River to the research station. My father called the station home for half the year. This was the first time I'd actually been in the vast Amazon rain forest. My father has spent his life studying the insects of the rain forest. However, I had always lived in Rio de Janeiro. This was the first time I had convinced my father to let me spend part of my school holidays with him at the isolated Amazon research station.

Orlando finally had the motorboat reasonably dry. He steered the boat into the main channel of the river. Once the rain stopped, the birds returned from their shelter in the trees. In front of us a pair of macaws swooped across the river. Their red, yellow, and blue tails streamed behind them. Through the thick vegetation we could see occasional glimpses of a flock of parrots. They wheeled and circled overhead. Their wings were flashes of yellow and green darting through the almost black shadows of the rain forest. Their harsh cries echoed down the still river.

Suddenly three *toninas*, Amazon river dolphins, appeared. They seemed to lead the way up the river. Their silvery skin shone in the sunlight. They were often so close I could see the patches of pink on their faces and backs. Every once in a while one of the dolphins would leap out of the water, spraying us. I thought they were merely being friendly. Orlando thought they were more interested in the fish our motorboat frightened out of the shallows along the riverbank. Dad told me later the *toninas* were once very plentiful in the Amazon rivers but now there are fewer and fewer. They are hunted in some parts of the Amazon for meat.

With the dolphins in the lead, we chugged up the river for another two hours. We passed a wall of unbroken forest. Occasionally the silver-gray skeleton of a dead tree would loom out of the forest. That was all that broke the solid wall of green. I was beginning to believe we were the only people in all of the Amazon. Suddenly a weathered building of rough boards and planks standing on stilts appeared in a small clearing hacked out of the forest. On the steps two small children shouted and waved. A man and a teenage boy worked on the shore loading bundles into a dugout canoe. They waved and shouted a greeting to Orlando and my father as we chugged by. It was hard to believe this family lived in so isolated a spot. I couldn't imagine what it would be like to live here in the middle of the rain forest, surrounded by nothing but the vast green forest.

The North

The North region includes the states of Pará, Amazonas, Acre, and Rondônia, as well as the territories of Amapá and Roraima. The major topographical features in the North are the Guiana Highlands and the Amazon Lowlands. The Amazon river system drains the entire North region.

Territory of Roraima

GUIANA HIGHLANDS

Territor of Ama

Amazonas

Pará

Acre

Rondônia

AMAZON LOWLANDS

Climate: Tropical Wet

The North region is located in the low latitudes of the world. The area between the Tropic of Cancer and the Tropic of Capricorn is called the low latitudes or sometimes the Tropics. The very warm/wet climate of the North reflects its position close to the Equator.

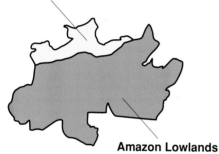

Guiana Highlands

Amazon Lowlands

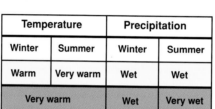

Tropical: Very Warm/Wet Climate

Equator

Tropic of Cancer
Equator
Tropic of Capricorn

	Temperature		Precipitation		
	Winter	Summer	Winter	Summer	
	Warm	Very warm	Wet	Wet	GUIANA HIGHLANDS
	Very warm		Wet	Very wet	AMAZON LOWLANDS

The North region has two types of climate: Tropical Climate and Equatorial Climate.

Tropical Climate

(Guiana Highlands)

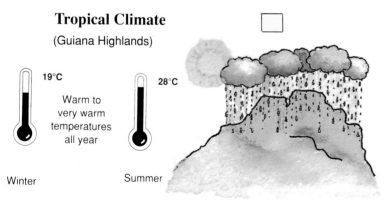

19°C

Warm to very warm temperatures all year

28°C

Winter

Summer

Yearly Rainfall: 2 000 mm

The Guiana Highlands experience a tropical climate. Temperatures for a tropical climate range from 19°C to 28°C. The higher elevation of the Guiana Highlands produces cooler temperatures than the lower elevation of the Amazon Lowlands.

Try to Imagine!

Rainfall in the Tropics is as high as 2 500 mm per year. This is higher than an average door!

Equatorial Climate

(Amazon Lowlands)

25°C

Very warm temperature all year

25°C

Winter

Summer

Yearly Rainfall: 2 500 mm

The climate of the Amazon Lowland areas of the North is equatorial. Equatorial climates are a response to low elevation and a position close to the Equator. Equatorial climates show little difference between winter and summer temperatures. Although it will often rain all through the year, equatorial climates do have a rainy season and a dry season. During the season of heavy rains, many parts of the Amazon Lowlands flood. For several months large areas of the rain forest are flooded.

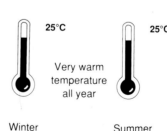

Natural Vegetation

Rain Forest

The natural vegetation of the North region is rain forest. This rain forest covers most of the North region and nearly 40% of Brazil. Since it covers the Amazon Lowlands, this area is usually called the Amazon rain forest. Rain forests consist of trees up to 70 or 80 metres high that grow so closely together their crowns form a continuous canopy of leaves.

From the air, a rain forest resembles an unbroken sea of green.

Rain forests contain an abundance of plant and animal life. The rain forest of the Amazon Lowlands has more species of trees, birds, insects, fish, animals, and plant life than any other place on earth. Scientists estimate that 700 species of mammals, 1 800 types of birds, and 1 500 species of fish live in the Amazon rain forests.

The Amazon rain forest is the world's largest remaining rain forest. Vast areas of the rain forest are currently being cleared and burned. Many people in the world are concerned about destruction of the Amazon rain forest and the effect this massive burning will have on the ecology of the world.

Emergents
(70–80 m high)

Continuous Canopy
(40–50 m high)
Broad leaf with trees that are green all year provide shade and break rainfall.

Middle layer of Trees

Lower level of Shrubs
Few plants grow on the floor of the forest because it is shaded from the sunlight.

23

Soil: Rain Forest

The soils of the rain forest in the North region appear to be soils of low fertility. Rain forest soils are very acidic and contain few nutrients. This makes them unsuitable for growing many food crops.

Rain forest soils can sustain crops on freshly cleared areas for only two or three years. After this time the nutrients in the soil will have been lost through erosion or leaching. The soil will no longer be able to grow crops. Substantial amounts of fertilizer are needed to maintain high crop yields on rain forest soils. Vast areas of the rain forest have been cleared for farming and cattle ranching. This means that knowledge of soil conditions in the North region is particularly important.

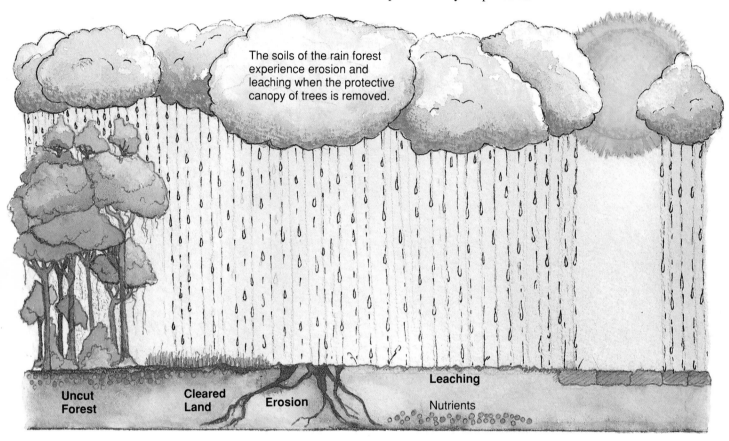

The soils of the rain forest experience erosion and leaching when the protective canopy of trees is removed.

Leaching

Nutrients

Uncut Forest　　**Cleared Land**　　**Erosion**

Erosion occurs when the heavy rains wash away the thin top layer of soil. This layer contains most of the nutrients.

The heavy rains also cause the nutrients in the soil to be washed deep into the earth far from the reach of plant roots. This process is called LEACHING.

The soils of the rain forest can also harden into brick-like blocks. This happens once the natural vegetation is removed. The soil is then exposed to repeated dry and rainy periods.

Large amounts of the rain forest are being cleared for farming and cattle ranching. Rain forest soils are of low fertility. This presents special problems for farmers and ranchers.

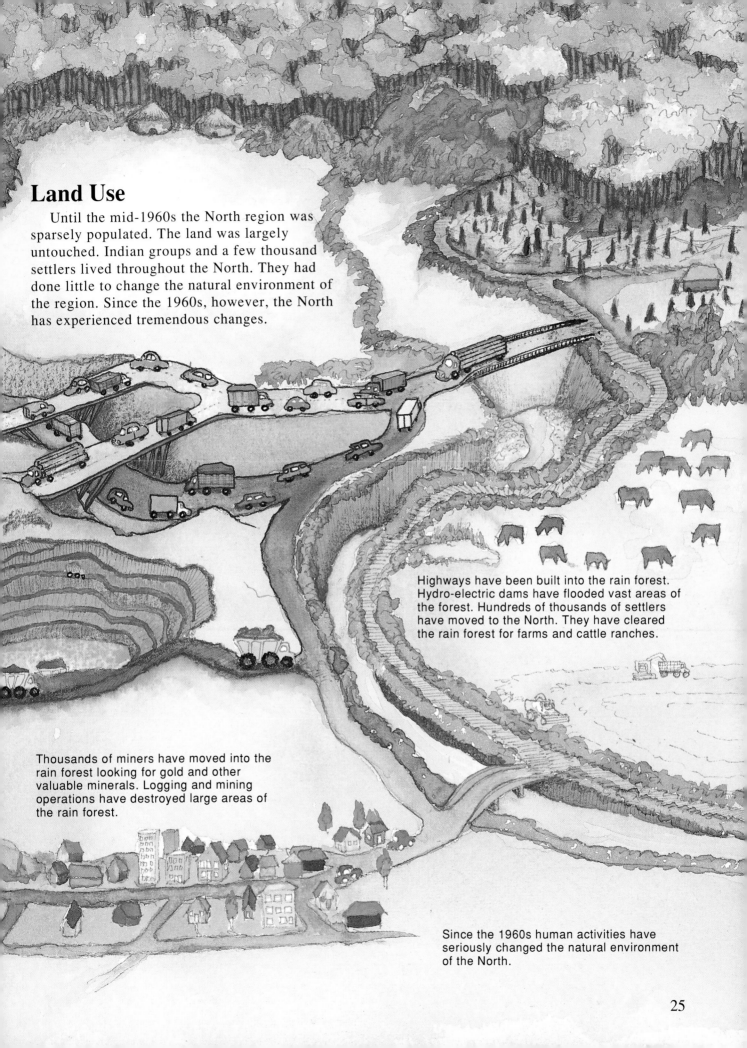

Land Use

Until the mid-1960s the North region was sparsely populated. The land was largely untouched. Indian groups and a few thousand settlers lived throughout the North. They had done little to change the natural environment of the region. Since the 1960s, however, the North has experienced tremendous changes.

Highways have been built into the rain forest. Hydro-electric dams have flooded vast areas of the forest. Hundreds of thousands of settlers have moved to the North. They have cleared the rain forest for farms and cattle ranches.

Thousands of miners have moved into the rain forest looking for gold and other valuable minerals. Logging and mining operations have destroyed large areas of the rain forest.

Since the 1960s human activities have seriously changed the natural environment of the North.

25

Center West

The Center West region includes the states of Mato Grosso, Mato Grosso do Sul, Goiás, and the Federal District of Brasília. Brasília replaced Rio de Janeiro as the capital of Brazil in 1960.

The main topographical features of the region are the high plateaus and low mountains that cover most of Mato Grosso, Goiás, and Mato Grosso do Sul. They form part of the Brazilian Highlands. The Pantanal and a small section of Amazon Lowlands in northwestern Mato Grosso are the areas of low elevation in the region.

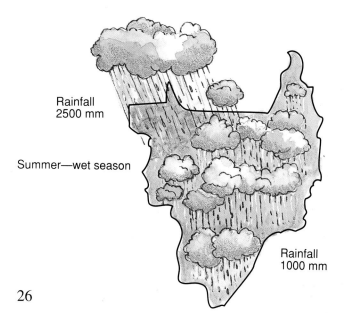

BRAZILIAN HIGHLANDS

AMAZON LOWLANDS

Mato Grosso

Goiás

Federal District of Brasília

PANTANAL

Mato Grosso do Sul

Climate: Tropical Wet & Dry

The climate of the Center West is wet-dry tropical. Wet-dry tropical climate has warm temperatures all year. It has a wet rainy season and a dry rainless season.

Temperatures for wet-dry tropical climates are generally warm all year, between 19°C and 28°C.

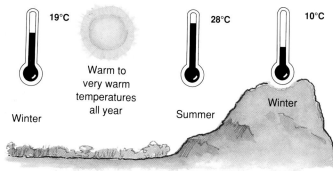

19°C

Warm to very warm temperatures all year

28°C

10°C

Winter

Winter

Summer

Winter

Places on the higher plateaus, however, can experience cooler winter temperatures. During the winter months temperatures can drop to 10°C in places.

Rainfall 2500 mm

Summer—wet season

Rainfall 1000 mm

The Center West region has a dry winter season with little rain and a wet summer season with rainy weather. The amount of rain, however, varies throughout the region. The southeastern portion of the region receives 1 000 mm while the northwest section can receive up to 2 500 mm of rain.

Brasília—number of days each month with rain

Jan	Feb	Mar	Apr	May	Jun	Jul	Aug	Sep	Oct	Nov	Dec
15	18	13	12	3	<1	<1	<1	4	16	18	21

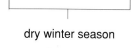

dry winter season

26

Natural Vegetation

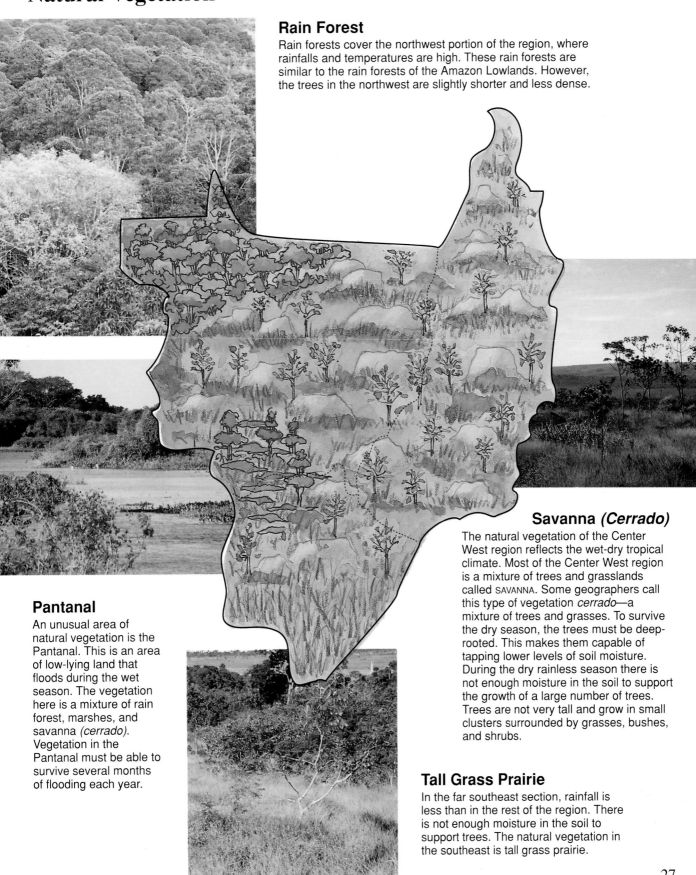

Rain Forest

Rain forests cover the northwest portion of the region, where rainfalls and temperatures are high. These rain forests are similar to the rain forests of the Amazon Lowlands. However, the trees in the northwest are slightly shorter and less dense.

Savanna *(Cerrado)*

The natural vegetation of the Center West region reflects the wet-dry tropical climate. Most of the Center West region is a mixture of trees and grasslands called SAVANNA. Some geographers call this type of vegetation *cerrado*—a mixture of trees and grasses. To survive the dry season, the trees must be deep-rooted. This makes them capable of tapping lower levels of soil moisture. During the dry rainless season there is not enough moisture in the soil to support the growth of a large number of trees. Trees are not very tall and grow in small clusters surrounded by grasses, bushes, and shrubs.

Pantanal

An unusual area of natural vegetation is the Pantanal. This is an area of low-lying land that floods during the wet season. The vegetation here is a mixture of rain forest, marshes, and savanna *(cerrado)*. Vegetation in the Pantanal must be able to survive several months of flooding each year.

Tall Grass Prairie

In the far southeast section, rainfall is less than in the rest of the region. There is not enough moisture in the soil to support trees. The natural vegetation in the southeast is tall grass prairie.

27

Soil Conditions

The soils of the Center West region are low in nutrients. They are easily eroded by wind and rain once the covering vegetation of trees and grasses is removed. The soil of the Center West region requires heavy fertilization to continue to produce high crop yields.

Uncleared   Cleared   Wind Erosion   Heavy Fertilizaton   High Yield Crops

Some areas of the savanna (*cerrado*) have been overcropped and overgrazed by cattle. They are showing signs of desertification. DESERTIFICATION is the process where land changes to become more like a desert. Vegetation becomes sparse. Desertification occurs when soil loses its ability to support plant growth.

Land Use

Since the 1960s the Center West region has experienced increased settlement and agricultural development. A new highway has been built across the region. A new capital city, Brasília, has been constructed in Goiás State. These have encouraged settlement and development of the region. There are, however, consequences of this development.

Large areas of the rain forest and savanna (*cerrado*) are being cleared for farms and cattle ranches. Erosion and heavy use of fertilizers is seriously affecting the physical environment of the region. Gold mining in the region has also caused some environmental damage.

Center West—Changing Landscape *(Factual Narrative)*

The Cessna skimmed low over the river. I could spot several groups of 10 and 20 alligators sunning themselves on the sandbanks. The trees lining the riverbank were so filled with birds they looked as if they were covered with a blanket of snow. This was the low-lying land in southern Mato Grosso called the Pantanal. During the rainy season the area is flooded. The floodwaters drain down from higher land in the northern plateaus. These flooded marshlands provide an ideal breeding ground for thousands of birds.

Turning away from the river, my uncle made a low pass over one of the many marshes. Below us were hundreds of ducks and wading birds. They were foraging for food in the shallow water-filled fields. A particularly spectacular sight was a flock of 40 **tuyuyú** storks. As the Cessna turned for another pass of the marsh, the noise of the engine startled the storks. Suddenly the entire flock skittered across the marsh and took flight.

Flapping their huge wings, the storks rose swiftly into the air directly in front of the Cessna. The sudden movement of the storks sent the other birds swirling skyward. In a matter of moments the air filled with birds. Frantically my uncle pulled the plane's nose higher into the air. He banked sharply away from the circling birds. An encounter with birds this close to the ground could be extremely dangerous. The birds could easily crash into the motor or go through the windscreen. Luckily my uncle was able to manoeuvre the plane away from the birds. Despite the danger, the sight of hundreds of birds circling and wheeling below us was an incredibly thrilling sight. As the birds gradually settled back onto the marshes, I wondered if they would be able to survive the drastic changes going on in the region. This was my first trip back to Mato Grosso in 15 years. I'd been overwhelmed by the changes in the countryside.

I'd expected Mato Grosso to have changed. But I hadn't expected the dramatic differences I'd found. The changes were noticeable as soon as the plane flew over the plateaus west of Goiás. I had last flown over this region 15 years earlier. Then the view from the plane had been one of rivers, rain forest, and grassland. On the flight this time I could still see the rivers twisting like immense gray serpents across the plateaus. But I could also see large areas where grassland and rain forest had been cleared.

In the last decade thousands of hectares of grassland and rain forest have been cleared. This makes way for highways, mines, pasture land for cattle, and fields for soybeans, rice, and coffee. During the dry season there is smoke from the burning of trees and grass. It is so thick that it closes many airports in the Center West region.

Fifteen years ago most roads in the Center West region were dirt. Now I could see many new paved highways stretching out in all directions across the plateaus. Eventually they disappeared into the distant brown hills. Even the 1 800-kilometre BR-364 Highway from Brasília to Porto Velho is paved.

At last we landed in Cuiabá. I found that it had changed even more than the countryside. I remembered Cuiabá as a small, dusty frontier town. I was surprised to find a modern airport. My aunt was waiting with an air-conditioned car to take us to a luxurious new hotel in the center of the city. Instead of traveling on dusty dirt roads, we drove along paved streets filled with new cars, jeeps, buses, and motorcycles. We even had to negotiate a traffic jam.

Fifteen years ago it had been common to see groups of gold and diamond miners and ranch hands strolling down the dirt street of Cuiabá. They wore guns and holsters. As a thirteen-year-old from Rio de Janeiro, I had been dazzled by the exciting frontier life in Cuiabá. Today Cuiabá is a bustling business center with a population of nearly 200 000. Everywhere I looked there seemed to be new office towers, hotels, banks, theaters, apartment blocks, and department stores. This was definitely a different Cuiabá!

The Rio de Janeiro newspapers often contain stories of the successful new cattle ranches, soybean farms, and gold discoveries in Mato Grosso. It is exciting to visit what once was an empty and undeveloped region. Today it is one of Brazil's most prosperous areas.

Tuyuyú—pronounced two-you-you

The South

The South region includes the states of Paraná, Santa Catarina, and Rio Grande do Sul.

There are two main topographical features of this region. The high plateaus of the Brazilian Highlands cover the interior of these states. The coastal plain is along the eastern coast.

Climate: Humid Subtropical

The South region is located south of the Tropic of Capricorn. This places the South region in the mid-latitudes. The climate of the South is called humid subtropical. It reflects a location farther from the Equator.

A small section of northwest Paraná state has a wet-dry tropical climate with a dry rainless season.

The South region experiences warm summer temperatures up to 28°C. There are noticeably cooler winter temperatures.

Rainfall through most of the South region is spread fairly evenly throughout the year.

SUMMER   FALL   WINTER   SPRING

Jan   Feb   Mar   Apr   May   Jun   Jul   Aug   Sep   Oct   Nov   Dec

1 000 to 2 000 mm each year

Frosts and even light snowfalls can occur in the plateau and mountain areas.

The winds from the South Pole area sweep along the southern coast during the winter months. They produce some of the cooler temperatures. Winter temperatures in the South can drop to below 10°C. The mountains and plateau areas of the South have cooler temperatures because of the higher elevations.

Natural Vegetation

Subtropical Forests and Grasslands

The natural vegetation of the South reflects cooler temperatures and higher elevations. On the higher plateaus the most noticeable vegetation is the araucaria pine. This tall, unusual-looking pine once covered all the plateau areas of the South.

In the far south of the region the major vegetation is grasslands called tall grass prairie. These vast stretches of grasslands extend well into Uruguay and Argentina.

The natural vegetation along the coastal plain is a mixture of rain forest and palms. Much of this vegetation has been cleared for growing coffee and other food crops.

Logging operations in the last century removed most of the pine forests. Only few isolated stands of these pines remain.

Soils

The South contains some of the most fertile soil in Brazil. The rich brown soil is high in nutrients. It will grow a wide variety of crops, from soybeans to wheat. It is particularly suitable for growing coffee.

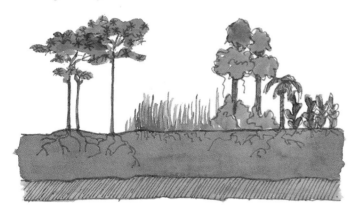

The rich soil of the South also produces some of South America's finest grasslands for cattle ranching.

Land Use

The South is one of the largest agricultural areas in Brazil. Coffee, soybeans, and wheat are grown in northern Paraná. Tobacco, potatoes, wheat, and a variety of fruits such as apples and grapes are grown in Santa Catarina and Rio Grande do Sul. The main activity in the far South is cattle ranching. Much of the natural vegetation of this region has been cleared for agriculture and to provide timber.

The plateau region of Paraná has a combination of cool temperatures and rich soil. This makes it one of the best coffee growing regions in the world.

The Southeast

BRAZILIAN HIGHLANDS

Minas Gerais

Espírito Santo

COASTAL PLAIN

Rio de Janeiro

São Paulo

The Southeast region includes the states of Espírito Santo, Minas Gerais, Rio de Janeiro, and São Paulo.

The main topographical features of the Southeast are the coastal plain, and the mountains and high plateaus of the Brazilian Highlands.

Climate: Tropical

The climate of the Southeast is tropical. It has warm temperatures most of the year and heavy rainfall. There are, however, climate variations in the region. These reflect differences in elevation, closeness to the Atlantic Ocean, and distance from the Equator.

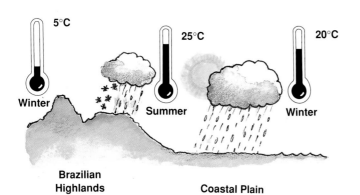

5°C Winter

25°C Summer

20°C Winter

Brazilian Highlands

Coastal Plain

Much of Minas Gerais State and the western portion of São Paulo State have a wet-dry tropical climate.

In the highlands of Minas Gerais and São Paulo, frosts are common. Temperatures may drop below 5°C during the winter months. There were light snowfalls and heavy frosts in São Paulo State during the winter of 1988, for example. They ruined much of the year's coffee crop.

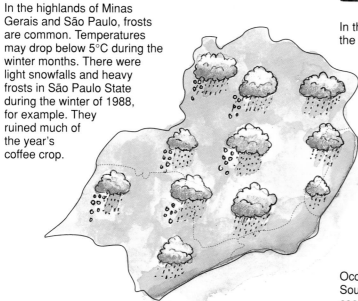

In the mountains and plateaus of the Brazilian Highlands, the higher elevations can produce a subtropical climate.

The coastal plain of the Southeast has heavy rainfall. Its warm temperatures generally do not drop below 20°C even in the winter months.

During the summer the coastal plain has slightly cooler temperatures than areas inland. This is caused by the cooling effect of the ocean winds.

Occasionally cool winter winds from the South Pole area sweep along the southeast coast, causing temperatures to drop to 15°C.

32

Natural Vegetation

The areas of Minas Gerais and São Paulo State with a wet-dry tropical climate produce savanna (cerrado) vegetation.

On the plateaus and mountains the rain forest is mixed with deciduous trees, palms, and some evergreen trees.

Along the coastal plain the natural vegetation is a mixture of rain forest and palms.

The rain forests in the Southeast region are similar to the rain forests in the Amazon Lowlands. However, the trees in the Southeast are shorter and less dense.

Soil

The soil along the coastal plain is very fertile. It is heavily used for agriculture. The plateau regions of São Paulo State have very fertile soil. It is ideal for the cultivation of coffee and other food crops. However, once the covering of natural vegetation on the steep hillsides is removed, the soil is easily eroded by the winds and heavy rains.

The soil of the savanna (cerrado) is low in nutrients. It requires extensive fertilization to maintain high crop yields. With fertilization, however, it becomes rich and can produce a wide variety of crops.

Much of the area around São Paulo and Rio de Janeiro has been extensively eroded. Now it is no longer able to support crops.

Land Use

Little remains of the natural vegetation in the Southeast region. Most of it has been cut down for timber or replaced by agriculture. The cultivation of coffee in São Paulo State and Rio de Janeiro State in the 1800s resulted in the clearing of vast areas of the forest for coffee plantations. Large cities have grown and industries have developed in the Southeast region. This has resulted in a reduction of the natural vegetation.

The Northeast

The Northeast region includes the large states of Bahia, Piauí, and Maranhão as well as the small states of Ceará, Rio Grande do Norte, Paraíba, Pernambuco, Alagoas, and Sergipe.

The main topographic features of the Northeast region are the wide coastal plain, a small section of Amazon Lowlands, and the mountains and plateaus of the Brazilian Highlands.

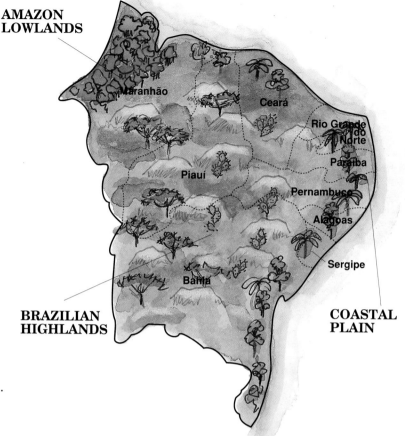

AMAZON LOWLANDS

Maranhão

Ceará

Rio Grande do Norte

Paraíba

Piauí

Pernambuco

Alagoas

Sergipe

Bahia

BRAZILIAN HIGHLANDS

COASTAL PLAIN

Climate

Tropical Climate

The Northeast region is very large. It contains several different climates.

The northern states are close to the Equator. They have a tropical climate with warm temperatures and high rainfall.

Much of the southeastern portion of the region has a tropical climate. This means temperatures are warm and rainfall is abundant.

Areas in the higher mountains and plateaus of the Brazilian Highlands have tropical climates with cool winter temperatures.

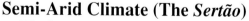

- Equatorial
- Tropical
- Semi-Arid
- Coastal

Semi-Arid Climate (The *Sertão*)

The interior of the region is called the SERTÃO. It has a semi-arid climate. A semi-arid climate has very warm temperatures and a long dry season. The dry season in the *sertão* lasts from July to January. The annual rainfall is less than 800 mm. There are frequently years when there is no rain. A long period with no rain is called a DROUGHT.

Sertão—pronounced sair-tow to rhyme with now

34

Natural Vegetation

Rain Forests
Along the coastal plain the natural vegetation is rain forests mixed with many varieties of palms. Part of the Amazon rain forest extends across the far north of the region. The Amazon rain forest is more dense than the rain forest along the coast. The Amazon rain forest contains taller trees.

Caatinga
In the semi-arid interior the natural vegetation is CAATINGA. *Caatinga* vegetation is a combination of small bushes, grasses, cacti, and thornbushes.

Soil
The soil of the Northeast region, especially the soil of the coastal plain, is very fertile. Even the soils of the semi-arid interior can produce good crops when they are properly irrigated. The soils of the interior are easily eroded by wind and rain if the covering of natural vegetation is removed.

Land Use

The Northeast is one of the oldest settled regions in Brazil. The land here has been used for agriculture and cattle ranching for hundreds of years. The first sugar cane plantations were established in this region as early as 1600. Much of the natural vegetation was removed many years ago. This provided timber and fuel for sugar cane plantations. It also made room for farms and cattle ranches. Much of the interior has been overgrazed by cattle and overplanted. It can no longer be used for farming or ranching.

The frequent droughts of the semi-arid interior have also made life very difficult for millions of small farmers in the Northeast. Many of the people in the Northeast region have left the interior. They have moved to cities along the coast or to other regions in search of jobs and farmlands.

The Northeast—*Sertão*

(Factual Narrative)

A long drought lasting from 1979 to 1984 forced thousands of people to leave the interior of the Northeast region.

The blazing midday sun beat down on the battered truck rattling along the dirt road. Claudio shielded his eyes against the bright sun. He searched the horizon. The landscape flashing past was familiar enough but they were beyond any landmarks Claudio knew. This was the farthest he had ever been from his small village in southern Ceará.

Suddenly the truck began jerking forward. Black smoked sputtered from the tailpipe. A few moments later the truck shuddered to a halt. The cloud of thick brown dust that had trailed behind slowly engulfed the truck. It covered the 30 men standing and sitting in the open back. The driver jumped out angrily, hitting the side of the truck several times with his straw hat. He flung up the hood. Then he shouted at his helper for the tool kit.

The men in the back of the truck jumped off. This was an unexpected opportunity to stretch their legs and escape the dust. A few men managed to squeeze into the small patch of shade created by the truck. Most just stood or squatted by the roadside. They talked or watched the driver bent over the engine.

Around them were hot, dry, scrub grasslands of cactus, thornbushes, and a few scattered, leafless trees. They seemed to stretch endlessly to the flat brown hills in the far distance. This was the *sertão*, the dry backlands of the Northeast interior.

The *sertão* occupies the interior of the Northeast. It has a small amount of rainfall. This comes at irregular times. Some years the rains come during a short rainy season. Then the corn and bean crops grow well. The brown, dry land turns green. The small herds of cattle and goats grow fat on the new grass. Leaves appear on the short, twisted trees and thornbushes. But most years in the *sertão* are not good. Either the rains come at the wrong time or not at all. Every eight to fifteen years a devastating drought hits the *sertão*. These droughts can last several years. That was the problem now. There had been no rain in the *sertão* for four years.

At first Claudio's family had survived on their small patch of beans and corn. They had a few scrawny chickens, and made a little money working on a cotton plantation. In the last six months, however, there had been no work. The long drought had finally forced Claudio and his neighbor, Luis, to leave their small farms. They decided to try their luck finding a job in Fortaleza, on the coast. They weren't the only ones forced by desperation to leave the *sertão*. The long droughts in the *sertão* regularly force the **Nordestinos** to leave their homes. They migrate to other parts of Brazil to look for work and to outwait the droughts.

For Claudio, Luis, and the other men from southern Ceará, it was a week's trip to Fortaleza. The first four days had been on the dirt roads of the interior. By nightfall today they would reach the paved highways nearer the coast. Here the land received more rain. It was always green with palms and sugar cane. Claudio and Luis had never seen this part of Brazil. They had never been farther than twenty kilometres from their small farms and village. For many of the men, however, this was the second or third time they had been forced to leave the *sertão*. Despite the harsh life in the *sertão*, Nordestinos fiercely love the land. They always hoped to return when they had saved enough money or when the rains returned. This was the hope Luis and Claudio held. They would work for a year in the city. Then they hoped they could return.

It was over an hour before the driver was able to prod and wire some life back into the truck. Reluctantly Claudio and the other men climbed into the back. In a few minutes the truck was once again rattling along the dirt road. Claudio watched the road, the distant hills, and the *sertão* disappear in the thick brown dust.

Nordestino—a person from the Northeast

CHAPTER SUMMARY

Brazil is located in the Southern Hemisphere and is the largest country in South America. Brazil has many connections with the countries in South America, North America, Europe, Asia, and Africa.

Brazil's five regions have distinctive physical features. The topography of the Northeast, South, Southeast, and Center West consists of coastal plains, low mountains, and plateaus. Lowlands cover nearly all of the North region. Brazil has very few high mountains compared to other places in South America.

Nearly all the regions in Brazil have a tropical climate with warm temperatures throughout the year and heavy rainfalls. Many regions experience a wet season of heavy rains and a dry season of little rain. The natural vegetation of the five regions reflects the tropical climate. All of the North region and parts of the other regions are rain forest. Savanna (*cerrado*) vegetation is a combination of trees and grasslands that covers large portions of the Center West region. Much of Southern Brazil is grasslands. A large area of Northeast Brazil is semi-arid *caatinga* vegetation: small bushes, grasses, cacti, and thornbushes. Soils along the coastal plain and plateau areas of the South and Southeast are very fertile. The soils of the North are low in nutrients.

Large areas of the rain forest and savanna (*cerrado*) vegetation in the North and Center West regions have been removed for farms, cattle ranches, logging and mining operations, and hydro-electric dams. Many people are concerned that the development of natural resources in the North and Center West regions will seriously damage the physical environment of Brazil.

Natural Resources and Industries

NATURAL RESOURCES are the raw materials of the environment. Air, land, soil, water, mineral deposits, oil, animals, fish, and natural vegetation are considered natural resources. Regional natural resources are being used to develop different types of industries throughout Brazil.

Bauxite—mineral containing aluminum

Primary Industries

Primary industries take their products from the environment. Fishing, forestry, agriculture, and mining are all examples of primary industries. In recent years the Center West and North regions have been the center of new forestry, mining, and agricultural development. The North, for example, has some of the world's largest deposits of iron ore, gold, tin, copper, and **bauxite**. The vast rain forests and rivers of the Amazon give Brazil one of the largest hydro-electric potentials and forest resources in the world.

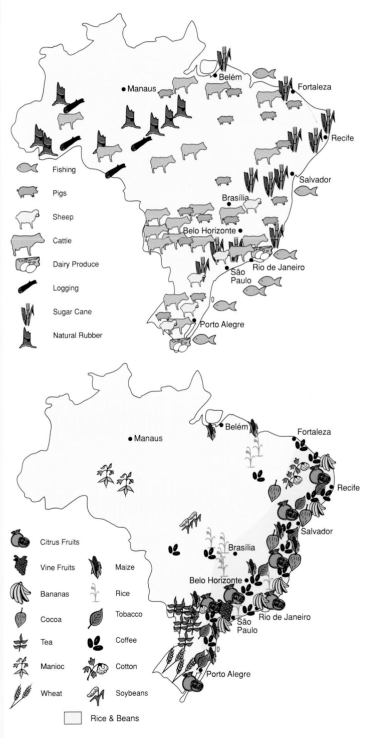

Fishing

Pigs

Sheep

Cattle

Dairy Produce

Logging

Sugar Cane

Natural Rubber

Citrus Fruits

Vine Fruits

Bananas

Cocoa

Tea

Manioc

Wheat

Maize

Rice

Tobacco

Coffee

Cotton

Soybeans

Rice & Beans

37

Industry In Brazil

Symbol	Industry		Symbol	Industry
	Diamonds			
	Timber (paper & pulp)			
	Oilfields			
	Oil Refineries			
	Leather Goods			
	Sugar Refining			
	Rubber Products			Chemicals
	Iron & Steel			Mechanical Engineering
	Gold			Textiles
	Motor Vehicles			Shoes
	Shipbuilding			Coal Mining

Belém
Fortaleza
Manaus
Recife
Salvador
Brasília
Belo Horizonte
Rio de Janeiro
São Paulo
Porto Alegre

Secondary Industries

SECONDARY INDUSTRIES use the products from primary industries and manufacture them into finished goods. Some secondary industries manufacture goods for other secondary industries. Most of Brazil's secondary industries are located in the Southeast region near São Paulo and Rio de Janeiro or in the large cities along the eastern coast. Transporting raw materials the great distances from the North and Center West regions to the industries along the eastern coast presents many problems.

Service Industries

SERVICE INDUSTRIES provide services that help in the running of other industries, or make our lives more pleasant. The greatest concentrations of services are in the large cities along the eastern coast. Service industries employ more and more of the Brazilian workforce each year. The Brazilian government is one of the largest service employers in the country.

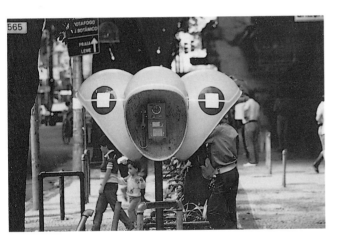

Quaternary Industries

QUATERNARY INDUSTRIES include people who plan a country's economy, provide financial advice, and make investments, or are scientists who research and develop new products. Most of Brazil's quaternary industry is located in the universities and financial centers of Brazil's large cities such as Rio de Janeiro and São Paulo, or in the capital city, Brasília.

CHAPTER REVIEW

For Your Notebook

1. In your notebook, copy and complete the retrieval chart* on the right. Use information gathered from this chapter.

2.  Using the information from the retrieval chart on page 3, develop a concluding statement to the problem: **What are the Physical Features of Brazil?** Your concluding statement may be in the form of a short paragraph. A sample opening sentence for your paragraph might be: Brazil has a varied physical environment.

3. There is a map on the inside of the front cover of this book. Use it as you make a list of the physical features of South America. Underline the physical features found in Brazil.

Exploring Further

1. Using the information gathered from this chapter, prepare a travel brochure for each of Brazil's five regions. Fold paper as shown. Include information about the topography, climate, and natural vegetation. List any information that would attract tourists to the region. Sketches and maps would also be useful additions to brochures.

2. Compare the physical features of Brazil with the country where you live. Comparing shows how places are alike and how places are different. Copy and use the Venn Diagram* shown on this page. List in A and B the physical features of Brazil and your country that are different. In C list the physical features common to both countries. Evaluate the information. Are the physical features of your country more similar to or more different from those in Brazil?

Retrieval Chart

REGION	Location	Topography	Climate	Natural Vegetation	Soils	Rivers
1.						
2.						
3.						
4.						
5.						

Travel Brochures

Venn Diagram

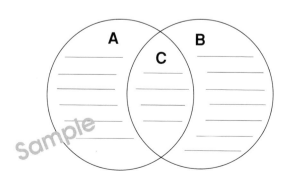

---

*Retrieval Chart/outline map/Venn Diagram available as blackline masters in the Teacher Resource Package.

40

4.

Decision Making

Decision making is an activity to resolve an issue. An issue is a discussion or disagreement about possible courses of action. In decision making, a choice is eventually made from among several alternative plans or courses of actions. As you work through this text, you will be asked to use the decision making strategy to resolve the issue:
To what extent do you think Brazil considers its physical environment as it develops its natural resources?

Decision making involves
- considering alternatives,
- predicting the possible consequences of the alternatives,
- evaluating the advantages and disadvantages of the alternatives, and
- eventually choosing the best course of action. The steps in a decision making strategy are shown in the chart on the right.

You will be asked to develop alternatives. Then you will evaluate the advantages and disadvantages of consequences resulting from those alternatives. At the end of the text you will be asked to make a decision on the issue. You should be prepared to justify your decision. Then you should state what plan of action would best support your decision.

Getting Started

Copy and use the Decision Making Form* shown on this page. The issue is already written at the top of the form. Brainstorm alternative courses of action. Predict the possible consequences of those alternatives. Consider what action plans might be put into place to support each of the alternatives. Record your ideas on the Decision Making Form.

Decision making is a continual evaluation of new information. Read through the next chapters. Consider how the information presented may be used to develop alternative courses of action or to evaluate consequences.

A Model for Making Decisions

- Identify an issue.
- Identify possible alternatives.
- Devise a plan for research. Gather, organize, and interpret information.
- Using collected information, evaluate the alternatives.
- Make a decision. Plan or take action on the decision.
- Evaluate the process, the decision, and the action.

Each time you see the Decision Making logo in this book, you will be asked to continue the Decision Making process as outlined in the above model.

There are many excellent decision making models you may use. This textbook uses the above model for making decisions. You may either use this model or any other model that you prefer. As you get more practice in decision making, you may wish to design your own model.

Decision Making Form

Issue: To what extent do you think Brazil considers its physical environment as it develops its natural resources?			
Alternatives	Consequences (Pros and Cons)		Action Plan
1.	+		
	−		
2.	+		
	−		
3.	+		
	−		

*Decision Making Form available as black-line master in the Teacher Resource Package.

PART II:
Settlement Patterns 1500–1890

CHAPTER 2
People and
Their Environment

SETTLEMENT PATTERNS show where people live and what use they make of the natural or physical environment. Geographers try to understand the factors that influence the location of settlements, why settlement patterns change over time, and how human settlement activities affect the natural environment.

The early settlement of Brazil was influenced by factors of physical and human geography. The physical environment provided natural vegetation, agricultural land, climate, water, minerals, and other useful items. Characteristics of human geography such as economics, politics, and religion also affected the location and activities of the early settlements in Brazil.

1. Who were the first inhabitants of Brazil?
2. What use did these first inhabitants make of the natural environment? How did these first inhabitants affect the natural environment?
3. When did Portuguese explorers come to Brazil?
4. Where were the first Portuguese settlements? What use did the Portuguese make of the natural environment?
5. What factors influenced the settlement of Brazil by the Portuguese?
6. What effect did the Portuguese settlements have on the natural environment of Brazil?
7. What effect did the Portuguese have on the natives of Brazil?
8. What settlement patterns were established in Brazil from 1500 to 1890?

42

Problem Solving

Problem Solving Strategy*

1. Explore possible answers to the question:

   What has been the interaction between the early settlements of Brazil and the physical features?

2. Develop a hypothesis. The chart on the right indicates some of the reasons for early settlements in Brazil. Predict how these early settlements might have altered Brazil's physical environment.

3. There are many ways of organizing ideas and information. For this problem solving activity, organize your ideas by copying and using the Fishbone Chart** shown at the bottom of this page. Your teacher will explain how to record information on a fishbone chart. The large "bones" of the fish are the main events and the smaller "bones" are the details.

4. At the end of the chapter you will be asked to use the information you have collected. Make a concluding statement about how the early settlement of Brazil altered the physical environment.

Fishbone Chart

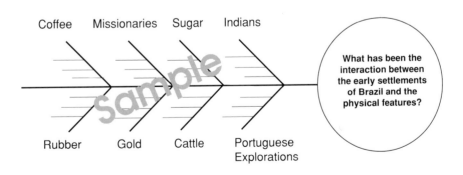

Coffee   Missionaries   Sugar   Indians

Sample

Rubber   Gold   Cattle   Portuguese Explorations

What has been the interaction between the early settlements of Brazil and the physical features?

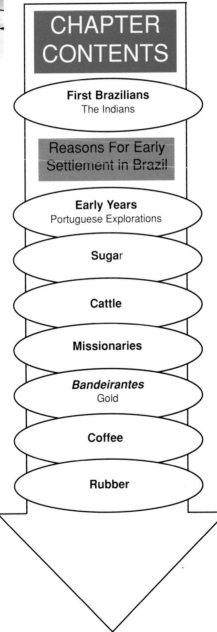

CHAPTER CONTENTS

First Brazilians
The Indians

Reasons For Early Settlement in Brazil

Early Years
Portuguese Explorations

Sugar

Cattle

Missionaries

Bandeirantes
Gold

Coffee

Rubber

---

* Refer to page 3 for problem solving strategy details.
** Fishbone Chart available as black-line master in the Teacher Resource Package.

THE FIRST BRAZILIANS

The original inhabitants of what is now Brazil were groups of Amerindians. AMERINDIAN refers to the native groups who lived throughout North and South America. It is estimated that the entire Indian population in Brazil was four million in 1500. This was when the first Europeans came to Brazil.

Indian Settlements

Brazilian Indians lived in villages throughout the rain forests and along the rivers and seacoasts. The style of Indian villages varied throughout Brazil. However, it was common in many Indian villages for several families to live together in a longhouse made of palm thatch and poles. In some villages individual families lived in small palm and thatch homes. Indian houses were often built around a cleared area of ground. This open area was used for group gatherings, meetings, and special village celebrations.

The availability of food was a factor in determining the size of Indian villages. Along the main rivers and seacoasts, where food was plentiful, the villages often had populations of

1 000 to 2 000 people. In the rain forests, food was more difficult to obtain. Indian villages there had populations of 100 to 200 people. Some villages in the Amazon rain forest consisted of only one extended family with 15 to 100 people.

Indian villages were usually located many kilometres apart. The Indians' means of obtaining food by hunting, fishing, gathering, and farming required large areas of land. Indians from one village often had little contact with other villages.

Occasionally, however, Indian villagers fought one another over good hunting, fishing, or farming areas. Sometimes Indian groups raided other villages. They captured slaves and

food. Indians living along the main rivers and seacoasts had little friendly contact with each other. Indians living deep in the Amazon rain forests were even more isolated. Many Indian groups knew of the existence of other people in the rain forests. However, most never made contact with anyone outside their own village.

Some Indian groups in Brazil shared a common language and CULTURE or way of life. But many Indian groups developed their own distinctive languages and customs. These were often very different from other Brazilian Indian groups. The lack of contact between Indian groups resulted in individual groups developing their own languages, religious beliefs, and social customs.

Indians and the Physical Environment

The native Brazilians lived as **nomadic** tribes. They depended on the forests and rivers to meet all of their needs. The forests provided the natives with material for houses, canoes, sleeping hammocks, clothing, bows and arrows, axes, and other tools. Forest plants also provided the Indians with a vast array of medicines. Indians did fish and hunt. However, most relied on gathering nuts, fruits, and insects in the forests and growing vegetables in small garden plots for food.

Nomadic—moving from place to place

Manioc
Manioc (also called cassava) is a plant with a root something like a sweet potato. Manioc roots are grated, pressed to remove all liquid, and then roasted to produce a starchy flour. Tapioca is also made from manioc.

Slash-and-Burn Agriculture
Most Indian groups living in the Brazilian rain forests practiced a farming method called "slash-and-burn." This type of agriculture involved cutting down and burning the trees. Soils in the rain forest do not contain many nutrients. Fertilizer provided by the ash helped increase the nutrients in the soil. Crops were planted among the charred trunks and roots of the trees. The main food crop grown by the Indians was manioc. They also grew a variety of crops including sweet potatoes, bananas, beans, squash, and corn.

Every two or three years the Indians abandoned one garden plot and cleared a new area. They repeated the process of cutting, burning, and planting. Slash-and-burn agriculture is often called shifting agriculture because the garden plots are constantly being moved.

The Indians would regularly abandon an entire garden plot area and move to a new location in the forest. At this new location, the cycle of cutting, burning, planting, and harvesting would continue. Finally the soils in that location could no longer produce sufficient crops.

Cutting and Burning

Planting

Harvesting

45

Amazon Indians Today

There are many Indian groups living in the Amazon rain forest.* The struggle of two Indian groups to defend their land against development and settlement has recently attracted world attention. The **Yanomami** and the Kayapó are often mentioned in North American newspapers and on television. The map indicates where these groups live in the Amazon rain forest.

The Yanomami

Yanomami are a group of people living in the highland areas on the border between Brazil and Venezuela. The Yanomami live in one of the most remote locations in the Amazon rain forest. In the past, the Yanomami have had little contact with the outside world or other Indian groups. They are thought to be the largest group of Indians in the Amazon that still follow **traditional** ways of life.

The way of life of the Yanomami centers on the forest and the rivers. The Yanomami feed themselves mainly from garden plots they clear in the rain forest. Their main food crops are bananas, **plantains**, and sweet manioc. As well as tending the garden plots, the men hunt for birds, monkeys, and small forest animals. They use darts and arrows poisoned with **curare**. This is a poison made from a rain forest vine. Curare makes the muscles of the animal relax. The animal falls from the trees or dies when the lung muscles are unable to function.

The women fish in the rivers. They gather fruits, nuts, and insects from the forest. The nuts and insects are an important source of protein for the Yanomami.

All the Yanomami in a village live in one large building called a *shabono*. It is built around a central clearing. Each Yanomami family has an area inside the *shabono* for their cooking fires and sleeping hammocks.

Contact with other cultures in recent years has begun to change the Yanomami way of life. Guns, axes, and knives brought by missionaries, miners, loggers, and settlers have changed how the Yanomami live. This contact has also brought epidemics of diseases previously unknown to the Yanomami. Hundreds of Yanomami have been killed by measles and influenza. These diseases were brought into their land by the settlers and miners.

Since the 1970s Yanomami territories have been exposed to greater activity. Road builders, settlers, and gold miners want Yanomami land. In the 1980s this activity increased with the discovery of large gold and tin deposits in the heart of Yanomami territory. The Yanomami have begun to speak out about what is happening to them. They have joined with several Brazilian and international human rights organizations. They are campaigning for recognition of their right to keep their land free from mines and settlers.

There are often violent clashes between the Yanomami and gold miners, road builders, and settlers. You may have seen stories about these clashes in North American newspapers.

Yanomami—pronounced yan-oh-mam-ee
Traditional—based on the beliefs, customs, and stories that are passed on from one generation to another
Plantains —an edible fruit similar to a banana
Curare —pronounced kyu-ra-reh

---

* Brazilian scientists estimate that there are more than 180 different Indian groups living in the Amazon rain forest. These groups often consist of less than 200 people. They have their own distinctive languages and customs. The actual number of Indian groups living in the rain forest is difficult to determine because some areas of the rain forest are still unexplored by people from the outside world. There may be many other groups living in the more remote areas of the rain forest. Two Indian groups are presented on pages 46 and 47. You may wish to independently research the lifestyles of other Indian groups in Brazil.

The Kayapó

The Kayapó are a group of people living in the rain forest at the very center of Brazil. Like the Yanomami, the Kayapó have had clashes with miners, loggers, cattle ranchers, and settlers moving onto their lands. New roads are now reaching into land that was once extremely inaccessible to other peoples. Rough dirt landing strips for helicopters and light aircraft are being cleared in even the most remote rain forest locations.

As with all Amazon Indian groups, the life of the Kayapó is closely linked to the rain forest and the rivers. When the forest and rivers are changed, so are the Kayapó. More and more of the Amazon rain forest is cleared by settlers, miners, loggers, and cattle ranchers, or flooded by hydro-electric dams. The Kayapó have become determined to keep control of their lands. They want to keep their forest intact and uncut. Several Kayapó groups have taken over gold mining areas. They have evicted the miners.

Recently the Kayapó were involved in an international demonstration in Altamira to protest the proposed building of hydro-electric dams on the Xingu River. This demonstration was the first time Brazilian Indians and **international environmentalists** gathered together to protest what was happening to Indian lands. One Kayapó leader, Chief Payakan, has toured Canada and the United States several times. He was campaigning for international support to save Indian lands from development. The Kayapó are often featured in television and magazine news stories because they are using modern tools such as video cameras, tape recorders, airplanes, and motor boats. They want to keep control of their lands and protect their traditional way of life. The photo shows several Kayapó at the Altamira meeting.*

Kayapó—pronounced k-eye-a-poh
International environmentalists—people from all over the world who are concerned about protecting and preserving life on the planet

* The hydro-electric issue will be examined again on pages 158 and 167.

Poison Fishing

In the darkness the Kayapó men left their village. They paddled their narrow dugout canoes up the river. They paddled in quick short bursts that sent the canoes darting silently over the dark water. Their strokes barely rippled the smooth black surface.

The river where the Kayapó lived was a narrow, watery passage. It made tunnels through the thick Amazon rain forest. For two hours the Kayapó silently paddled through these dark tunnels. Massive tree roots reached out into the water, forming small twisted islands. Above them the thick foliage of the trees blocked the sky and stars. By dawn the Kayapó had reached a narrow, reedy inlet branching off from the main river.

In the early morning darkness the Kayapó silently left the canoes. They carried a fence of reeds and branches to the entrance of the inlet. Yesterday morning a group of Kayapó had built a fish trap in the inlet. They had constructed a fence of branches across the entrance to the inlet. They left only one small opening. Now they used the second reed fence to close the opening. The fish trap was closed.

Once the entrance to the fish trap had been closed, the Indians broke their silence. As they strung their hammocks between the trees, they shouted to each other. They laughed and teased the young boys organizing the campfires. Laying back in the hammocks the older, married Kayapó men told stories of previous hunting and fishing trips. The young, unmarried men sat around the fires listening quietly to the stories. They were carefully making new spear tips from sharpened splinters of palm wood and monkey bones. The young boys were sent into the forest to collect firewood. The Kayapó were organized into age groups with specific jobs and responsibilities. The older, married men were the leaders. They supervised the group of young, unmarried men. The young boys worked together as a team and obeyed the unmarried men.

In the morning the sky brightened and light filtered steadily through the canopy of leaves. The younger men and boys took the bundles of dried *timbo* from the canoes. They laid the timbo out on the river bank. TIMBO is a green vine that twists and climbs up the trunks of trees. Two weeks before the women of the tribe had gathered the *timbo*. They carefully dried it in the sun. Under the direction of the elders the younger men took sharp rocks. They began beating the dried *timbo* vines.

Soon all the *timbo* vines had been pounded into long, stringy fibers. The men took the bundles and waded into the water. The water splashed around their waists as they beat the timbo bundles in the water. Soon a soap-like foam spread across the inlet. The young boys jumped up and down, spreading the poisonous foam throughout the inlet. The older men on the river bank shouted and sang encouragingly.

After a few minutes, fish began drifting to the surface. They gasped for air, their white and yellow bellies glinting in the sunlight. Some of the fish began a frenzied leaping into the air. A few of the stronger fish managed to hurl their bodies over the reed fence. They landed in the canoes tied to the fish trap fence. Several fish even managed to hurl themselves completely over the fence and the canoes. They escaped in the main channel of the river.

As the fish began their wild leaping, the older men gathered at the edge of the trap. At first only the young boys were allowed to shoot at the fish with their bows and arrows. This was a time for the older, experienced hunters to watch the skills of the young boys. The older men shouted comments to the boys. They threw small pebbles at their feet to encourage them to take greater care with their aim. Soon the boys had had time to practice their shooting skills and to make a kill. Then the rest of the Kayapó men gathered up their spears and joined the boys. They balanced in the canoes and on the tree limbs that reached over the water. They began spearing the fish with careful, deadly strokes. In less than an hour, the Kayapó had filled the large reed baskets in the canoes.

One of the younger boys was barely taller than his spear. There was great excitement when he struck a large brown-speckled fish. The fish was one of the Kayapó favorites. It was not usually caught in such small inlets far from the main river channel. The Kayapó men shouted their approval. The catch marked the inlet as a good fishing spot. It earned honor for the older Kayapó hunter who chose the hidden inlet for the fish trap. That evening there would be much singing, laughing, and story telling. The older men would recount other successful fishing trips. They would comment on the fishing skills of the younger men and boys.

Effect of Indian Settlement on the Physical Environment

The lifestyle of the Brazilian Indians did not change the natural vegetation, land, or animal life in Brazil. The areas cleared for their garden plots were not large. The Indian villages were moved every few years. Then the forest was able to grow back over the cleared patches. The Indian diet was mainly vegetables, fruits, and nuts. Hunting and fishing activities killed only a small number of animals. The Indians had little impact on the animal populations.

Indian settlements were generally temporary. They did not remain in any one area for long enough to permanently change the natural environment. The Indian population was small in comparison to the vastness of the land. This meant the Indians would have little impact on the physical environment. In thousands of years of settlement, the way of life of Brazilian Indians did not alter the physical environment of Brazil.

Indian in Hammock

Wooley Monkey

Toucan

Dugout Canoe

Berries on Bark Tray

Field Basket Woven from Leaves and Vines

Plantain

Grubs on Leaf

Papayas

Ground Manioc and Scored Grating Board

Fish

Peccary

Armadillo

Manioc

For Your Notebook

1. The Brazilian Indians developed a way of life that used the resources of their environment to meet all their needs. List examples to illustrate this statement.
2. The Brazilian Indians practiced slash-and-burn agriculture. Explain why it was given this name. Write an explanation of slash-and-burn agriculture.
3. List reasons why the garden plots were moved to a new site every few years. Use information from this section and from Chapter 1.
4. How did the physical environment of Brazil affect the Indian way of life?
5. Summarize why the Brazilian Indians had little impact on the land, natural vegetation, and animal resources of Brazil.

PORTUGUESE: Exploration and Settlement

The Portuguese began to arrive in Brazil soon after the 1492 voyage of Christopher Columbus, who explored for Spain. At first the Portuguese were only interested in taking from Brazil any valuable natural resources that could be found along the coast. Gradually agricultural settlements replaced the coastal trading posts. However, Portuguese settlement of Brazil remained small and limited to the immediate coastal areas in the Northeast.

The Early Years

Treaty of Tordesillas

In the late 1400s most spices and other goods from India and China were brought overland to Europe by Arab merchants. Italian ships then carried the spices and goods to European ports. This spice trade with India and Asia was very profitable. People from Spain and Portugal hoped to find a sea route to India and China. They wanted to bypass the Arab and Italian traders.

Spanish and Portuguese explorers kept attempting to find this sea route. They often reported discoveries of land "to the west." To keep peace between these countries, the Pope prepared the Treaty of Tordesillas in 1494. The Treaty of Tordesillas gave each country a specific area of the "new world in the west." They were allowed to explore and settle only their area.

For the Treaty of Tordesillas, a north-south imaginary line was drawn 370 **leagues** west of the Cape Verde Islands. All newly discovered lands to the east of this line would belong to Portugal. All newly discovered lands to the west of the line would go to Spain. As the map indicates, only the northeast of Brazil was given to Portugal by the Treaty of Tordesillas. Over the next two hundred years, Portuguese settlers would push into the interior of the new land. They extended Portuguese land claims far beyond the limits of the Treaty of Tordesillas.

Spain, Portugal, and the other European countries competed for land in North and South America. They did not consider that the native Amerindians had any claim to the land. The natives were not considered when treaties were prepared. These treaties divided North and South America among Spain, Portugal, France, Holland, and Britain.

Tordesillas—pronounced tor day see yahs
League—measure of distance, approximately 3 miles or 4.8 kilometres

Treaty Line of Tordesillas 1494

Portuguese Trading With Indians
Early 1500s

The Portuguese

On April 22, 1500, Pedro Alvarez Cabral, a Portuguese explorer, landed on the eastern coast of what is now Brazil. He claimed the land for Portugal. Cabral named the land Terra da Vera Cruz, "land of the true cross." Within a few years, however, that name was forgotten and the land quickly became known as the land of "Brasil."

Brazilwood Trading Forts 1500–1530

For the first thirty years after Cabral's landing, Portuguese settlement in Brazil was limited to isolated trading forts along the northeast coast. The first Portuguese settlements in Brazil were established by traders. They wanted brazilwood logs to send back to Europe. Brazilwood, called pau-brasil, produced a reddish-purple dye. This was highly valued by European cloth-makers. Indians of the coastal rain forests cut brazilwood logs from the rain forest. They brought the logs to the Portuguese forts along the coast. The Indians traded the brazilwood logs for pots, axes, hatchets, knives, and other European goods.

The brazilwood trading forts were not intended to be permanent settlements. The traders were there only to collect the brazil-wood logs from the Indians. The Portuguese government was not interested in establishing permanent settlements in Brazil. The Portuguese were more interested in developing their spice-trading colonies in India and Asia. Then the threat of losing Brazil to the French developed. That forced the Portuguese government to establish permanent settlements in Brazil.

The French Threat

The successful brazilwood trade attracted the attention of French traders. They soon arrived in Brazil and set up their own trading forts. The French and Portuguese often attacked each other's forts and ships. Several times the Portuguese navy tried unsuccessfully to clear Brazil's coast of French trading ships. By 1530, the Portuguese government realized that if it wanted to keep Brazil it needed permanent settlements. The Treaty of Tordesillas had not included French claims in the New World. The French, however, were prepared to ignore the treaty. They had already established settlements to the north of Brazil. These settlements were in what was supposed to be Spanish territory.

The Captaincy Settlements

The Portuguese government wanted the entire Brazilian coast settled and under Portuguese control. The Portuguese government divided Brazil into fifteen strips of land (see map). Each strip extended from the Tordesillas Line to the coast. Each section was called a CAPTAINCY. A captaincy was given to a wealthy Portuguese family for life. The people receiving the land grants were called donatories. The granting of large areas of Brazil to individuals is sometimes called a DONATORY SYSTEM. The family was expected to use its own money to settle the region. They were expected to develop agriculture and provide defenses against French and Indian attacks. The Indian tribes along the coast frequently attacked the Portuguese trading posts and settlements. The Indians wanted to prevent the Portuguese from taking over their lands.

Only a few of the captaincies were successful. The brazilwood trade was declining. The few captaincies that were successful were the ones that began planting a new crop from Africa. This crop was called sugar cane.

Brazilwood Trading

French Threat

Captaincy Settlements

Line of Tordesillas

51

Economic Booms

Throughout Brazil's early settlement, specific agricultural products or natural resources determined settlement patterns. These products became very popular for a short period of time. This meant they attracted a lot of attention and provided opportunities for people to make a great deal of money. The period when these particular resources or agricultural products are in high demand is called an ECONOMIC BOOM. Brazilwood trees had been the first product to determine where settlements would be located. Sugar cane was the next economic boom product. It also influenced the early settlement patterns in Brazil.

The Sugar Colonies

SUGAR CANE is a tall grass that grows in tropical climates. It produces sturdy stalks from two to five metres high. These stalks contain a large amount of sweet juice. Sugar and syrup can be made from this juice.

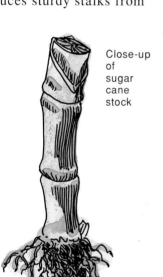
Close-up of sugar cane stock

In the 1500s, world demand for sugar was increasing. This made sugar a highly priced product.

Sugar cane could be grown along the entire length of the Brazilian coast. The northeast coast became the center of sugar cane production.

The southern coast was actually more suitable for sugar cane. However, the northeast had better ports. It was much closer to European markets. In the days of sailing ships, distance was an important consideration. The closer the sugar cane plantation to ports and to the markets in Europe, the greater the profits. There were steep highlands along the southern coast. These made access to farming areas several kilometres inland difficult. In the Northeast, the coastal plain is wider. There are small rivers providing access to farming areas many kilometres in from the coast.

Sugar Cane Plantations

Sugar Cane Plantations

Sugar cane was usually grown on large estates. They were farmed by paid workers or slaves. These estates were called PLANTATIONS. Sugar cane plantations required large areas of land. A large labor force was needed to work the fields and mill the sugar.

At first plantation owners tried to use Indian slaves. They soon found, however, that this was not possible. The Indian population was small and scattered. Indians did not want to be slaves and retreated into the rain forest areas. Expeditions were organized to capture the Indians. Once captured, the Indians fled at every opportunity. The work of the plantations was too different from the Indian way of life. Contact with the Portuguese settlers also brought epidemics of diseases. These diseases were previously unknown to the Indians. Thousands of them died from epidemics of measles and influenza. In 1560, for example, a smallpox and measles epidemic killed thousands of Indians in the Northeast.

The plantation owners attempted to use Indian slaves from 1540 to 1600. It soon became apparent that the Indians could not be acquired in large enough numbers to meet the enormous labor needs of the sugar cane plantations. By 1560 the plantation owners had started buying African slaves.

African Slaves

Wealthy landowners in the United States and Europe, including Portugal, had been buying African slaves for several decades. Slaves were brought from Africa by the English, Spanish, and Portuguese slave traders. African slaves were not immediately used in Brazil because of the great expense. Only wealthy plantation owners could afford to buy hundreds of African slaves. The Brazilian plantation owners had hoped to use the native Indians. This way they could avoid the high cost of importing African slaves.

All records documenting the African slave trade in Brazil were destroyed in 1891 by the government. Without these records it is impossible to know exactly how many Africans were brought to Brazil. It is estimated that at least 4 million people were captured and shipped from Africa to Brazil.

Most Africans were settled in the Northeast region of Brazil. For many years the number of Africans in the Northeast was more than the number of Portuguese settlers. Because of their large numbers, Africans had a substantial influence on life in northeast Brazil. They influenced the music, language, food, religion, and festivals in Brazil. They married Portuguese settlers and Indians. This added to Brazil's population mix.

Decline of Sugar Production

The production of sugar reached a peak between 1650 and 1700, and then declined. Lower crop yields and competition from other countries contributed to this decline. The sugar cane areas had been extensively cultivated for many years. Because fertilizers and other methods of preserving soil fertility had not been used, soil fertility dropped. The land produced less sugar cane. The Dutch on their sugar plantations in the West Indies used newer machinery and more efficient methods to produce sugar. They were able to produce sugar and sell it at a lower cost than the Brazilian plantations.

For Your Notebook

1. On an outline map of Brazil draw in the Line of Tordesillas. Explain how this line affected settlement patterns in the new land of Brazil.
2. Summarize how the brazilwood trade and the development of sugar cane plantations affected the settlement of Brazil.
3. What effect did the sugar cane industry have on the Indians of Brazil?
4. Write a definition of economic boom.

Cattle Ranching

Cattle ranching was introduced into Brazil early in the 1600s. The large sugar cane plantations used many oxen to haul cane and firewood to the sugar mills. They also hauled processed sugar to the seaports. A growing number of sugar cane plantations and new coastal ports and towns developed to service the sugar industry. They created a large demand for fresh meat.

Sugar plantations occupied the coastal plain. The cattle industry was forced to move farther inland for pasture lands. Ranchers and their cowboys moved inland from the coast. They drove the Indians from the land and cleared large areas of coastal rain forest. They established fortified cattle ranches. The ranching areas were first established along the rivers since these were the easiest transportation routes inland. By 1700 the cattle ranches had spread into the Rio São Francisco valley.

Cattle Ranches 1700

Settlements grew in southern Brazil. The demand for oxen and mules for transportation increased. Gradually cattle ranches were established on the grasslands of southern Brazil. The Portuguese government encouraged the establishment of ranches in southern Brazil. They wanted to ensure that this area would be controlled by Portuguese settlers, not taken over by the Spanish settlers from Uruguay. Cattle ranching in southern Brazil helped to establish Portuguese claims to more territory. Some of this territory was beyond what was originally granted by the Treaty of Tordesillas.

The establishment of cattle ranches had a substantial effect on the land. Ranchers cleared the forest to make more pasture lands. They burned off trees, shrubs, and grasses each year to encourage the growth of new grass for their cattle. In many areas this regular burning and overgrazing quickly exhausted the soil. When the soil could no longer produce grasses for cattle, the grazing area was abandoned. New areas were continually being cleared.

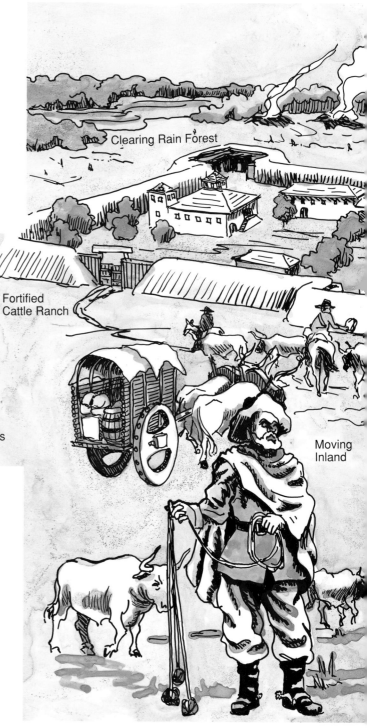

Clearing Rain Forest

Fortified Cattle Ranch

Moving Inland

Brazilian cowboys are called *vaqueiros* in the north and *gauchos* in the south.

54

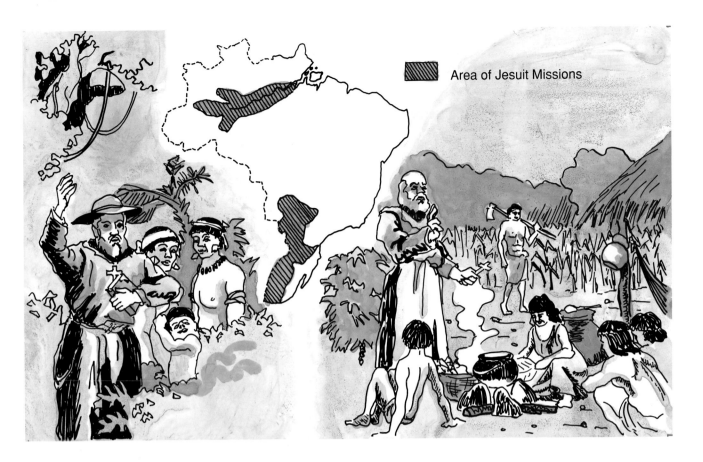

Area of Jesuit Missions

The Jesuit Settlements

The JESUITS are a Roman Catholic religious order. They were active in many areas of South America. They began arriving in the area of Brazil in 1549. The Jesuits' goal was to establish the Roman Catholic Church in South America. They wanted to convert the Indians to the Catholic religion and protect the Indians from Indian slave hunters. The Jesuits believed that the best way to protect the Indians was to set up protected mission settlements. They believed the Indians needed to live under the supervision of the Church. The Church could provide protection and education. In many areas the Jesuits established their own plantations. They taught the Indians farming skills. They discouraged the Indians from learning Portuguese. The Jesuits tried to prevent the Indians from making contact with other settlers.

Jesuit settlements came into conflict with Portuguese settlers in Brazil. The Jesuits were unpopular because they opposed the slavery of Indians. The Jesuit plantations also competed with Portuguese plantations. The Portuguese government believed that the Jesuits were trying to establish areas that would be controlled by the Roman Catholic Church, not by the government of Portugal. The Jesuits denied they were competing against the Portuguese government. Portugal did not believe this. In 1759 the Portuguese government ordered the Jesuits to leave all territories under Portuguese control.

The Jesuit missions did affect the settlement of Brazil and the final establishment of Brazil's borders. The Jesuit settlements in the far interior regions guaranteed that the Portuguese could claim possession of these interior areas from the Spanish. These were areas that were given to Spain in the Treaty of Tordesillas. In 1750 a new agreement was reached between Spain and Portugal. This was called the Treaty of Madrid. In this treaty it was agreed that occupation was the factor that would decide what territory each country could claim. All lands with Portuguese settlements would become part of the Portuguese claim. The Jesuit settlements helped the Portuguese establish a claim to a large area of southern Brazil and areas along the rivers of the Amazon region.

The *Bandeirantes*

For the first one hundred years of the Brazilian colony, the major settlements and agricultural developments were along the northeast coast. The growing cities and towns, prosperous sugar cane plantations, successful cattle ranches, and active trading seaports were along the northeast coast. The capital city, Salvador, was a major northeast seaport. The Portuguese settlers in the northeast were wealthier than those in other areas of the colony. The Portuguese **immigrants** attracted to the northeast were usually from well-off families. They had the finances to develop large plantations. They could purchase machinery and African slaves, build luxurious homes, and support the development of cities.

The southern areas of Brazil remained relatively undeveloped. The Portuguese settlers in southern Brazil were not from wealthy families. They could not afford to develop large plantations, buy expensive machinery, or purchase African slaves. As a result southern Brazilians, particularly the residents of São Paulo, were forced to find other ways to make a living in Brazil. Many chose to explore the interior looking for Indian slaves, gold, **emeralds**, and other mineral wealth.

These adventurers who set off into the interior were called *bandeirantes*. The term *bandeirante* means "flag bearer." The *bandeirantes* were often organized into small semi-military units. They carried the Portuguese flag into Spanish territory. Brazilians think of them as the real founders of Brazil. Most *bandeirantes* were from São Paulo. Many were financed by a resident of São Paulo who provided them with guns and supplies. In return the *bandeirantes* gave a share of the profits from the sale of Indian captives to the resident.

Many of the *bandeirantes* were of mixed Indian and European background. They adopted Indian ways. This permitted them to survive in the interior rain forest. They dressed, ate, and lived like the Indians. They spoke Indian languages. With their Indian background and skills they were able to use Indians friendly to the Portuguese to help capture other Indians. Indians also acted as guides through the interior territory.

Routes of *Bandeirante* Exploration

Salvador

São Paulo

The *bandeirantes* often spent months and sometimes years in the interior. They traveled enormous distances on foot or by canoe. They followed the river valleys inland. By the early 1600s, the *bandeirantes* had captured most of the Guaraní Indians in the region surrounding São Paulo.* Then the *bandeirantes* began to look at the vast interior as a source of Indian captives. Here the *bandeirantes* came into conflict with the Jesuit missionaries. The Jesuits had established protected mission settlements in the interior. Many of the missions were raided by *bandeirantes*.

The *bandeirantes* were largely responsible for the westward expansion of Brazil's frontiers. Eventually they settled the interior areas. The *bandeirantes* explored the interior of the present-day states of Minas Gerais, Goiás, and Mato Grosso and as far north as the Amazon River. The presence of *bandeirantes* in the interior allowed Portugal to claim these lands from the Spanish. In fact they were well beyond the limit set by the Treaty of Tordesillas. The explorations of the *bandeirantes* also shaped the settlement patterns of Brazil for the next two hundred years. While searching for Indian captives, the *bandeirantes* also searched for gold and mineral wealth. In the mountains of Minas Gerais in the 1690s the *bandeirantes* discovered large gold deposits. Their discovery started the next major economic boom in Brazil—a gold rush. This gold rush changed the settlement patterns in Brazil. It helped the rapid development of southern Brazil.

Immigrant—a person from another country who has come to a new country to live

Emerald—a bright green precious stone
* An Indian tribe from the southeast region of Brazil

The Discovery of Gold

The discovery of gold in southern Brazil started Brazil's first gold rush. This was Brazil's first economic boom centered on a mineral. Previous booms had centered on agricultural products.

The *bandeirantes* had made Indian hunting raids into the interior. These became opportunities to search for gold. In the 1690s gold discoveries were made in the streams not far from the present-day city of Belo Horizonte. The site of this discovery was named *Villa Rica* which means "rich village." In 1729 diamonds were discovered in the same area. This started a diamond rush. For a short while Brazil became the leading world source for gold and diamonds. By 1760 nearly half of the world's gold was coming from Brazil. This mineral wealth was shipped back to Portugal. There it enriched the Portuguese king.

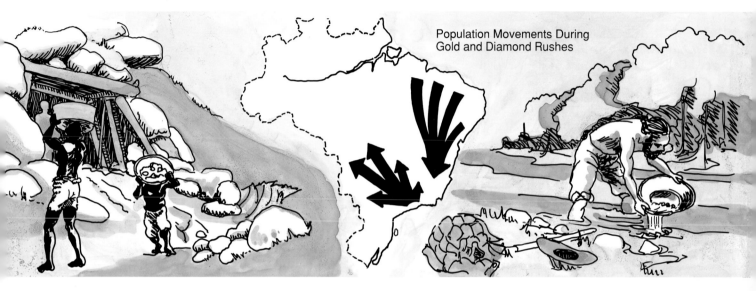

Population Movements During Gold and Diamond Rushes

Settlement Patterns and the Gold Rush

The discovery of gold attracted people from all over the Brazilian settlements. This created the first population movement of large numbers of people from one region in Brazil to another. Gold discoveries also attracted people from other parts of the world. The gold and diamond booms had several long-lasting effects on settlement patterns in Brazil.

- Large numbers of people abandoned the sugar plantations and towns of the northeast coast. They flooded into the southern mining areas.

- Large numbers of people from the São Paulo area also moved into the interior regions of what is now Goiás, Mato Grosso, and Mato Grosso do Sul. They were looking for gold and precious stones.

- In the early 1700s nearly 400 000 Portuguese immigrants came to the mining areas in southern Brazil. Nearly half a million African slaves were shipped to work in the gold mines.

- By 1725, half the total population of Brazil was living in southern Brazil.

- Gold and diamond booms accounted for the first permanent settlements far from the coast. The gold and diamond rush created new mining settlements in the interior regions of what is now Minas Gerais, Goiás, and Mato Grosso.

- The gold rush affected the balance between rural and urban populations. During the gold and diamond booms, many people moved to mining camps and small towns from the plantations.

- The gold and diamond booms produced the first improvements to Brazil's transportation system. For the first time roads were built through the Brazilian Highlands. They linked the mining regions with the coastal towns and ports. Mules became the important pack animal along these routes. Many of today's modern roads were built along the routes of these early roadways.

By the beginning of the 1800s the gold and diamond booms were over. There were few new gold discoveries. The supplies of gold in the rivers and mines were showing signs of exhaustion. Brazil was ready for a new economic boom. This time the product would be coffee.

Coffee Boom

The next major economic boom was based on coffee. Coffee was a relatively new product in the 1800s. It was first introduced into Europe in the 1500s from Arabia. The Dutch and French began growing it in their South American colonies in the 1700s. Coffee rapidly gained popularity in Europe. It sold for a high price there, making it an attractive crop to cultivate in Brazil. By 1850 Brazil was producing nearly half of the world's supply of coffee. This later rose to nearly three quarters of the world coffee supply.

Coffee Cultivation

Coffee was first planted near Rio de Janeiro. It quickly spread to what is now the state of São Paulo. There the soil and climate conditions were ideal for coffee cultivation. More land was cleared for coffee cultivation. The plantations gradually moved westward into the interior areas of the state. The search for new lands where coffee could be planted gradually pushed settlement into Minas Gerais, Paraná, and even parts of Mato Grosso. Railway lines were built inland. This guaranteed that interior plantations had access to coastal seaports. This encouraged the movement of coffee plantations westward.

Effect on the Natural Environment

The coffee boom dramatically changed the natural environment of southern Brazil. It created a large demand for land. The hills and plateau areas of São Paulo and Rio de Janeiro States were quickly cleared of forest to make way for more coffee plantations. The rapid destruction of the coastal forest areas of southern Brazil was a direct result of the coffee boom.

Effect on Settlement Patterns

The coffee boom also substantially affected settlement patterns in southern Brazil.

The coffee boom made southern Brazil the wealthiest and most important area in Brazil. This wealth was concentrated in the cities of São Paulo and Rio de Janeiro. They became two of the world's most prosperous cities. Up to this point, the Northeast had been the economic and political center of the country. By the 1800s, southern Brazil had become more important. In 1863, Rio de Janeiro replaced Salvador as the capital of the country.

Coffee plantations required large labor forces. At first, African slaves were brought in to work on the plantations. Slavery was abolished in 1888 by the Brazilian government. This ended the use of African slaves. The demand for labor brought thousands of Europeans to southern Brazil as paid farm workers. From 1888 to 1920 Italian, German, Swiss, and Japanese immigrants came to southern Brazil to work on coffee plantations. In 1888 alone nearly 90 000 European immigrants arrived in São Paulo State. These immigrants brought farming skills, organizational abilities, new agricultural products, and new trade skills to Brazil. As a result of this massive European and Asian immigration, the economy and the way of life of southern Brazil changed. It became substantially different from the way of life in earlier settled areas of Brazil.

Coffee Plantation

Coffee Cultivation

Rubber Boom in the Amazon

The coffee boom continued into the 1900s. There was one other economic boom in Brazil before the 1800s ended. This was in the Amazon region of northern Brazil. It centered on the rubber tree.

The rubber tree is the source of natural rubber. It grows wild in the Amazon rain forest. Natural rubber, however, was difficult to use and not in high demand. It melted easily when warm and became brittle in cold weather. A process called VULCANIZATION was developed in 1839 by an American, Charles Goodyear. Vulcanization corrected these problems. It made rubber a more reliable material. Suddenly rubber was in great demand for rubber tires for cars, trucks, buses, and bicycles.* The world price of natural rubber rose quickly. The Amazon had its first economic boom.

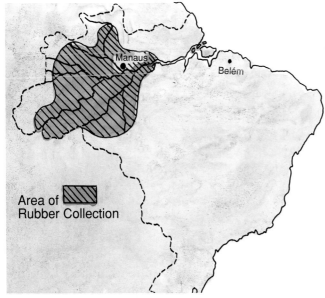

Area of Rubber Collection

Effect on Settlement Patterns

Before the rubber boom there had been no development and very little settlement in the Amazon region. A few military forts and missions had been established along the Amazon River. A few traders had posts along the rivers. They collected tropical forest products. At the end of the 1800s the population of the Amazon region was small and consisted of scattered groups of natives, a few slaves, and some missionaries, soldiers, and traders. The rubber boom changed all that.

As the price of rubber soared, the demand for labor to collect the rubber from the rain forest grew. Thousands of **poverty-stricken** farm workers came from the farms of the Northeast. The Northeast had suffered through several years of drought that ruined cattle ranches and farms. Thousands were without work or farmlands. It is estimated that from 1879 to 1910 nearly two hundred thousand people left the Northeast to work in the Amazon.

For a time the rubber boom drastically changed settlement in the Amazon region. Belém, at the mouth of the Amazon River, and Manaus, two thousand kilometres up the river, became bustling centers of the rubber trade. Manaus grew from a population of only five thousand in 1865 to a population of fifty thousand by 1900. The enormous profits of the rubber trade were spent on impressive buildings. These included private mansions, government palaces, theaters, and opera houses. Manaus also had electric lighting, elaborate public squares, and the latest in Paris fashions. For a time Manaus, at the heart of the Amazon wilderness, was transformed from a small outpost. It became one of the richest and most modern cities in Brazil.

The end of the rubber boom came quickly. There was competition from new rubber plantations in Malaysia, in Southeast Asia.** This ended Brazil's control of the rubber supply. Rubber from the Malaysian plantations was cheaper to produce. It was also of a higher quality than the wild rubber of the Amazon. On a plantation one person was able to collect the rubber from more trees per day than was possible in the Amazon. In the rain forest rubber trees grew far apart. The price of natural rubber dropped. By 1913 the Amazon rubber boom was over.

In Manaus and Belém the theaters closed and buildings began to crumble. Grass grew in the streets. Large numbers of people moved on to other regions. A few remained in the Amazon, attempting to develop cattle ranching and agriculture. It would be over sixty years before attention was again focused on the rain forests of the Amazon.

---

* Bicycles reached a peak of popularity in the 1880s. Automobiles appeared after 1900.
Poverty-stricken—very poor
** Seeds of the rubber tree were smuggled out of the Amazon to Malaysia.

Seringueiros tapping rubber trees for latex.

The Rubber Boom in Brazil

A fictionalized newspaper report* written by Walter Trenton, a reporter sent to Brazil to report on the rubber boom in the Amazon.

December 29, 1908
Manaus, Brazil

My first five days in Brazil are spent traveling up the Amazon River on a paddle-steamer. It is crowded with several hundred Nordestinos. They are from the Northeast region of Brazil. The Nordestinos are fleeing a devastating three-year drought in the *sertão*. It has ruined crops, killed cattle, and brought thousands to the point of starvation. Thousands of Nordestinos have been drawn to the Amazon rubber boom. It offers the promise of great fortunes to be made collecting rubber. This group is camped out on the deck with their hammocks and cooking pots. They are determined that the Amazon rubber boom will make them rich. Evenings on the ship are filled with the sound of their excited talk. They retell stories they have heard of rubber collectors making large fortunes in one or two years.

The arrival at Manaus can only confirm their stories of the great wealth to be made in the Amazon. Manaus is dazzling. It has a population well over one million. Manaus is one of the largest cities in Brazil. At the height of the Amazon rubber boom it is also the most modern, richest city in Brazil. People walking along the tree-lined avenues pass the luxurious homes of the wealthy **"rubber barons."** It is difficult to believe Manaus is in the heart of the Amazon wilderness. The city is filled with banks, mansions, shops selling the latest in Paris fashions, restaurants, and night clubs. The wealth of the rubber barons is difficult to imagine. They give lavish parties. Some send their laundry to Portugal, and their children to schools in Switzerland and France. They bring in vegetables from Europe. A favorite story in the city is about wealthy rubber barons who use 500 *milreis* notes ($200) to light their cigars.

Life in Manaus is quite different from the lives of rain forest rubber collectors. Renaldo Guias works an area a hundred kilometres up the Madeira River. He is typical of the many *seringueiros* working in the Amazon. Renaldo has been working this area for two years. Like the men I met on the Amazon steamboat, Renaldo was advanced passage money by a rubber company. The company supplied him with a few tools, a weapon, and some food supplies. He was dropped off at this isolated location. Renaldo has not made the promised fortune, however. He is deeper in debt than when he arrived.

---

* A fictionalized newspaper report is one that tells a story that didn't really happen. However, the background information in a fictionalized report is based on real situations. In this case, Renaldo is not a real person, but there are many *seringueiros* like him in the Amazon.

Rubber Barons—individuals who became extremely wealthy from the rubber trade
Seringueiro—Brazilian word for rubber tapper or someone who gathers rubber from the rubber trees

Renaldo lives alone at his riverbank camp. It consists of a crude lean-to shelter made of palm thatch. He has a hammock strung between the trees. Renaldo is expected to collect **latex** from a string of rubber trees. These trees are spaced throughout a large area of rain forest. Most of the rubber trees are at least a ten-minute walk apart. Each day Renaldo walks a great distance through the rain forest. He collects the latex that drips from the cuts in the trees. Then he heats the latex over the campfire, forming the rubber into large balls. He sells these rubber balls to the rubber trader who comes by his camp every six months.

Renaldo had hoped that the rubber he collected each season would produce enough money to pay off his debts to the rubber company. In fact, he hoped to make a profit. In the last two years, however, no money has changed hands. According to the books of the rubber trader, Renaldo now owes more than he did when he first arrived. At the end of a season Renaldo's payment for his rubber is usually not enough to cancel out his debt for food and supplies. Renaldo is forced to buy food supplies from the rubber trader. Renaldo must pay the outrageous prices he charges. Renaldo showed me the moldy bag of manioc

flour he'd recently purchased from the rubber trader. The price was five times the selling price in Manaus.

This is a fairly typical situation for *seringueiros*. The *seringueiro* has little hope of escape. He could flee to another part of the rain forest and begin again with a different rubber trader. But if he tries to leave the Amazon he faces arrest by authorities downriver. Most rubber *seringueiros* remain. They grow deeper in debt each year. Few manage to survive the **malnutrition**, diseases, and other hazards of living in the unfamiliar and dangerous rain forest for more than two or three years.

The day we arrived at Renaldo's camp he was too weak to hunt for food. He could not even make his daily rounds of the rubber trees. The hope and enthusiasm I saw on the faces of the men traveling with me up the Amazon quickly disappeared. They were seeing the reality of life in the rain forest. There is great wealth to be made from the Amazon rubber boom. However, the *seringueiros* like Renaldo are not destined to share in that wealth. They hope to make a fortune and return to their homes and families in the Northeast. For most this is nothing more than an illusion.

For Your Notebook

1. Explain how the introduction of cattle ranching affected settlement patterns and the natural environment.
2. How did the Jesuit settlements and the explorations of the *bandeirantes* help Brazil's land claims?
3. List four ways the gold rush and the coffee boom affected settlement patterns in southern Brazil.
4. How did the coffee boom affect population growth in southern Brazil?
5. Using information from Chapter 1, determine what climate and soil conditions made São Paulo an ideal location for the cultivation of coffee.

6. Using the topographical map on page 13 and the map of Brazil's rivers on page 15, determine why the miners didn't use the rivers to reach the gold fields in Minas Gerais.
7. List three effects of the rubber boom on the Amazon region.
8. On an outline map of Brazil, mark in the areas of brazilwood collection, sugar cultivation, cattle ranching, gold and diamond discoveries, coffee cultivation, and rubber collection. Examine the areas marked. Summarize the effect of economic booms on the settlement of Brazil between 1500 and 1890.

Latex—the raw rubber that drips from the rubber tree when the tree is cut

Malnutrition—lack of nourishment, physical problems caused by not eating enough good food

The Roman Catholic Church in Brazil Today

The Jesuits had an important impact on the early settlement of Brazil. The Roman Catholic Church continues to have a strong influence on modern-day life in Brazil.

Nearly 94% of Brazilians are Roman Catholics. This makes Brazilians the single largest group of Catholics in the world. The Catholic religion plays a major role in Brazilian society. Religious festivals are great public celebrations. Community chapels and churches are found throughout the countryside and the cities. The Roman Catholic churches in Brazil do more than serve the spiritual needs of the people.

Led by the National Conference of Bishops, the Catholic Church in Brazil has been one of the most active groups pressing for social changes to benefit the poor in Brazil.

In urban areas, the **clergy** work with labor organizations and with the poor. Community-based Catholic groups pressure the government to provide more government services, jobs, adequate housing, health services, and education for the poor. In rural areas the church has concentrated on land reform.* Catholic bishops in the Northeast, for example, have been active since 1966 supporting rural workers' organizations' demands for better wages and land reform.

The Catholic Church has also been one of the major groups providing education services in Brazil. In the late 1960s Catholic schools made up nearly 30% of the country's secondary schools. The church's Movement for Basic Education was aimed at increasing the number of adults in Brazil who could read and write.

The Catholic Church has also been involved in defending the rights of Brazilian Indians. They have opposed many government plans to settle and develop Indian lands.

The Catholic Church has supported union organizations, pressed the government for improved social services, and criticized many of the government programs. This has often placed the church in opposition to the Brazilian government. In recent years there has been increased conflict between the government and the Roman Catholic Church. At times the government has **deported** foreign priests and imprisoned church workers. Church workers have been threatened. A few have been killed by groups opposed to the church's involvement in land reform and other social issues.

Despite these difficulties, the Catholic Church in Brazil appears to be committed to improving the living conditions for the majority of Brazil's poor. The Catholic Church will likely play a significant part in any political and social changes in the next decade.

Clergy—people trained to do religious work; priests, ministers, rabbis
*Land reform is discussed in more detail in Chapter 5.
Deport—send out of the country

Contributions to Life in Brazil

Between 1500 and 1890, three groups of people made significant contributions to life in Brazil.

Indians

Native Indians of Brazil, especially the groups living along the eastern coast, have made significant contributions to life in Brazil. Indian languages contributed a vast vocabulary of names for animals, plants, and places. Indians introduced the Portuguese settlers to a variety of new fruits and vegetables. The Indians also shared their knowledge of plant medicines with the early settlers. They showed the early settlers how to clear and farm in the rain forest. This particular style of agriculture is still widely used in Brazil.

Indians also introduced the Portuguese to hammocks, a traditional Indian sleeping arrangement. Today, the hammock is the most common sleeping style in Brazil's interior. Indian folktales have become a part of Brazilian literature.

Manioc and a wide variety of fruits and vegetables were introduced to the Portuguese settlers by the Indians. These became important staples in the Brazilian diet.

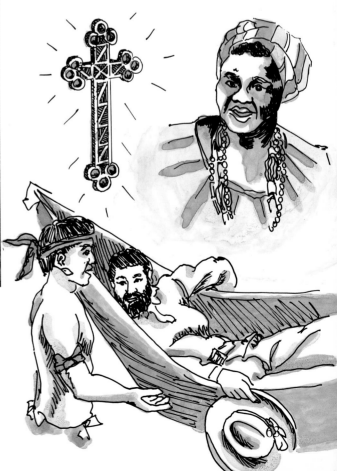

The Portuguese

The Portuguese have had great influence on life in Brazil. Brazil was originally a royal colony of the Portuguese government. It was considered part of the Portuguese empire. In 1549, Salvador became the capital of the Brazilian colony. It was the center of Portuguese control in Brazil. Portuguese Governors General ruled the Brazilian colony for many years. They used Portuguese laws and government regulations.

Another significant event was the arrival in Brazil of the **Prince Regent**, Joao. With him came the entire **royal court** from Portugal. Joao wanted to escape the invading French armies led by Napoleon. He moved to Rio de Janeiro.

For nearly twenty years, Rio de Janeiro was the capital of the entire Portuguese empire. During this time, the Portuguese lifestyle was transferred to Rio de Janeiro.

In 1821, Prince Joao returned to Portugal. He became King of Portugal. His son Dom Pedro was declared Emperor of Brazil in 1821. Portuguese Emperors ruled Brazil until 1889. Then Brazil proclaimed itself a republic with a president. There were close political and social connections between Portugal and Brazil. They helped transfer Portuguese influences to nearly every aspect of life in Brazil.

The most noticeable Portuguese influence is the language of Brazil. Brazil is the only Portuguese-speaking country in South America.

The other noticeable influence is religion. The Portuguese brought the Roman Catholic religion to Brazil. Today, nearly 94% of Brazilians are Catholics. Roman Catholic cathedrals, churches, and monasteries are found in all the early Portuguese towns and cities.

The Portuguese also brought to Brazil their love of family. Family life was very important to the early Portuguese settlers. It is still an important feature of life in Brazil today. Brazilians enjoy large family gatherings. Grandfathers and grandmothers, aunts and uncles, cousins and second cousins see each other as often as possible. Sometimes many generations of a family live together in one house.

Prince Regent—prince who reigned while real king or queen was unable to do so
Royal Court—all the government officials and advisors to the king

Brazilians follow many other Portuguese traditions. Many Brazilian festivals, cooking methods, foods, and styles of art and music are Portuguese. The way the government and the law courts of Brazil are organized follows systems used in Portugal. The early towns and cities in Brazil even followed a Portuguese plan. Salvador, Olinda, and Rio de Janeiro all follow the design of Lisbon in Portugal.

The Portuguese brought the Roman Catholic religion to Brazil. "The Christ" statue is located at Rio de Janeiro.

The early cities of Brazil resemble those in Portugal.

Carnival Time! Carnival is a festival brought to Brazil from Portugal.

The Africans

The African influences have given Brazil much of its unique character. No other country in South America is quite like Brazil.* Part of the reason is the strong African influence on life in Brazil.

The Africans brought their languages, religions, style of music, dances, folk tales, foods, and festivals to Brazil. Today, modern Brazilian music and dance styles reflect strong African traditions. The *samba*, Brazil's national dance, reflects a strong African influence. African words have been mixed with Portuguese to produce a very distinctive "Brazilian Portuguese." African foods and cooking styles are evident in Brazil, especially in the Northeast. African influences are also noticeable in religious customs in Brazil. African spirits have joined Catholic saints as part of religious worship. African religious festivals are celebrated along with those of the Catholic Church. African religions also enjoy a large following in Brazil. The African influence in Brazil is most widely felt in the Northeast. That is where the majority of the Africans were originally settled. African influences, however, can be found in daily life throughout Brazil.

* Many countries in Latin America also have strong African heritage (Columbia, Peru, Cuba, Haiti and most of the Caribbean).

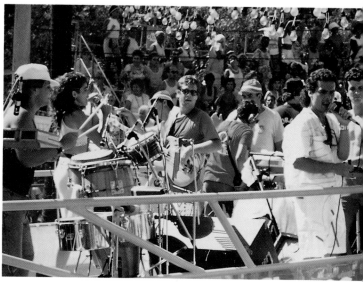

A band playing *samba* music in a carnival crowd. *Samba* is the most popular form of Afro-Brazilian music.

A *capoeira* demonstration—a combination of Afro-Brazilian dance and martial arts.

Feijoada is a mixture of rice, black beans, and meats. Originally an African slave dish, *feijoada* is now often considered Brazil's national dish. It is served at lunchtime on Saturday throughout Brazil.

CHAPTER SUMMARY

Settlement of Brazil
1500 to 1900

Native Indians of Brazil lived by hunting, fishing, farming, and gathering fruits and nuts from the forest. Most Indians practiced a form of agriculture called slash-and-burn. Indians relied on the natural environment to provide all of their basic needs. The Indian way of life did not harm the land, natural vegetation, or animal resources of Brazil.

The first European settlers in Brazil were Portuguese. They had been given the eastern coast of Brazil in the Treaty of Tordesillas with Spain. Early settlements were temporary trading forts. There Portuguese collected brazilwood and shipped it to Europe. There was a threat of the French taking over the territory. This prompted the Portuguese government to establish permanent settlements in Brazil. The eastern coast was divided into captaincies. Captaincies were awarded to wealthy Brazilian families to settle and develop.

From 1600 a series of economic booms influenced the settlement of Brazil. Sugar plantations and cattle ranching were the first developments in the Northeast. For many years the Northeast was the center of all economic and political activity in Brazil. The discovery of gold and the later cultivation of coffee attracted thousands of settlers from the Northeast and new immigrants to southern Brazil. Southern Brazil soon became the new political and economic center.

Portugal had been given only the eastern coast of Brazil by the Treaty of Tordesillas. However, by 1750 Portugal was able to claim a huge area of the interior. The Treaty of Madrid allowed Portugal to claim all lands that were occupied by Portuguese. The Jesuit missionaries had established mission settlements far in the interior. *Bandeirantes* from São Paulo had also explored well into the Amazon region. This exploration and settlement extended the borders of Brazil well into the interior areas of the continent. This made Brazil the largest country in South America.

Between 1500 and 1890, Brazilian Indians, Portuguese settlers, and Africans slaves made significant contributions to the way of life in Brazil. The Portuguese brought their language, religion, way of life, and form of government to Brazil. For a short time, Brazil was even the center of the Portuguese empire.

Brazilian Indians added new words to the Portuguese language. They introduced the Portuguese settlers to new tropical foods. They used the slash-and-burn style of rain forest agriculture.

The African influence in Brazil has contributed to Brazil's unique character. Africans brought their languages, religions, style of music, dances, folk tales, foods, and festivals to Brazil. Portuguese, Indian, and African influences contributed to life in Brazil between 1500 and 1890. These influences can still be felt today.

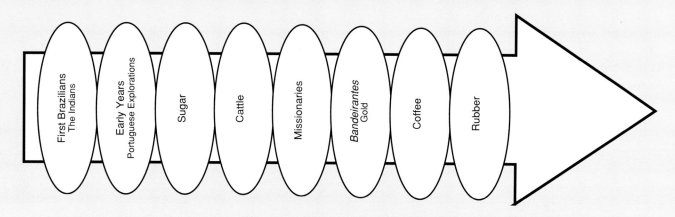

Settlement Patterns 1500 to 1890

By 1890 some definite settlement patterns were well established in Brazil.

- Most of the population lived within three to five hundred kilometres of the coast.
- Nearly all the major cities were along the eastern coast.
- Interior areas were sparsely populated and largely undeveloped.
- Economic booms centered on agricultural products or a natural resource influenced the location of settlements.
- Large shifts in population accompanied each of the economic booms.
- Large population movement from the Northeast region to the Southeast and South regions occurred.
- Southeast became more important than Northeast. Brazil's capital moved from Salvador to Rio de Janeiro.
- Agriculture was the main activity in Brazil.
- Most of the population lived in the countryside.
- Brazil's population was a mix of Portuguese, African, and Indian.
- Indians lived mainly throughout the rain forests of the interior. The descendants of Africans made up the largest part of the population in the Northeast. Most Portuguese settlers lived on plantations or in the small towns and cities along the eastern coast. The largest number of Portuguese settlers was in southern Brazil.

Settlement and the Indians

The settlement and development of Brazil had come at a high cost to the native Indians.

Contact with Portuguese settlers often proved fatal for Brazilian Indians. The Indian population rapidly declined as Portuguese settlement and development increased.

At first the Portuguese traded with the coastal Indians for brazilwood, furs, and other forest products. Later the Portuguese tried to use the coastal Indians as slave labor on their sugar cane plantations. Thousands were taken captive while many more died resisting capture. When captured, the Indians usually did not survive on the plantations. European diseases, such as small-pox, measles, and influenza, were unknown to the Indians. Many died from exposure to these diseases.

The Portuguese pushed farther into the interior in search of new farm land, grazing land, gold, or rubber. Interior Indian populations suffered a rapid decline in numbers. Portuguese settlers often raided Indian villages. They killed women and children and took men as slaves. Each of the economic booms that affected Brazil also affected Indian populations. The number of Indians along the Rio Putumayo, for example, dropped from 50 000 to 8 000 by the end of the rubber boom. Each tonne of rubber collected in this area cost nearly seven Indian lives.

Jesuit missionaries also disturbed the Indian populations and Indian way of life. The missionaries set up protected Indian settlements. They tried to teach the Indians religion and farming skills. This changed the Indian way of life. It altered their nomadic settlement patterns. The Indians were also exposed to European diseases at the missions. While attempting to protect the Indians from the slave hunters, the missionaries in their own way contributed to the death of many Brazilian Indians. The Jesuits contributed to the disappearance of the Indian way of life.

Even for Indian groups who survived the arrival of the Portuguese, the European settlements severely disrupted Indian settlement patterns and the Indian way of life. Some coastal Indians escaped from the slave hunters. They were forced to flee farther inland away from their natural hunting, fishing, and farming territories. They were forced to mingle with interior Indian groups. A fleeing coastal Indian group often forced an interior Indian group from its settlement areas. More Indians moved further and further inland. The competition for farming, hunting, and fishing areas increased. Hostility amongst Indian groups increased. Competing groups often raided other Indian villages in search of wives and children if their own numbers became too small.

European tools also affected Indian settlement and way of life. Steel axes and machetes were traded from one Indian group to another. These tools often reached Indians living far in the rain forest. These Indians had not yet been in contact with the Portuguese. The tools made it easier to clear larger areas of the rain forest, build canoes, and construct homes. With these European tools Indian villagers could build larger and more permanent settlements. European tools changed Indian settlement patterns.

Settlement and the Physical Environment

The Portuguese arrived in 1500. Before this, the Brazilian Indians had not changed the land or natural vegetation in Brazil. Portuguese settlement, however, had a substantial impact on the natural environment. This happened in a short period of time.

The Portuguese established settlements. They began to clear the forest lands for their sugar and coffee plantations, cattle ranches, towns, and mines. Between 1500 and 1890, vast areas of tropical forest were cleared. Forest that once covered most of the coastal areas rapidly disappeared.

The Portuguese plantation owners did not use any methods to preserve the fertility of the soils. Manure from cattle herds was not applied to farmland. Crops were not rotated to preserve fertility. Irrigation and drainage projects were not used to protect the cleared lands from erosion during the heavy rains. It was only the exceptional fertility of the coastal soils that allowed the settlers to continue to grow crops for so long.

Large herds of cattle were moved into the drier areas of the interior. This caused overgrazing problems. Again the land seemed endless. There was no **incentive** to utilize the land effectively. Ranchers merely cleared new areas and moved their herds when one area no longer produced good grasses for grazing.

The sugar mills also had a destructive impact on the coastal forest. The mills used great amounts of wood as fuel. Soon great gaps in the forest appeared around sugar mills. Many mills were forced to close when the wood supply ran out. The French, Dutch, and English sugar mills used dried sugar cane, straw, or grass as fuel for their mills. These methods were not utilized by the Portuguese plantations.

The Portuguese settlers used the Indian slash-and-burn farming method. This cleared land for their plantations and cattle ranches. The plantations and cattle ranches, however, needed large areas of cleared land. These larger areas of cleared forest were exposed to rapid erosion and depletion of soil fertility. Land was very plentiful. Plantation owners made no attempt to carefully utilize the land or preserve the soil fertility. Soon the land no longer produced high crop yields. New areas were cleared. Then these large areas of cleared forest were abandoned. The forest was not able to recover as it had done in the smaller Indian plots.

Incentive—encouragement or payment

CHAPTER REVIEW

For Your Notebook

1. List at least three reasons for the decline of Indian populations in Brazil between 1500 and 1890.
2. Make a time line or make a comic book page indicating the important events in the early settlement of Brazil. Use illustrations to highlight the important events and dates.
3. What could the Portuguese have done to better utilize the resources of the land and natural vegetation?
4. What physical features of Brazil influenced the settlement patterns in Brazil between 1500 and 1890? Using the information on the physical features of Brazil from Chapter 1, make a list of the factors that made early settlement in Brazil easier and which factors made settlement difficult.
5. Summarize features of the settlement patterns in Brazil between 1500 and 1890.

6.  Evaluate the information gathered on your Fishbone Chart and develop a concluding statement to solve the problem: What has been the interaction between the early settlements of Brazil and the physical features? A concluding statement may be in the form of a short paragraph. A sample opening sentence for a paragraph might be: "The early settlements in Brazil affected the physical environment in many ways."

Exploring Further

1. Pretend you are a newspaper reporter from Portugal. The year is 1695. Prepare a short newspaper article explaining the effect of the gold rush on Brazil. Include information about the emigration from Europe and the internal movement of people from the Northeast.
2. Prepare a chart illustrating one of the economic booms in Brazil's early history. Include illustrations and maps.

3. Chapter 2 presented information on the consequences of resource development in Brazil during the 1500 to 1890 period. Use the information gathered from this chapter to revise and add to the alternatives and the consequences on your Decision Making Form. Read the following questions. They will help you make your decision.
   • Were there consequences from early resource development that were advantageous?
   • Were there consequences that were disadvantageous?
   • Can the consequences of early resource development be used to predict possible consequences of modern resource development in Brazil?

(Continued from Chapter Review on page 41)

69

PART III
Settlement Patterns
1890–1990

ADVANCE ORGANIZER

Several events affected settlement patterns in Brazil during the 1890 to 1990 period. These events will be examined in detail in chapters three to five.

1. Immigration
2. Population Increase
3. Opening Up the Interior
4. Millions on the Move

1. Immigration

Large numbers of people from Europe, Asia, and the Middle East arrived in Brazil during the first part of the 1900s. They affected the settlement of southern Brazil. Immigrants helped establish new towns and communities in southern Brazil. Many of these new towns resembled the immigrants' home towns in Europe. Immigrants added to the population mix in Brazil. They also contributed foods, music, art, folk dances, languages, and **customs** of their home countries to everyday life in southern Brazil. Immigrants also improved and expanded farming in Brazil.

(Chapter 3)

Customs—something done by habit; tradition

2. Population Increase

The population in Brazil rapidly increased during the first half of the 1900s. Today Brazil is the most populated country in South America. It is the sixth most populated country in the world. This increase in population has had an impact on settlement patterns in Brazil.

(Chapter 3)

3. Opening Up the Interior

During the second half of the 1900s, the Brazilian government began several projects to open up and settle the vast interior of the country. They built a brand new capital city in the interior. They constructed thousands of kilometres of highways into the interior. These projects to settle and open up the interior had a major impact on settlement patterns in Brazil.

(Chapter 4)

4. Millions on the Move

During the second half of the 1900s Brazilians continued the pattern of mass movement. People went from one region to another. Millions of people from the countryside moved to the cities. Millions more moved from the Northeast to southern Brazil. Millions of people followed the newly constructed highways. They moved into the interior rain forests. The movement of large numbers of people is an important feature of settlement patterns during the second half of the 1900s.

(Chapter 5)

CHAPTER 3
Immigration and Population Increase

Settlement patterns show where people live and what use they make of the natural or physical environment. By 1890 some settlement patterns in Brazil were already well established. In this chapter, we will examine settlement patterns in Brazil between 1890 and 1990. These patterns were affected by immigration and population increases.

1. How did the settlement patterns in Brazil change between 1890 and 1990?
2. How did emigration from Europe, Asia, and the Middle East affect the settlement patterns in Brazil?
3. Why did large numbers of immigrants come to Brazil during the first part of the 1900s?
4. What is meant by the term "population explosion"?
5. How is a country's population growth rate calculated?
6. How do birth rates and death rates affect a country's population increase?
7. How might a rapid population increase affect a country?
8. Why did Brazil experience a large population increase between 1890 and 1990?

Problem Solving

Problem Solving Strategy*

1. Explore possible answers to the question:

   ### How did immigration affect the settlement patterns in Brazil?

2. Use what you know about the effect of immigration on Canada and the United States to develop a hypothesis about the effect of immigration on settlement in Brazil. Copy and use the Fishbone Chart** below to record your hypothesis. Your teacher will explain how to use a fishbone chart.
3. Record information on the fishbone chart as you read through the section on immigration.
4. At the end of the section, you will be asked to develop a concluding statement for the problem: How did immigration affect the settlement patterns in Brazil?

Fishbone Chart

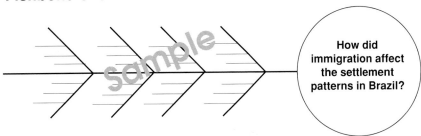

How did immigration affect the settlement patterns in Brazil?

* To review the steps of problem solving strategy, see page 3.
** Fishbone Chart available as a black-line master in the Teacher Resource Package.

IMMIGRATION

IMMIGRATION occurs when people from a foreign country come to a new country as permanent residents.* The immigration of large numbers of people to Brazil was an important feature of settlement patterns between 1890 and 1990. People from Portugal and other European countries had immigrated to Brazil before 1890. However, the numbers had usually been small.** After 1890 the number of **immigrants** increased. Between 1890 and 1990, over five million people from Europe, the Middle East, and Asia came to live in Brazil. They came from Portugal, Italy, Germany, Spain, Russia, Poland, Turkey, Lebanon, Japan, Switzerland, Holland, North Africa, Syria, Egypt, and the United States.

Reasons for Increased Immigration

Several reasons account for increased immigration to Brazil after 1890.

- **The end of slavery**. The slave trade ended in 1850 and slavery ended in 1888. After that, immigration to Brazil steadily increased.
- **Expansion of the coffee industry in southern Brazil.** Coffee plantations required thousands of farm workers. Without African slaves, plantations had to rely on immigration to provide workers.
- **Brazilian government's recruitment of farm workers.** Immigrants from Germany, Italy, Spain, Holland, Switzerland, Portugal, and Japan were encouraged to move to Brazil to be agricultural workers.
- **Development of fast, inexpensive ocean transportation.** Cheaper ocean travel made it possible for Europeans to come to North and South America.

- **Population increases in Europe.** The population of Europe was rapidly increasing. The continent was running out of farmland. Brazil offered an opportunity for poor, landless European farmers to own farmland.
- **World War I (1914-18) and World War II (1939-45).** Many people in Europe were homeless and without jobs after these wars. Immigrating to Brazil was a chance to start a new life.
- **Economic, social, and political problems.** Many Europeans immigrated to other countries to avoid problems in their home countries.
- **Adventure and wealth.** The coffee and rubber boom in Brazil attracted world attention. Many young Europeans believed that moving to Brazil would give them a chance to "make their fortune."

---

*The opposite term, emigration, applies to a person permanently leaving his or her home country.
**African slaves are not considered part of the immigrant totals.

Immigrant—a person from another country who has come to a new country to live

Immigration Totals

Immigration to Brazil was highest from 1890 to 1930. In 1934 the Brazilian government introduced a limit on the number of immigrants allowed into Brazil each year. This resulted in a decrease in immigration over the next ten years. The last period of high immigration occurred after World War II. Since 1970 immigration to Brazil has steadily decreased. Now there are less than 20 000 immigrants per year. Brazil has economic problems and high unemployment. Government immigration controls may also have discouraged potential immigrants. The graph below shows the pattern of immigration to Brazil between 1850 and 1989.

Immigration to Brazil 1850 to 1989

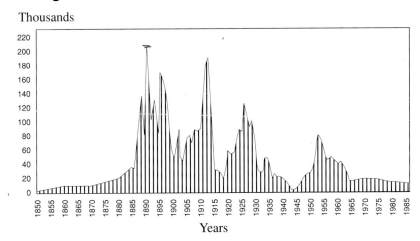

Immigration Totals 1890 to 1989

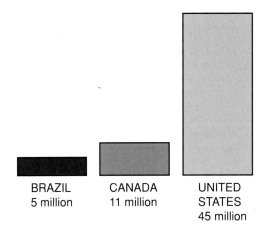

BRAZIL	CANADA	UNITED STATES
5 million	11 million	45 million

The total number of immigrants who came to Brazil from 1890 to 1989 is small when compared to the number of immigrants who came to Canada and the United States during the same time period.

Many immigrants did not stay in Brazil. Some immigrants were disappointed with conditions in Brazil. They returned to their home countries. Others moved to other countries. As many as 30% of the immigrants from 1890 to 1970 eventually left Brazil. Approximately 3.5 million of the 5 million immigrants to Brazil became permanent residents.

Modern day immigrants.

For Your Notebook

Use the graphs on this page to find answers to the following questions:
1. What observations can be made about immigration to Brazil since 1890?
2. What year was the peak year for immigration to Brazil? What years showed the lowest immigration to Brazil?
3. Two periods of low immigration for Brazil were the years during World War I and World War II. Locate these years on the graph.
4. Immigration to Brazil showed an increase in the years shortly after these two wars. What might account for these increases in immigration after World War I and World War II?
5. Compare the number of immigrants to Canada and the United States between 1890 and 1989 with the number of immigrants to Brazil during the same period. Based on the number of immigrants, predict what effect immigration might have on life in Brazil.

Settlement Patterns of Immigrants

Nearly all the immigrants to Brazil after 1890 settled in southern Brazil. Most settled in the states of São Paulo, Rio de Janeiro, Santa Catarina, and Paraná. Often groups of immigrants from one country settled in the same area of Brazil. These groups often kept the languages and customs of their home countries. They built new towns in Brazil that looked very much like the towns in their home countries. Many of the small towns in southern Brazil, for example, closely resemble small towns in Germany and Switzerland. The map below shows where many immigrant groups settled in Brazil.

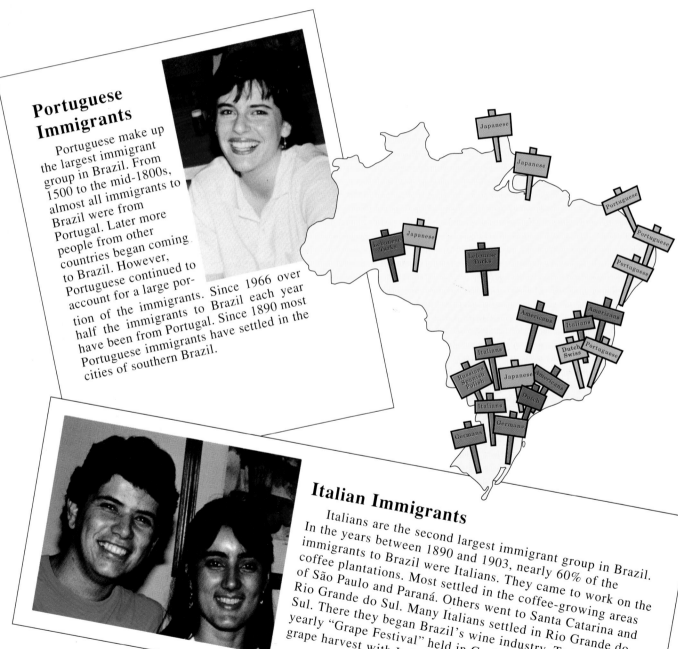

Portuguese Immigrants

Portuguese make up the largest immigrant group in Brazil. From 1500 to the mid-1800s, almost all immigrants to Brazil were from Portugal. Later more people from other countries began coming to Brazil. However, Portuguese continued to account for a large portion of the immigrants. Since 1966 over half the immigrants to Brazil each year have been from Portugal. Since 1890 most Portuguese immigrants have settled in the cities of southern Brazil.

Italian Immigrants

Italians are the second largest immigrant group in Brazil. In the years between 1890 and 1903, nearly 60% of the immigrants to Brazil were Italians. They came to work on the coffee plantations. Most settled in the coffee-growing areas of São Paulo and Paraná. Others went to Santa Catarina and Rio Grande do Sul. Many Italians settled in Rio Grande do Sul. There they began Brazil's wine industry. Today the yearly "Grape Festival" held in Caxias do Sul celebrates the grape harvest with Italian food, music, and folkdances.

Other European Immigrants

Most German, Dutch, Swiss, Polish, Russian, and Spanish immigrants were farmers. They settled in southern Brazil. Many Dutch and Swiss immigrants settled near Rio de Janeiro. There they started Brazil's dairy industry. German immigration to southern Brazil actually started in 1824. By 1914, nearly 50 000 Germans had settled in the southern portion of Rio Grande do Sul. For many years German was the only European language used in large areas of southern Brazil. Many German Brazilians did not learn Portuguese until they were drafted into the army during World War II. Distinctive German-style buildings are still found in the small towns throughout the south.

Japanese Immigrants

The first ship carrying Japanese immigrants arrived in Brazil on June 18, 1908.* Between 1908 and 1930 approximately 250 000 Japanese immigrated to Brazil. Like Italians, Japanese came to work on the coffee plantations in São Paulo and Paraná. Most Japanese soon moved to the cities to open businesses. Some bought their own farmlands on abandoned plantations that would no longer grow coffee. The Japanese built vegetable and fruit farms on this land. Japanese immigrants also went to the Amazon areas. There they established fruit, vegetable, black pepper, and jute farms. Today Brazil has one of the largest populations of Japanese outside Japan. The largest concentration of Japanese-Brazilians is in São Paulo.

Middle Eastern Immigrants

Several thousand immigrants from Syria, Lebanon, Jordan, Egypt, Palestine, and Turkey immigrated to Brazil from 1890 to 1990. Most opened businesses in the large cities in southern Brazil. Others opened businesses in the new towns in the interior. Several of Brazil's most important companies were started by immigrants from the Middle East.

American Immigrants

Several thousand people from the United States immigrated to Brazil in the 1870s, after the American Civil War. These immigrants set up American settlements in São Paulo, Espírito Santo, and in the Amazon. Between 1920 and 1950 about one thousand Americans a year immigrated to Brazil. In the decade between 1954 and 1963 nearly 12 000 Americans entered Brazil. These were mainly business people. They found living in Brazil convenient for their businesses. Since 1960 a few thousand Americans have immigrated to Brazil each year.

*In 1890 the Brazilian government passed a law forbidding Africans and Asians from entering the country without government approval. In 1903 the government allowed Asian immigrants to enter the country.

Contributions of Immigrants to Life in Brazil

The new immigrants to Brazil:

- brought the small family farm system to southern Brazil. Earlier Brazil had mainly a large plantation-style agricultural system.

- began the steady settlement of land away from the coastal area. Soon there was no longer enough unoccupied land along the coast to be divided among the settlers' sons. Then new settlements were established a few kilometres farther inland.

- contributed to the increase in the population of southern Brazil.

- contributed to the growth of cities in southern Brazil, especially São Paulo. Many immigrants preferred to live in cities rather than the countryside.

- brought improved agricultural skills to southern Brazil. These included use of fertilizers, contour plowing, farm machinery, and cattle breeding.

- started many new businesses and provided skills to construct new roads and railways. They provided the skilled workers for new factories in southern Brazil.

- established trade connections with Europe, the Middle East, and Asia.

- introduced new words to the Portuguese language. They added new foods, music, festivals, sports, and customs to everyday life in Brazil.

- brought the Protestant, Buddhist, and Islamic religions to Brazil.

- added to the ethnic mix in Brazil. In 1850, for example, nearly three million of the seven million people in Brazil were Africans. With the addition of nearly five million mainly European immigrants and the end of the African slave trade, the ethnic mix and balance in Brazil changed.

For Your Notebook

1. List at least five reasons why immigration to Brazil increased after 1890.
2. How could the Brazilian government encourage farm workers from Europe and Asia to settle in Brazil?
3. List at least three contributions immigrant groups made to life in Brazil.
4. How did immigrants change agriculture in Brazil?
5. How did immigration affect the ethnic mix in Brazil?
6. How did immigration affect regional differences in Brazil?
7. If you could look through a phone book in São Paulo, what kinds of restaurants would you expect to find in the city?

Using the information from your Fishbone Chart on page 73, write a concluding statement about how immigration affected settlement patterns in Brazil. Your statement may be in the form of a short paragraph. An opening sentence for your paragraph might be: "Immigration to Brazil between 1890 and 1990 affected settlement patterns in several ways."

POPULATION INCREASE

Population

In the second half of the 1900s the population in Brazil increased rapidly. By 1989 nearly half of all the people in South America lived in Brazil. Many people believe that this population increase has created serious problems for Brazil. In order to discuss population problems, it is important to understand how to use population terms. It is also important to understand how changes in population can affect a country.

Population Terms

POPULATION is the total number of people in a country, region, city, or specific area. The population of a country does not stay the same over periods of time. Populations can increase or decrease. Populations can change slowly or rapidly. There are several factors that influence whether a country's population will increase, decrease, or stay the same. But first it is important to define some terms used to describe population.

1. Birth Rate

BIRTH RATE is the number of babies born for every thousand people in a country.

2. Death Rate

DEATH RATE is the number of deaths for every thousand people in a country.

3. Infant Mortality Rates

INFANT MORTALITY rates are a way of showing how many babies under one year of age die each year. This figure is usually an indication of the health care, **sanitation services**, and **nutrition** available to mothers and babies. Infant mortality rates are usually included with death rates.

4. Life Expectancy

LIFE EXPECTANCY is the average age to which most people in a country can expect to live. Life expectancy rates are often very different for men and women. Life expectancy rates may vary from one part of a country to another. They vary for people in the city or in the countryside. Life expectancy rates are usually an indication of the health care, sanitation services, and nutrition available in a country. Longer life expectancy rates in a country mean that people live longer. This means they add to the country's population totals for longer periods of time.

5. Immigration

IMMIGRATION occurs when people from a foreign country come to another country as permanent residents.

6. Emigration

EMIGRATION occurs when people leave their home country to move permanently to another country.

Sanitation services—disposal of sewage and refuse from homes
Nutrition—food that supplies necessary nutrients for good health

7. Growth Rate

GROWTH RATE is the overall increase in population each year. Growth rate is calculated by subtracting total deaths each year from total births, then adding the number of immigrants moving to a country and subtracting the number of emigrants leaving. Growth rate is expressed as a per cent. If a country's growth rate is 2.5%, it means that the country's population is increasing by 2.5% each year.

Geographers use growth rate to determine how many years it will take for a country's population to double. The fewer the number of years needed to double a country's population, the faster its population growth.

Growth Rate Formula

Births - Deaths + Immigration - Emigration = Population Growth

$$\frac{\text{Population Growth}}{\text{Total Previous Population}} \times 100 = \% \text{ Growth}$$

Brazil's Population Explosion

Brazil has experienced a large increase in population over a short period of time. This rapid increase in population is often referred to as a "POPULATION EXPLOSION."

The graph below illustrates the increases in Brazil's population from 1890 to 1990. Brazil's population more than doubled from 14 million in 1890 to 30 million in 1920. It doubled again from 50 million in 1950 to 100 million in 1972. Geographers predict that Brazil's population will double again from the 100 million recorded in 1972 to 200 million by the year 2000.

Population Increases 1890–1990

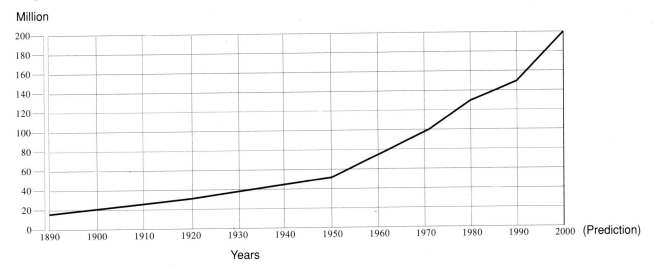

Years

81

Population of Brazil 1990

By the beginning of 1990, Brazil's population was estimated to be 153 million.* Brazil is the sixth most populated country in the world. It is the most populated country in South America. Over half of all the people in South America live in Brazil.

The three charts on this page compare Brazil's population with the population of other countries in South America and the rest of the world.

Population of Brazil and South America	
BRAZIL	153 000 000
SOUTH AMERICA	282 200 000

Brazil's Population Compared to Other Countries in South America

COUNTRY	POPULATION
BRAZIL	153 000,000
ARGENTINA	32 000 000
COLOMBIA	30 600 000
PERU	21 300 000
VENEZUELA	18 000 000
CHILE	12 000 000
ECUADOR	10 200 000
BOLIVIA	6 900 000
PARAGUAY	4 400 000
URUGUAY	3 300 000
FRENCH GUYANA	1 000 000
GUYANA	800 000
SURINAM	400 000

Brazil's Population Compared to Other Countries

COUNTRY	POPULATION
CHINA	1 087 000 000
INDIA	816 800 000
USSR	286 000 000
UNITED STATES	246 100 000
INDONESIA	177 440 000
BRAZIL	153 000 000
JAPAN	122 000 000
MEXICO	83 500 000
FRANCE	55 900 000
CANADA	26 100 000
CUBA	10 580 000

For Your Notebook

1. Using the Population Increases graph on page 81, calculate how many years it took for Brazil's population to double between 1890 and 1920, between 1950 and 1972, and between 1972 and the year 2000. What is the average doubling time for Brazil's population since 1890?
2. Compare the years of rapid population increase with the peak years of immigration to Brazil. The immigration graph is on page 75. What effect did immigration have on Brazil's population increases?
3. Using the information presented in the Population Terms section on pages 80 and 81, predict what events might have caused the rapid increases in Brazil's population since 1890.
4. Predict what effect the rapid increase in population might have on the settlement patterns in Brazil.
5. What problems might occur when a country experiences a population explosion?
6. Brazil is one of the world's largest countries. How does its population compare to other large countries? Compare the population of Brazil with that of Canada and the United States.
7. With a population of 153 million, what population problems do you think Brazil might have?

*The last census was taken in 1980.

Reasons for Brazil's Population Explosion

Brazil's population explosion is the result of several factors. The numbers refer to the population terms on pages 80 and 81.

1. Birth Rate

Brazil's large population increase has not been the result of an increase in birth rate. Since 1900 the birth rate in Brazil has actually decreased. The chart below shows the decrease in Brazil's birth rates from 1890 to 1989.

Birth Rates in Brazil
1890 to 1989

PERIOD	BIRTH RATE (per 1 000 people)
1890-1900	46
1901-1920	45
1921-1940	44
1941-1950	43
1951-1960	44
1961-1970	37
1971-1980	35
1981-1989	30

2. Death Rate

Brazil's large population increases were produced mainly by a steady decrease in the death rates. Fewer people died each year, so Brazil's population increased. The chart below shows the decreasing death rates in Brazil between 1890 and 1989. In 1901, for example, for every 45 babies born at least 26 people died. The population increased by about 19 people for every 1 000 in the population. In 1970, however, for every 37 babies born only 10 people died. The population increased each year by about 27 people for every 1 000 in the population. As the death rate dropped, Brazil's population started to show large increases.

Death Rates in Brazil
1890 to 1989

PERIOD	DEATH RATE (per 1 000 people)
1890-1900	28
1901-1920	26
1921-1940	25
1941-1950	19
1951-1960	15
1961-1970	10
1971-1980	9
1981-1989	8

Birth and Death Rates for Selected Countries
1988

COUNTRY	BIRTH RATE	DEATH RATE
BRAZIL	30	8
CANADA	15	7
UNITED STATES	16	9
CUBA	18	6
USSR	19	10
CHINA	18	7
INDIA	32	12
MEXICO	29	6
JAPAN	12	7
FRANCE	14	10
ARGENTINA	24	9
CHILE	24	6
PERU	32	10
CHAD	51	28
GHANA	47	14
UGANDA	50	18
NIGERIA	46	18

Why the Decreasing Death Rates?

The death rates in Brazil decreased because of improved health care and sanitation services. Diseases, infections, and **parasites** used to kill hundreds of thousands of adults and children each year in Brazil. After World War I better sanitation services were built in most of Brazil's large cities. New medicines were available to treat diseases. After 1930 these new medicines also became more readily available in the countryside. The new medicines and better sanitation services greatly reduced the number of deaths caused by diseases and infections. The widespread use of **antibiotics** to treat infections, and the vaccination programs to prevent smallpox and diphtheria, for example, have enabled more infants to survive the first year of their lives.

Parasites—animal or plant that takes its food from another living body without having to kill it
Antibiotics—substances that kill harmful microorganisms

3. Infant Mortality Rate

Brazil's infant mortality rates have steadily declined since 1900. In 1900, for example, it was common for 250 infants out of every 1 000 born to die within their first year. Today, approximately 65 Brazilian infants out of every 1 000 die within their first year. In some areas of the countryside and in some of the crowded cities, however, the infant mortality rates are much higher than the Brazilian national average of 65. In some cities in the Northeast, the infant mortality rate is nearly 150 infant deaths for every 1 000 born. The chart below compares Brazil's average infant mortality rate with those of other countries.

Infant Mortality Rates For Selected Countries 1988

Country	Infant Mortality Rate (per 1 000 people)
Brazil	65
Canada	10
Cuba	13
United States	10
USSR	29
China	35
India	86
Mexico	48
Japan	6
France	8
Argentina	34
Chile	22
Peru	90
Chad	140
Ghana	98
Uganda	105
Nigeria	127

4. Life Expectancy Rates

Not only are more infants surviving childhood, but the adults in Brazil are living longer. Recent years have seen the introduction of better health care and sanitation facilities. Now life expectancy rates for Brazilians have steadily increased. The chart at the top right shows that the life expectancy of an adult male Brazilian increased from 40 years in 1890 to 62 years by 1988. The next chart compares the life expectancy rates in Brazil with those of other countries.

Life Expectancy Rates In Brazil 1890 to 1988

Year	Males	Females
1890	40	40
1900	40	40
1930	45	45
1960	55	56
1970	57	61
1988	62	68

Life Expectancy Rates for Selected Countries 1988

Country	Males	Females
Brazil	62	68
Canada	73	80
Cuba	72	76
United States	71	79
USSR	65	74
Mexico	65	72
China	68	70
India	57	56
Uganda	46	49
Argentina	66	73
Chad	43	45
Nigeria	48	54
Japan	75	80

5. Immigration

Immigration accounted for only a small part of Brazil's large population increases. The period of peak immigration was before 1940. The years of large population increases were after 1940. Since 1940 immigration has produced less than 2% of the yearly increase in population. In 1960, for example, when the annual increase in population was more than two million people, only about 40 000 were immigrants.

Growth and Doubling Rates		
	Growth Rate %	Doubling Time Years
Brazil	2.2	32
Canada	1.1	65
United States	1.0	72
France	.5	144
Sweden	.1	720
Japan	.7	102
India	2.2	32
Ghana	3.2	22
Mexico	2.2	32
China	1.2	60
Argentina	1.5	48
Peru	2.6	27
Paraguay	2.8	25
Venezuela	2.6	27
Chile	1.8	40
Colombia	2.3	31
USSR	.9	77

6. Emigration

In the past emigration has not been an important feature of Brazil's settlement patterns. Since 1985, however, almost 1.5 million Brazilians left Brazil. They went to live in North America, Europe, Australia, and New Zealand. Unfortunately, many of those emigrating to other countries are Brazil's most capable and best educated professionals. They are moving to other countries to find jobs and better living conditions. Several hundred leading Brazilian science researchers, for example, are working in Europe and the United States. This happens because the Brazilian government and most Brazilian industries do not invest enough money in research. Many Brazilians consider the loss of some of their best educated people a "brain drain."

The number of emigrants, however, is very small compared to Brazil's annual increase in population. Very few Brazilians can afford to move to another country. Emigration has had little effect on slowing down Brazil's population increase.

7. Growth Rate

The rapid increase in Brazil's population is due to the high growth rates between 1940 and 1970. For several of the years between 1950 and 1970, Brazil's growth rate was over 3.0%. By 1990 Brazil's growth rate had dropped to 2.2%. This is about the same as the growth rate of other countries in South America. It is higher than the world average growth rate.

WORLD GROWTH RATE	1.7 %
YEARS TO DOUBLE WORLD POPULATION	41

For Your Notebook

1. Explain in your own words how a country's yearly population growth rates are calculated.
2. In 1988 Brazil had a birth rate of 30 and a death rate of 8. In your own words explain what these rates mean.
3. Compare Brazil's birth and death rates with those of selected countries in Europe, North America, Africa, and South America.
4. Explain how a decrease in death rates can produce large population increases.
5. What factors might account for the different infant mortality rates throughout Brazil?
6. Compare Brazil's infant mortality rates and life expectancy rates with those of selected countries in North America, Europe, Africa, and South America.
7. Compare Brazil's life expectancy rates with those of selected other countries.
8. Predict what problems a "brain drain" might cause for a country.
9. Which countries have the highest growth rate? The lowest?
10. Compare Brazil's growth rate to that of Canada, the United States, and several European and African countries.
11. If Brazil's growth rate is 2.2% in 1989 with a population of 153 million, calculate how many more people will be added to Brazil's population by the end of 1990.
12. Which factor do you think most influenced Brazil's population explosion?

The White Coffins

(Factual Narrative)

Father Bernardo waited for a moment. The young mother knelt down to the white coffin. She gently stroked the soft cheeks of the infant. She tucked a few more flowers around the tiny body. Sobbing quietly, she knelt at the coffin, whispering her goodbyes. She was only nineteen. This was her first loss. After a few moments, two of the women put their arms around her. They pulled her back into the group of relatives.

As Father Bernardo continued the **rites**, the workman secured the lid. Then they lowered the white coffin into the grave. The women dabbed at their faces with tissues. The men stood grim-faced. The mother sobbed openly. Her husband watched sadly as the workman shovelled the red earth over the coffin of his young son.

After the family left, Father Bernardo remained at the grave for a few minutes. He stared at the scattered rows of small white crosses. They stretched across the dusty field. The workmen had already started digging new graves. They usually had a dozen graves dug and waiting in the area set aside for children. Each week Father Bernardo was called on to perform the burial rites for several children from the *favela*. Some were young children under six years. Most were infants less than one year old.

Father Bernardo left the graveyard. He trudged slowly back toward the lines of huts marking the *Favela* Jardim Sentiha. He had been working in the *favelas* surrounding São Paulo for the last ten years. In those years the *favelas* around São Paulo had grown enormously. In the 1970s there were less than 40 000 people living in *favelas* near the city. Now over 600 000 people lived in shacks and huts on the outskirts of the city. *Favela* Jardim Sentiha, 25 kilometres outside the city, was home to over 5 000 people. The number of people crowding into the *favela* seemed to grow larger each month.

Like most *favelas*, Jardim Sentiha had started with an invasion of homeless families. They moved onto unused, swampy land outside the city. First there were a few huts of discarded cardboard and tin. Those had expanded into thousands of shelters. Today in Jardim Sentiha thousands of families were crammed into a jumble of shacks. They built the shacks of packing cases, flattened oil drums, and sheets of iron and cardboard. There were no proper sewage facilities or running water. Water was carried in kerosene tins from several public taps and fire hydrants often half a kilometre away. Sewage and used water flowed in open ditches along the narrow alleyways. Garbage accumulated in piles behind the homes. Most of the families were poorly fed. Many suffered from malnutrition. These conditions resulted in waves of disease sweeping through the *favela*. In the crowded *favela* with poor water and no sewage systems, the effect of disease was disastrous. The ones most vulnerable to disease and malnutrition were the babies.

Father Bernardo found the deaths of the infants the most difficult to bear. Most of the babies died of **dehydration** caused by weeks of diarrhea. The infection was brought on by bacteria in the contaminated water and from poor sanitation facilities. Father Bernardo knew the source of the problem. In the past it had been beyond his ability to do more than provide limited medical care at the church's clinic. He also provided some comfort to the grieving parents.

In the last year, however, there had been hope that things would change. With church support, the women in Father Bernardo's section of the *favela* had organized their own women's health clinic. They were even able to get a government-funded nurse to help vaccinate their babies against diseases. Several associations in the *favela* had organized mass demonstrations. They hoped to convince the government to provide sewage facilities, running water, and electricity to the *favela*. The city government had finally agreed to fund a water project. Work on a water system had already started in the eastern part of the *favela*. It was hoped that by next year all of the *favela* would have clean water. The next major project would be to fight for a proper sewer system.

Father Bernardo knew that these improvements would make a great difference to the children. As the health and sanitary conditions improved in the *favela* he hoped that they would need fewer graves for small white coffins.

Rites—ceremonies, especially religious

Dehydration—the excessive removal of water

86

Effect of Population Increases

Food
A large population increase means that there are a great many more people to feed. This causes problems for countries that lack good soil and climate resources for growing food crops. They may have difficulty providing adequate food supplies for a growing population.

Land
Population increases can affect the natural environment negatively. A large population increase means agricultural land must be shared by an increasing number of people. This may result in shortages of agricultural land and a large number of landless farmers. Farms may become too small to grow enough food to feed a family. New areas may have to be cleared and developed to provide more farmland. Dams, which are built to provide electricity for a growing population, flood and destroy vast areas. Garbage and sewage from large populations can damage the natural environment.

A larger population, however, can also be an advantage. It can provide the people needed to settle and develop sparsely populated, undeveloped regions.

Housing
A large population increase means an increased demand for housing and services. Many countries lack the resources to build adequate housing. They cannot provide electricity, running water, and sewers for their rapidly increasing populations. The housing demands of a large population can result in increased clearing of the natural vegetation. This is often done to provide building materials or to make room for more homes.

Education
Educating a young, rapidly increasing population requires thousands of new classrooms and teachers each year. It is very difficult for many countries to provide enough books, schools, and teachers.

Employment
Swiftly growing populations create a tremendous demand for new jobs. Without new jobs, a large percentage of the population will be without work and incomes. New industries, mines, and logging operations may be started just to provide jobs. These activities also have a damaging effect on the natural environment.

Age Structure
Rapid population growth can result in a large percentage of the population being very young. The age structure of a population influences the demands for housing, jobs, education, and medical care.

Industrial Development
A rapidly increasing population can be both an advantage and a disadvantage for industrial development. The addition of several million new people to the population each year can provide the needed workers for new factories. It can also provide the people needed to buy the goods produced by industries. However, it also means that a large part of the total income of the country is required just to maintain the current level of services. Governments must often choose between providing services and developing natural resources. They must decide between building railways, highways, or hydro-electric dams, and expanding industries and agriculture.

How Population Increases Affected Brazil

There are not enough new jobs created each year to meet the employment needs of a growing population. Many young children must work to help support their families. Emillio shines shoes to help support his family.

A 2.2% population growth means that there are nearly 10 000 more people to feed each day in Brazil. Food is very costly. Many people in Brazil suffer from malnutrition.

In Brazil the number of children not attending school increases each year. In many areas of the country children only go to the first few primary school years. This boy has worked at the market since he was ten.

The population increased in the rural areas. Finally there was no longer enough good farmland available. The problem of lack of land is made more difficult by the fact that most of the good farmland is owned by a few people. Nearly 80% of all agricultural land is owned by only 4% of the population. Many poor landless families are unable to work their own farmland. They have moved to the cities.

People crowd into the cities looking for jobs. This creates a tremendous shortage of housing. Thousands of people live in homes made of cardboard, metal, and wood salvaged from the city dump. Many housing areas in the cities have no running water, electricity, or sewage systems. These areas of poor housing are called *favelas*.

The rapid increase in Brazil's population has produced a large population of young people. This has created a huge demand for housing, employment, health care, and education. The graphs below illustrate the age distribution of Brazil's population compared to that in Canada and the United States.

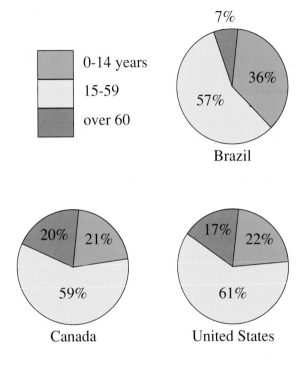

Legend:
- 0-14 years
- 15-59
- over 60

Brazil: 7%, 36%, 57%

Canada: 20%, 21%, 59%

United States: 17%, 22%, 61%

Brazil's rapid population increase has created a shortage of farmland and food. The government has also found it difficult to provide the people's basic needs. Better housing, health care, education and sanitation services are necessary for an increasing population. The government hoped to solve these problems by opening up new areas of the interior. The government helped develop farms, cattle ranches, mines, logging operations, and build hydro-electric dams. It believed that opening the interior would provide land for landless farmers. It also hoped that these new undertakings would provide money. This money could then be used to improve living conditions for Brazil's increasing population.

favela—pronounced fah-**vehl**-ah

89

A Government Official's Viewpoint on Population

A few people in Brazil and in other countries believe that Brazil has a population problem. They think that a population of 153 million is too large. This is not necessarily the view of the Brazilian government or other Brazilians. The problem of overpopulation is not simply a large population. The United States, Japan, and the U.S.S.R. have very large populations. They are not considered overpopulated.

Population problems are linked to the physical environment of a country. In part, population pressures depend on the capacity of the environment to support a number of people. Sometimes the physical environment of a country cannot provide the basic needs of drinking water or food to feed all the people. Then there is a population problem. This is not the case in Brazil.

Brazil is a large country with a vast land area. It has a great wealth of natural resources. We have plenty of land to develop for agriculture and to grow food. We have natural resources. They provide jobs for our people and wealth for the country. Brazil has the natural environment needed to support a large population.

People forget that large populations can be good for a country. The population increases have solved Brazil's labor shortage. In the past Brazil had a shortage of workers. In the early part of the 1900s, Brazil had to recruit farmworkers from Europe and Asia. Brazil did not have enough people to develop new coffee plantations and farms. Now Brazil has enough people to work on plantations, farms, and ranches. There are enough people to work in new factories and service industries. As well, for the first time in its history, Brazil has a large enough population to fully settle and develop the resources of our vast **interior** regions.

Brazil does have some population problems. These problems are not necessarily too many people. One problem is that too many people live in the cities. Living conditions are

unsatisfactory when too many people are crowded into cities. City services include housing, transportation, hospitals, schools, electricity, running water, and sewers. Cities cannot afford to build services for rapidly increasing populations. The government must encourage people to move to the interior areas. This reduces the crowding in the cities.

Providing basic needs include housing, food, health, education, sanitary services, and jobs. The government has a problem providing basic needs for all the people. This does not mean the population is too large. It does indicate that the government lacks the money at the moment to provide these services.

We can solve this problem by developing more of Brazil's natural resources. Developing mining, logging, cattle ranching, farming, and secondary industries could produce the money needed to improve living conditions. Developing Brazil's resources could produce jobs for the people. That could provide wealth for the country.

There is a solution to Brazil's problems. It is not a program to reduce our population. We need to develop more of our resources. This would help improve the living conditions of the people. We need to open up more of the vast interior for settlement and resource development. Brazil is a vast country with unlimited potential. Brazil needs a large population to fully develop these resources.

Interior—a term that usually refers to the North and Center West regions

Working at the El Dorado

(Factual Narrative)

Carlos hurried across the parking lot to the entrance of the supermarket. It was a few days before Christmas. The parking lot at the El Dorado shopping center was packed with cars. El Dorado was one of the four huge shopping centers in São Paulo. Even though Carlos came six days a week to El Dorado, he had never bought anything at the mall.

Carlos was one of four hundred boys who worked as porters at El Dorado. He pushed grocery carts from the supermarket. He loaded the bags and boxes of groceries into shoppers' cars. Carlos didn't get a salary. His only pay was the tips he collected from the shoppers.

Carlos was very pleased to see all the cars in the parking lot. It was the last week before Christmas. The well-off residents of São Paulo were shopping for Christmas presents and holiday food from the supermarket. There would be lots of shoppers wanting porters today. Carlos hoped there would be lots of tips.

Carlos hurried across the parking lot to the porters' station. He picked up one of the brown jackets all the porters wore. Carlos hated to be late and miss time at work. The traffic today had been so bad that the bus had taken over an hour to get from the *favela* on the outskirts of the city to the shopping center. Luckily, the supermarket was busy. Carlos had a customer even before he could button up his jacket.

His first customer had two shopping carts. Both were loaded with bags of groceries. When Carlos was feeling hungry, the groceries in the bags looked very good. He'd look at the food and wish he could eat it. He had to keep reminding himself that he couldn't afford it and to stop wasting time thinking about it. He did wonder if some of it was as wonderful as the advertisements he saw on the television. He often told himself that one day he was going to have enough money to buy some of the food he helped load into the cars. One thing he really wanted to buy was a can of real American Coca-Cola.

Whenever he had a break between customers, Carlos chatted with his friend Luiz. Luiz worked all day at El Dorado. Most of the boys working at El Dorado worked all day. Carlos worked only in the afternoons. In the mornings he went to school. Carlos's family was very keen that he continue going to school. It would be easier for the family if he worked all day and brought home more money. His parents, however, believed that if he kept trying, worked hard, and studied, he would one day get a good job. Then the family would be better off. Carlos's parents would have liked him to go to school all day but there were too many children in the *favela*. There was only one teacher. The *favela* school had one class of 50 students in the morning. There was another class of 40 students in the afternoon.

Carlos wasn't convinced that learning how to read and write would help him get a better job. There were so many people looking for work. There were so few jobs. He did enjoy school, even though he was one of the few older students. Most youngsters in the *favela* dropped out of school when they were nine or ten. They had to earn money and help support their families. The small wages of working children helped feed and clothe most families. Most of Carlos's friends worked. They were servants for well-off families, office messengers, or delivery boys. Others sold things on the streets.

Luiz and the other porters told Carlos the tips had been good that morning. They thought that everyone was in a good mood. It was so near Christmas! Inside the shopping center the stores were decorated with Christmas lights and displays. Christmas music was playing over the loud speakers in the supermarket.

Carlos listened to the song playing on the loud speaker. He thought of his morning at school. It was the same Christmas song his teacher had used for their reading lesson. Sometimes his teacher would print the words to songs on the classroom chalkboard. She would use the words for the day's reading and writing lesson. Carlos loved to sing. He had been complimented many times on his good voice. This morning he'd spent an hour carefully copying out the words to the song in his notebook. At the end of the lesson the class had practiced the song. Carlos stood at the front, leading the singing.

The song kept running through Carlos's mind as he wheeled a particularly heavy cart out to the parking lot. The car was at the far end of the lot and the cart was piled high with

91

boxes and bags of groceries. It took all of his strength to keep the wire cart moving. To take his mind off the hard work, Carlos hummed the Christmas song to himself as he pushed. Before he knew it he was singing the song out loud in his strong clear voice. Several shoppers turned to look and smile. Carlos didn't notice. He was too busy pushing and trying to steer the cart. He was quite relieved to hear the man point out his car.

Carefully Carlos loaded the heavy boxes and bags into the trunk. As the man reached into his pocket for the tip he said, "That was always a favorite song of mine. Nice to hear it again." To Carlos' surprise the tip was twice as much as he usually got.

Carlos tucked the **cruzados** into his shirt pocket. He headed back to the supermarket. By putting one foot on the cart and using his other foot to push, he was able to work up enough speed to ride the cart back to the mall. "Maybe going to school will be useful," thought Carlos. "At least the songs might be ..." he said to himself. He patted the tips in his shirt pocket.

CHAPTER SUMMARY

The immigration of large numbers of people to Brazil was a feature of Brazil's settlement patterns in the early part of the 1900s. The highest period of immigration was 1890 to 1930. Millions of people from Europe, Asia, and the Middle East came to Brazil. The influence of this massive immigration to Brazil can still be seen. For example, Brazil has one of the largest populations of Japanese outside of Japan.

Immigration affected the settlement patterns of the South and Southeast far more than any other regions of Brazil. Nearly all the immigrants who came to Brazil between 1890 and 1930 settled in southern Brazil. A large percentage of these immigrants were farmers. They brought new farming methods and new crops. They also brought the small family-run farm system to southern Brazil. This system was different from the Brazilian plantation system. The plantation system was more common in the Northeast. Immigrants also pushed settlement in the South and Southeast farther inland. They established new farming areas, settlements, and towns away from the coast. Many of the immigrants were business people. They set up new businesses in the southern cities. These immigrants substantially added to the growth of southern cities. They added to the ethnic mix. They also brought new languages, new foods, and new religions. These changed daily life in southern Brazil.

The most important change to settlement patterns during the early part of the 1900s, however, was Brazil's rapid population increase. Brazil's population doubled between 1890 and 1920. It doubled again between 1950 and 1972. The population increase occurred over such a short period of time that it is often called a "population explosion." Geographers predict that Brazil's population could reach 200 million by the year 2000.

The rapid increase in population was the result of several factors. There was a high birth rate. It was combined with a decrease in death, including infant mortality, rates. Life expectancy rates for males, for example, increased from 40 years in 1890 to 62 years by 1988. There was improved health care, sanitation services, and disease prevention after World War II. All these factors helped reduce Brazil's death rates. This contributed to the rapid population increase.

Brazil is experiencing the effects of a large, very young population. The Brazilian government is faced with a huge demand for housing, food, employment, education, health care, and farmland. The population increase has given Brazil a much-needed work force. It has created the consumers need to buy Brazilian-made manufactured goods. It has also meant that much of the total income of the country is needed to meet the basic needs of the population. In the coming years the Brazilian government will be faced with a difficult choice. Brazil must either invest money in developing Brazilian industries or attempt to meet the basic needs of its increasing population.

Cruzados—(kroo-zah-dohs) Brazilian money

CHAPTER REVIEW

Problem Solving

For Your Notebook

1. How can immigration affect settlement patterns and way of life in a country?
2. How can an increase in population affect a country? List at least three advantages of a rapid population increase. List three disadvantages.
3. Why do many children in Brazil need to work?
4. Write the headings Life in Brazil, Settlement Patterns, and Natural Environment. Give several examples of how the population increase has affected each of these.
5. Explain in your own words how Brazil's population increase affected settlement patterns.
6. Many people believe that Brazil's larger population will help settle and develop the vast interior of the country. Use your knowledge of the physical features of Brazil (Chapter 1). Make a list of the physical features that will make settlement and development of the interior difficult. What physical features will make settlement and development easier?

Exploring Further

1. **Examining Opposite Points of View**
   One of the important critical thinking skills is the ability to examine both sides of an issue. People often look at only one side of an issue. Others form an opinion based on what they've heard from friends. People often do not examine the strengths and weaknesses of both sides of an issue before making up their own minds. Use the information presented in this chapter to carefully examine these two opposite points of view. In your notebook make a recording chart like the one shown on this page. In the + box list the possible benefits. In the − box list the possible drawbacks. The ? box indicates questions that may need to be answered before you form an opinion on the issue. Evaluate the possible negative and positive effects of a large population increase. Then complete the following statement: "In my opinion, Brazil's large population increase has been a ....because........................"

2. Chapter 3 presented information on Brazil's population increases. Many people believe that population increases contribute to the development of Brazil's natural resources. Use information gathered from this chapter to revise and add to the alternatives and consequences on the Decision Making Form you started on page 41.

Two Points of View

The large population increase in Brazil has been a benefit for the country.

The large population increase in Brazil has been a disadvantage for the country.

Has the population increase been a benefit or a disadvantage?		
+	−	?

Decision Making

(Continued from Chapter Review on page 69)

CHAPTER 4
Opening Up the Interior

In the 1950s the North and Center West regions of Brazil were sparsely populated. The many natural resources of these regions were not developed. The Brazilian government believed that opening up these **interior** regions for settlement and development of the land and the natural resources would create great wealth for the country. This would improve living conditions for the people. This chapter examines the government's program to open up the interior. We will look at the effect this program had on settlement patterns and the Brazilian Indians.

1. Why did the Brazilians feel it was important to open up the interior of the country to agricultural development and settlement?
2. How did the building of a new capital city in the interior affect settlement patterns in Brazil?
3. Why were highways such an important part of the program to open up the interior?
4. How did the Brazilian government encourage settlement in the interior?
5. What natural resources in the interior did the government hope to develop?
6. How did the settlement and development of the interior affect settlement patterns, the physical environment, and the Brazilian Indians?

Interior—a term that usually refers to the North and Center West regions. In the 1960s, the term interior meant the Center West region: Brasília, Mato Grosso, and Mato Grosso do Sul. By the 1970s, the term interior included Rondônia, Acre, Amazonas, Roraima, and Pará.

Problem Solving

1. Explore possible answers to the question:

   How did the opening up of the interior affect the physical environment of Brazil?

2. Skim through this chapter. Look at the photographs, illustrations, and the headings in bold type. Call on your knowledge of the physical environment of Brazil, the information gathered from skimming through the chapter, and your knowledge of North American settlement. Develop a hypothesis about how the opening up of the interior affected the physical environment of Brazil.

3. Copy and use the circle chart to the right to record your problem and your hypothesis.*

4. As you read through the chapter, record information about how opening up the interior affected the physical environment. You may need to revise your hypothesis as you gather information.

5. At the end of the chapter you will be asked to evaluate the information you have gathered and develop a concluding statement that solves the problem.

Sample

How did the opening up of the interior affect the physical environment of Brazil?

---

* Circle Chart available as a black-line master in the Teacher Resource Package.

The Interior

In Brazil in the 1960s, the term "interior" referred to the Center West region. By the 1970s the term "interior" included the states and territories of the North region. In this textbook "interior" refers to the states and territories that make up the North and Center West regions. Brazil's interior is shaded on the map below.

In the early 1960s the interior of Brazil was a sparsely populated, undeveloped wilderness. There were no roads providing access into much of the interior. Rivers provided the only transportation route through much of the area. Only small groups of settlers, rubber collectors, missionaries, and Brazilian Indians lived in the interior. Manaus, on the Amazon, was the only major city.

Interior States and Territories

96

Should the Interior of Brazil be Developed?

Brazilians of the 1950s said:

The cities are becoming too crowded. Many people from the countryside have moved to the cities looking for jobs. They can't find work in the countryside. If we open up the interior, we can encourage these people to move to the countryside. Fewer people will move to the cities if they can move to another part of the country. They want work or to own their own piece of farmland.

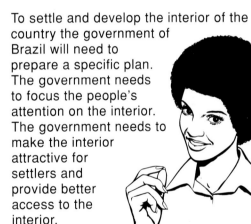

The interior wilderness has land for the growing population. Finally Brazil has enough people to settle the interior. There are hundreds of thousands of rural families in Brazil who are without land. These families need land to support their families. There is no more farmland available in the already-settled coastal areas. The interior of the country will provide farmland for thousands of Brazilians.

Brazilians have always had a special feeling for the interior. Many of us believe that the future economic **prosperity** of Brazil is connected to the vast agricultural and natural resource potential of the interior. The interior is like a bank vault filled with riches. Brazilians only need to open up this interior to secure its riches and wealth.

To settle and develop the interior of the country the government of Brazil will need to prepare a specific plan. The government needs to focus the people's attention on the interior. The government needs to make the interior attractive for settlers and provide better access to the interior.

The interior is Brazil's future!

✓ Yes
○ No

Prosperity—success, financial well-being

ADVANCE ORGANIZER

"MARCHA PARA O OESTE" (MARCH TO THE WEST)

The government of Brazil decided to open up the interior of the country. Their plan was referred to as the *"Marcha Para O Oeste"* (march to the west). The Brazilian government hoped to expand settlement westward from the eastern coast into the interior.

To open up the interior, the government of Brazil focused on three objectives:

Objective 1. Building a new capital city in the interior
The country's capital was to be moved from Rio de Janeiro to a new city to be built somewhere in the interior.

Objective 2. Building roads to open up the interior
This highway system was to connect the new capital city with the important cities along the coast. It was to provide access into all areas of the interior.

Objective 3. Encourage people to settle the interior
People were to be encouraged to move from the coastal areas to the interior with promises of free land. Agriculture and natural resources in the areas that the highways opened up were to be developed.

Objective 1: Building a New Capital City in the Interior

Requirements for the site of the new capital city:

- location somewhere in the interior
- level terrain to make construction easier
- adequate water supply for 500 000 people
- comfortable climate
- easily reached from the largest cities along the coast
- easy transportation to other regions
- nearby forested area for wood needed for construction
- land nearby with soils suitable for agriculture
- high enough to avoid the risk of **malaria**

Malaria—a disease carried by mosquitoes that causes high fevers and eventually death. Malarial mosquitoes cannot survive in the cooler temperatures of higher elevations.

Brasília, the New Capital City

The construction of a new capital city in Brazil's interior wilderness is an example of how government decisions can change the settlement patterns in a country. The new capital city, called Brasília, was planned, designed, constructed, and settled by the Brazilian government.

The Brazilian government decided to relocate the capital city of Brazil from Rio de Janeiro to a location in the interior. The government wanted to focus attention on the vast interior. Rio de Janeiro faced the Atlantic Ocean. It was cut off from the interior by the steep Brazilian Highlands. With the government offices in Rio de Janeiro, it was easy for the government to ignore the interior. Having the government offices in the interior would focus government attention on the plan to open up the Center West and North regions.

Building a capital city in the interior would help develop an unsettled area of the country. Hundreds of thousands of office workers and government officials would be moved to the new capital. The new city would require thousands of people to run restaurants, hotels, banks, supermarkets, and shops. Farms would need to be established to supply the new city with fruits and vegetables. Roads and airports would need to be built to provide access to the new capital.

Building a modern new city in the interior would help convince people that the interior was not isolated wilderness. The new modern city would show people that it was possible to live comfortably in the interior. The government hoped that people from the coastal cities would decide to move to the interior. This would help reduce the rapidly increasing population in the cities.

In 1947 the government sent out a team of surveyors to study the interior. They selected a suitable location to build a new capital city. In 1956 the government announced the final selection of a site. In April 1960 Brasília officially became the new capital of Brazil.

In a country as large as Brazil there were many possible sites for the new capital. The site selected, however, did meet all of the requirements the government considered important for the new capital.

. Brasília

The site selected for the new capital city of Brasília was an isolated, undeveloped location in the central plateau.

Objective 2:
Building Roads to Open Up the Interior

Highways

Before the 1960s the interior of Brazil was almost completely lacking in roads. The movement of goods and people to the interior was by river or air transportation. After the building of Brasília, the new capital city, there was a second major project to open up the interior. It was a massive road-building program. The chart below shows the increase in the number of kilometres of highway between 1930 and 1988.

New Roads

The new roads connected Brasília to Belém at the mouth of the Amazon, to Porto Velho in Rondônia, and to the important cities along the eastern coast. Locate the places on the map inside the back cover of this book. Two major highways were the Trans-Amazonian Highway and the BR-364. The Trans-Amazonian Highway cut through 4 300 kilometres of rain forest in northern Brazil. It runs from the Atlantic to Brazil's border with Peru. The BR-364 Highway connected Brasília with the remote areas of Rondônia and Acre.

The highways built in the late 1960s and early 1970s were often narrow dirt roadways. Many of the new interior highways were impassable for part of the year due to heavy rains.

During the rainy season they became thick red mud. Sections were regularly washed away during heavy rainstorms. The highways did not provide reliable, year-round access to the interior until they were completely paved. Before the BR-364 was paved, it often took 30 days to travel the length of Rondônia during the rainy season. After the highway was paved in 1984, the same trip took two days. Most of the Trans-Amazonian Highway, the Belém to Brasília Highway, and the BR-364 between Brasília and Porto Velho are paved. The photograph below shows a section of the BR-364 outside Brasília.

For Your Notebook

1. Using the information presented in Chapter 1: Location and Place, determine what difficulties the road-building crews might encounter as they tried to build the new interior highways.
2. What difficulties would the road-building crews encounter building the highway between Brasília and Rio de Janeiro?
3. What effect might the climate of Brazil have on road construction and the maintaining of highways?
4. How might the building of highways affect the natural vegetation and the settlement patterns of a region? Are there disadvantages to building highways into **inaccessible** areas? Are there advantages?

Development of Highways in Brazil	
Year	Numbers of Kilometres of Highway (paved and unpaved)
1930	113 000 km
1940	258 000 km
1964	548 000 km
1974	1 298 338 km
1981	1 400 584 km
1988	1 594 000 km

Inaccessible—difficult or impossible to reach

Building the BR-364 Highway

The early evening skies darkened to a purple glow. Clouds of mosquitoes began swarming around the construction crew. Alvaro tucked his pantlegs into his boots. He rolled down his sleeves and tightened the cotton scarf around his neck. Even with his hat pulled down, the mosquitoes managed to fill his eyes, ears, and mouth. Few men on the road crew paid much attention to the mosquitoes. Mosquitoes were only one of many difficulties of working in the Amazon rain forest.

Alvaro's road crew was the frontline of a massive road-building operation. Slowly Alvaro's construction crew was cutting a path for the BR-364 Highway through the Amazon wilderness. Ahead of them lay a dark wall of rain forest stretching for hundreds of kilometres into Rondônia and Acre. Behind them a narrow dirt road stretched nearly 500 kilometres back to Cuiabá.

Alvaro watched as a bulldozer pushed into a stand of trees. It toppled five or six of the fifty-metre trees. The rain forest trees had such shallow roots that a bulldozer could easily push over a group of trees in a few minutes. In some places the crew merely wrapped a chain around a clump of trees. Then they attached the ends of the chain to a bulldozer. As the bulldozer backed up, the trees were pulled out of the ground like a gardener pulling up weeds.

Today they'd cleared another eight kilometres of forest. Another road crew worked behind them, grading and leveling the rough clearing. Soon it resembled a road. Alvaro unfolded his survey map. He carefully marked in today's progress. On the map the BR-364 was an impressive thick red line. It extended from Cuiabá into the wilderness of Rondônia. In reality Alvaro knew the line was often nothing more than a thin dirt track hastily slashed through the forest. In the rainy season the road became a muddy ditch. Trucks and vehicles had to be regularly dug out of the thick red mud. During the dry season, traveling the road was a spine-jolting, incredibly dusty trip.

As the skies continued to darken, the men began packing up their equipment. They climbed into the trucks to take them the 20 kilometres back to their camp. Over the shouts of the men, Alvaro could hear the shrieks of the monkeys and birds. They were protesting this unwanted invasion.

More worrisome to Alvaro, however, was the possibility of human watchers. The road was pushing into territory occupied by several Indian groups. Many of these Indians had experienced little or no contact with the outside world. Alvaro knew his road crew was a frightening and unwelcome invasion of their lands. There had already been a few instances where Indians had attacked road crews. Several workers had been wounded. A few times Indians had attacked construction equipment. They broke windshields with their clubs and slashed tires. Only this morning Alvaro's road crew found three brightly feathered arrows stuck in the ground between the bulldozers. Alvaro had felt uneasy enough to post three additional guards. Today six men with rifles guarded the crew working this section of the road.

Alvaro packed up his maps. He stood for a few moments staring into the dark forest around him. Then he followed the other trucks rattling and bouncing over the rough roadway. For several minutes the thick clouds of red dust swirled from the trucks. It hid the clearing, the bulldozers, and the forest. As the dust slowly began to settle, a dozen Indians moved silently from the dark shadows of the forest into the clearing. They stared for a long while in the direction of the departing trucks.

Objective 3:
Encourage People to Settle the Interior

To encourage settlement and development of the interior, the government offered settlers free land. They had to clear an area of forest, build a house, and start farming. Most of this free land was offered in the new state of Rondônia. Wealthy Brazilians and large Brazilian- and foreign-owned companies were offered lower taxes and free land. They had to develop mineral resources or establish cattle ranches. Large sections of the new interior highways were paved to provide better access to more areas of the interior. New airports were built to provide access to remote locations.

There were several reasons why the government of Brazil encouraged the settlement of the interior.

Reasons Why the Government Encouraged Settlement

1. Opening up the interior for farming would provide land. Land was needed for the hundreds of thousands of landless poor in the rural areas.

2. Encouraging settlement would develop the wealth of natural resources in the interior. Agriculture, logging, and mining could be developed.

3. To develop mineral and forest resources requires labor. The major mineral and forest resources of the interior were far from Brazil's large populations. Large numbers of people needed to be moved to the interior to develop these resources.

4. There were timber, mineral, and hydro-electric resources in the interior. These could be sold to other countries. This would provide new wealth for the country.

5. The interior was considered Brazil's "bank vault of wealth." Members of the government thought that all they had to do was open up the area for settlement. Then Brazil would become a wealthy country.

6. The mineral and hydro-electric resources in the interior could provide the power and raw materials needed to develop industries in Brazil.*

7. The Brazilian government was concerned that another country might try to take over the sparsely settled North region. Another country might claim all the mineral and forest resources.

---

*Chart on page 177 outlines what conditions are needed before a country can become an industrial nation.

For Your Notebook

The interior of Brazil has been opened for settlement and development. This has affected the physical environment. It has changed settlement patterns and the Brazilian Indians' way of life. **Environmentalists** are not all pleased with the government decisions. Hearings are often held where environmentalists present their ideas. The following are articles by an **agronomist**, a geographer, an **anthropologist**, and an **economist**. They discuss how the *Marcha Para O Oeste* has changed Brazil. The land, the Indians, and the settlement patterns have all been affected.

Read through these interviews. Record the negative and positive consequences of the plans to open up the interior. A sample recording sheet is shown below.

Effect of Opening Up the Interior		
Effect on the Natural Environment	+	
	-	
Effect on Settlement Patterns	+	Sample
	-	
Effect on Brazilian Indians	+	
	-	

Effect of the Opening of the Interior—Viewpoints

Viewpoint from an Agronomist

The construction of Brasília, the new highways, and the increased settlement and development of the North and Center West regions since 1960 has substantially affected the physical environment. Thousands of hectares of savanna (*cerrado*) and rainforest were cleared. Farms, cattle ranches, and logging operations were developed. They have damaged the soil and natural vegetation of these regions. The natural vegetation is cleared, logged, or burned. Then the land is exposed to erosion from winds and rain. During the rainy season, heavy rains wash the exposed surface soil away. This results in a loss of the thin layer of soil containing the nutrients. Gradually the soil loses all its ability to sustain plants. Of particular concern is the rapid clearing and burning of the Amazon rain forest in the North region.

Sergio Andrade
Agronomist

Environmentalist—someone who is concerned about protecting and preserving life on the planet
Agronomist—someone who studies soils and crop management

Anthropologist—someone who studies the origin, development, and customs of people and their societies
Economist—someone who studies the way people and countries make and spend money. Some economists concentrate on the growth and development of industry and business.

Environmentalists fear that this vast rain forest may completely disappear by the year 2000.

Chemicals used on the farms in the Center West Region have **contaminated** the natural environment. The soil in the Center West region is low in fertility. It must be heavily fertilized to produce good crops year after year. Farmers also use chemicals to kill weeds and insects that damage crops. During the rainy season these chemicals are washed away and flood into the rivers. Many of the rivers of the Center West region contain high concentrations of chemicals that are harmful to plants, wildlife, and humans.

Gold miners who have come to the North and Center West region have also contaminated the physical environment. The mercury used to extract gold is being washed away into the rivers and streams. Mercury is particularly deadly to fish, wildlife, and humans.

These problems do not just affect the immediate area. Areas hundreds or even thousands of kilometres away from the mining, farming, ranching, and logging operations are also affected. The environment of the Pantanal, an isolated area in the far southern corner of Mato Grosso, is being seriously damaged by settlement activities in the northern part of the state.*

Viewpoint from a Geographer

The population in the interior areas has risen dramatically since the construction of Brasília and the new interior highways. This is especially true for the states of Goiás, Mato Grosso, Rondônia, and Acre.

The construction of Brasília had a noticeable effect on settlement in Goiás. In 1956 the site chosen for the new capital was in a sparsely populated area of Brazil. There were no cities or towns nearby. The huge labor force needed to build Brasília had to come from other parts of the country. Over 45 000 workers eventually came to work on the construction of Brasília. Most workers remained in the area after Brasília was completed. The population of Brasília and surrounding towns grew from 0 in 1956, to 550 000 in 1964. By 1989 the population had reached 1.5 million.

The new highways opened up vast new areas of the interior for settlement. People were attracted from all parts of Brazil. They came from the dry, overpopulated Northeast. They also came from the farms in the south where machinery was beginning to replace human labor. These **migrants** came to the interior looking for land, jobs, and a better life. The movement of large numbers of people to the interior substantially changed the settlement patterns in Rondônia and Acre. Before 1980 Rondônia was largely unsettled and unpopulated. By 1989 Rondônia had a capital city of half a million, and hundreds of new towns followed the BR-364 Highway. Towns like Ouro Prêto do Oeste, which did not exist in 1960, now have populations of over 100 000.

Today, the largest growth of population is in Acre Territory. As people become discouraged with trying to farm in Rondônia, or find that there is no more free land, they move on to more remote locations in the interior.

Most of the migrants to the Center West and North regions came as farmers. However, it is the cities and towns, not the rural areas, that have received the bulk of the population increases. Most of the migrants to the interior now live in the cities and towns. The cities of the interior have become very crowded.

Denise Costa
Geographer

Contaminate—pollute
Migrant—someone who moves from one area or country to another

* CASE STUDY: THE ENDANGERED PANTANAL at the end of this chapter explores the problems associated with settlement activities in the Center West region.

Viewpoint from an Anthropologist

The government programs to settle and develop the North and Center West regions have seriously affected the Brazilian Indians and their way of life. Highways have been built across their lands. Settlers have taken over their land for cattle ranches and farms. Gold prospectors have moved into their hunting areas. Hydroelectric dams and mines have damaged large areas of their rain forest.

It is not just the Indian lands that are threatened by the settlement activities. Contact with settlers has already killed thousands of Indians. Settlers and miners have carried measles, chicken pox, smallpox, influenza, and tuberculosis to the Brazilian interior. The Indians have had no chance to build up any resistance to these diseases. When Indians contact these diseases, the result is usually fatal. The same thing happened to people in Europe and North America until their bodies were able to develop some resistance to these diseases. In the last two decades disease has killed thousands of Indians. Estimates are that the population of Brazilian Indians is now 187 000 to 200 000. Some anthropologists believe the Indian population may be as low as 100 000. In Rondônia, for example, the population of Indians may have dropped from 35 000 in 1950 to only 5 000 in 1989.

Thousands of Indians have also experienced a sudden disruption in their **traditional** way of life as other cultures have come into contact with their isolated settlements. Anthropologists call this sudden change CULTURE SHOCK. The sudden introduction of new tools, new clothing, new foods, and new hunting equipment has caused great confusion in Indian groups who have lived isolated from the outside world for thousands of years. Traditional ways of farming, hunting, and living are affected when an isolated tribe makes contact with the modern world. Today, only a handful of Indian groups living in very remote and isolated areas of the rain forest have survived with their way of life unchanged by the modern world. These Indians have been mainly in very isolated areas beyond easy river access and beyond the reach of the roads. Even these groups, however, are no longer safe from the problems of development. The use of airplanes has made even their isolated areas accessible to

Silvia Alvarez
Anthropologist

scientists, government agents, hydro-electric engineers, and mining companies. New roads are being built even in the most remote areas of the interior.

Most of the Indian population in Brazil lives in government-assigned areas called RESERVES. Reserves are large areas of land that are for the exclusive use of the Indians. Outsiders are not allowed onto the Indian lands without permission from the Indians or the Brazilian government. Most of these Indian land reserves are in Amazonas, Rondônia, Mato Grosso, Acre, and Roraima. The government has indicated it will continue to support these Indian land reserves but there is a great deal of opposition to this plan from settlers, mining companies, prospectors, and the Brazilian military.

In recent years Indians have come into conflict with settlers, ranchers, prospectors, and engineers who want access to Indian lands to develop mines, dams, ranches, farms, and hydro-electric dams on Indian lands. In the last five years a number of Indians have been killed by gold miners invading Indian areas. The Indians believe the government is not doing enough to keep everyone out of the Indian reserves.

The government of Brazil will have to find a solution to the conflict between the Indians' demands to maintain their land reserves and the demands of the settlers for access to more areas of the interior.

Traditional—based on the beliefs, customs, and stories that are passed on from one generation to another.

Eliane Zarate
Economist

Point of View from an Economist

Opening up the interior areas of Brazil has benefited Brazil. Brazilians are able to utilize the land, forest, mineral, and hydro-electric resources of the interior. For so many years, we just talked about our country's great wealth of resources. Now that we are developing these resources, the country and the people will benefit.

Thirty years ago Brasília was built in the wilderness of Goiás. This marked the start of the program to open up the interior. At that time, the Center West was undeveloped and basically unsettled. Today the Center West is one of Brazil's most productive agricultural areas. In a few short years Brazil has become a leading producer of soya beans. Exporting soya beans to other countries has generated a great deal of money. Clearing land for farms in the Center West has also increased the production of wheat, rice, manioc, and beans.

The Center West is helping to feed Brazilians. It is also providing food to people in other countries. Clearing the interior has provided farmland for thousands of landless families. Now these families can grow food and feed themselves. They have more food and eat a more nutritious diet.

In the last thirty years, the development of the mineral resources in the interior has been substantial. Brazil has become one of the world's leading gold producers. Most of the gold is mined by individuals working small claims. These gold deposits have provided good incomes for thousands of individual miners. Brazil has vast deposits of iron ore, tin, bauxite, manganese, copper, and nickel. Development of these resources has created thousands of jobs and generated a great deal of money for the country.

Brazil has started to build dams and develop the hydro-electric potential of the interior rivers. Now the country has enough cheap electricity to fuel industries and homes. With cheap electric power, industries can expand and produce more goods. This is very good for the country. Industries create many new jobs and provide thousands of workers with steady incomes. This helps improve living conditions for the workers.

Brazil has had to lose some of the rain forest to develop these resources. The benefits for the people and the country, however, outweigh the loss of trees and animals.

SUMMARY: OPENING UP THE INTERIOR

In the 1950s the North and Center West regions of Brazil were sparsely populated and undeveloped. In the 1960s, the government of Brazil began the *Marcha Para O Oeste* (March to the West) program to open up the interior. The government hoped that this would result in development. New agricultural areas and development of the vast natural resources were the goals. The government hoped that the interior would provide land for the landless farmers in Brazil. This would reduce the flow of people to the already crowded cities. As part of its March to the West plan, the government built

a new capital city, Brasília, in the interior. It also built an extensive system of highways through the interior. Settlement was encouraged by the government's offer of free land.

The plan to open up the interior did change settlement patterns in Brazil. The population in Mato Grosso, Goiás, and Rondônia increased substantially. New towns sprung up almost overnight along the BR-364 Highway. Much of the increase in population in the interior has been to the new cities and towns. The rural areas have not grown as quickly.

Opening up the interior has greatly benefited Brazil. Developing the land, timber, mineral, and hydro-electric resources of the interior has created new jobs for thousands of people. It has also produced a great deal of money for the country. The development of inexpensive hydro-electric power has contributed to the building of new industries in Brazil. Opening up the interior has, however, seriously affected the physical environment and the Brazilian Indians.

Vast areas of the savanna and rain forest are being cut and burned for farming, logging, mining, and cattle ranching. The most serious concern is the rapid destruction of the Amazon rain forest. Environmentalists in Brazil and across the world fear that the world's largest rain forest may disappear by the year 2000. The interior rivers are also being polluted. Chemicals washing away from farms and gold mining operations are causing the pollution.

Opening the interior to settlement and development also affected the Brazilian Indians. Thousands have died from exposure to the diseases brought by settlers and gold prospectors. Many have died in clashes with settlers and prospectors who want access to Indian lands. In 1989 the Brazilian government was still working on a solution to the problem. It is trying to protect Indian lands while also developing and settling the interior.

CHAPTER REVIEW

For Your Notebook

1. On an outline map of Brazil, label the states and territories that are considered the interior of Brazil. Find Brasília on the map. Label it as well.
2. How have highways, airplanes, and electricity affected the interior?
3. Use your knowledge of the physical features of the interior. What predictions can you make about the success of farming and cattle ranching in the interior?
4. In your opinion, will opening up the interior have a lasting effect on the settlement patterns in Brazil? Will the interior regions eventually be successfully developed and heavily populated?
5. Evaluate the information gathered on your recording chart (page 103): Effect of Opening up the Interior. Develop a concluding statement that reflects your opinion as to whether the *Marcha Para O Oeste* had largely positive or negative results.
6. What might the government do to protect the land, rivers, and Indians?

Effect of Opening Up the Interior		
Land	+	
	−	Sample
Settlement	+	
	−	
Indians	+	
	−	

Exploring Further

1. Pretend you are working for the Brazilian government's *Marcha Para O Oeste* plan. Write a TV or newspaper advertisement encouraging settlement in the interior. Include the physical features that would attract people and encourage them to move to the interior.

2.  Evaluate the information gathered and develop a concluding statement for the problem solving activity you started on page 95: How did the opening up of the interior affect the physical environment of Brazil?

3.

(Continued from Chapter Review on page 93)

Chapter 4 presented information as to how Brazilians interacted with the physical environment of the interior to develop its resources. Evaluate the information gathered from this chapter. Add or make revisions to your Decision Making Form.
   • Does the information in this chapter suggest alternatives?
   • Does the information in this chapter provide positive and negative consequences of development that can help you in making a decision on the issue?

? Problem Solving

Brasília is one of the few totally planned cities in the world. What is it like living in a city that was designed on an **architect's** drawing board? The interviews in this case study present different points of view about life in Brasília.

As you read through the interviews consider the advantages and disadvantages of life in a planned city. This case study uses Brasília as an example. However, many of the arguments would apply to planned cities built anywhere in the world. Record the advantages and disadvantages of life in a planned city on a chart like the one to the right. At the end of the case study, evaluate your data and state your own opinion on planned cities.

Life in a Planned City

Advantages	Disadvantages

Evaluation

Sample

Brasília: The New Capital

By building Brasília, the government dramatically changed the settlement patterns in Brazil. The above photograph shows the spacious, open design of Brasília. The twin towers and bowl-shaped buildings house Brazil's Senate and Chamber of Deputies. They are separated from other government office buildings by a large area of grass. Other large, open areas of parkland are found throughout Brasília.

Architect—designer of buildings

A Planned City

Few cities in the world have been as completely planned as Brasília.* Brasília was a totally planned city. The site selected for the new capital city was an isolated, undeveloped location on the central plateau. It was a wilderness of trees, grasslands, and wild animals nearly 1 000 kilometres inland from the coast. Every road, every building, every park was built according to the plans drawn up by a team of architects. The feat of constructing an entirely new city in the interior wilderness attracted worldwide attention. In less than five years, construction crews, working nearly eighteen hours a day, built an entire city where once there had been only grasslands and trees.

When completed, Brasília was a new city complete with government buildings, courthouses, the President's residence, office blocks, apartments, houses, schools, shopping centers, supermarkets, restaurants, bus stations, churches, hospitals, movie theaters, playgrounds, parks, hotels, a university, and golf courses. A large artificial lake was even built to add moisture to the air during the dry winters. Everything in Brasília had been designed and planned by the team of architects.

The master plan for Brasília was drawn up by Brazilian architect Lucio Costa. Numerous buildings were designed by Brazil's most famous architect, Oscar Niemeyer. Many of these buildings are still considered to be some of the most beautiful examples of modern architecture in the world. They are now more than twenty years old. However, their bold, abstract designs continue to attract worldwide admiration.

Brazil's Senate and Chamber of Deputies' buildings are excellent examples of the modern architecture which makes Brasília famous.

Brasília was designed like a bow and arrow pointing into the interior. Along the curve of the bow are the residential and business areas. Along the arrow are the government buildings.

*Brasília is not the only planned city in Brazil. Goiâna, founded in 1933, was a planned state capital city.

CASE STUDY: **Life in Brasília**

Modern superhighways cut through the city, providing efficient transportation routes to all parts of the city. Roads pass under or over other roads to avoid intersections. There are very few traffic signals in Brasília to hold up traffic.

Brasílian architecture is modern. It is often stark, but graceful.

Each residential area includes several large apartment blocks called superquads. It also contains an elementary school, shops, church, movie theaters, and parks.

Oscar Niemeyer said he wanted to create a city that appealed to the imagination of the people. He was particularly fond of dramatic, curving shapes. The National Cathedral is one of Niemeyer's most modern designs.

Living in Brasília: Several Viewpoints

Denise, 16

High School student in Brasília

My family has lived in Brasília for the last six years. Before my father was transferred to Brasília we lived in an apartment in Ipanema. Ipanema is a suburb of Rio de Janeiro. I have had a hard time getting used to living in Brasília.

I think Brasília is too much the same. Every street seems exactly like every other street. All the residential areas and apartment blocks look the same. Our shopping area, supermarket, theater, park, and elementary school are identical to those in other residential areas. The neighborhoods don't even have names. They're numbered and labeled by the section of the city where they are located. We live in the 110 South residential neighborhood. Our residential area looks exactly like the 120 South residential neighborhood. In Rio every street was a little different. The neighborhoods had interesting shops, restaurants, and parks. The apartment buildings were different

designs and sizes. Here, everything is the same. Brasília is not a very interesting place to live.

Walking is another thing I miss. I am used to living in a city where people could walk to restaurants, movies, and shopping. Brasília is not a city for pedestrians. This is a city designed for cars. In our residential area, I can walk to the few shops. In the main part of the city, walking is almost impossible. Everything is spread out in separate areas. The city has specific areas for shopping, restaurants, banks, hotels, and recreation and sports centers. All the government offices and buildings are in one section of the city. These special sections are separated by large grassy fields. There are no paved walkways across these grassy fields. People who are without cars have made their own dirt walking trails across the fields.

The wide avenues also make walking difficult. The streets are too wide and busy to cross safely. At most of the main intersections there are traffic underpasses and **cloverleafs**. These were designed so there would be fewer accidents at intersections. It also means that it

is impossible to cross the streets. There are no traffic lights to stop the traffic. To get from one area to another you really need a car.

Brasília is so isolated that we can't even go anywhere for a short holiday. Everything is so far away that it is impossible to take a week-end holiday in the car. We have to fly if we want to go anywhere. Brasília is just too far away from the rest of Brazil.

My father has an excellent job here with the government. However, I know my parents would like to be back in Rio. If we could, my family would move back to Rio. Even the girls in my school who were born in Brasília want to move to Rio de Janeiro or São Paulo when they are older.

I can't wait to move back to Rio.

Julia, 21

Works at a radio station in Brasília

My husband and I live in **Taguantinga**, one of Brasília's seven SATELLITE CITIES. Satellite cities are located far outside Brasília. They are cities for workers. We live in Taguantinga because we cannot afford an apartment in Brasília. My husband works at a camera shop in the Conjuncto Nacional Shopping Center and I work at the radio station. We both have jobs in Brasília but we cannot afford to live there.

Brasília is not a city for workers. Brasília was built for the wealthy, the government politicians, and the government employees with good salaries. You have to have a very good wage to afford an apartment. Even if we did have enough money there are few apartments available.

Cloverleaf—a highway structure which allows traffic to curve upward or downward to join traffic on other highways without having to stop for traffic lights

Taguatinga—pronounced ta-wa-ching-uh

CASE STUDY: Life in Brasília

Building companies need government permission to build new apartment buildings. The city planners do not want many more apartments built in the city. The city planners want to keep Brasília's population less than a million. Someone at the radio station told me the government wants Brasília to have a population of only 500 000 people. They don't want Brasília to become overcrowded like other cities in Brazil. But the planners don't care how crowded we are in the satellite towns.

Taguantinga is 25 kilometres away from the city. For my husband and me it is a ninety minute bus ride into work each day. The buses are so crowded that I usually have to stand for the entire trip. The long ride means I don't see my children as much as I would like. My two little girls stay with a neighbor when we are working in Brasília. It is very late when I get home most days. If we could live closer to our jobs, we could spend more time with our daughters. We are still lucky. Many people live in satellite cities farther away. They have a very long bus ride each day to get to work in Brasília.

Even though we can't live in the city, my husband and I are very happy we moved to Brasília. We grew up and married in Teresina in northern Brazil. There was no work for us. It was very hard on our family. My husband's brother moved here two years before us. He helped get my husband the job in the camera store. We are very lucky that we both have jobs.

We also have a better place to live than we had in Teresina. Last year we moved into a government-built house outside Taguantinga. Now we have electricity and there is a tap with running water. Many who come to Brasília are not as lucky as we are.

Antonio, 20

A student at the University of Brasília

Brasília is the most wonderful city in the world. Everything here is ahead of its time. When you look at these buildings it is difficult to remember that they are nearly thirty years old. No where in the world are there buildings like the ones here.

Brasília is truly a wonderful place to live. It is so well planned. Buildings are not crowded together. There are many open, grassy areas between the buildings. In most cities, the buildings are crowded together and there are few open spaces. In Brasília, there are many parks and open spaces.

The architects have organized the city into sections for different functions. All the hotels are in one section, all the banks in another, and all the restaurants in another. This is much better than having them spread out over the city. In most cities there are hotels, banks, shops, restaurants, and schools everywhere. It is so difficult to find anything. Here, everything is very well organized.

The wide avenues and streets have room for several lanes of traffic. With only a few traffic lights to stop the flow of traffic, Brasília does not have many traffic problems. In other cities it is impossible to drive from one part of the city to another in a few minutes. There are always traffic problems. In Brasília, it is very easy to travel right across the city in a few minutes.

Brasília is an example for other countries to follow. The cities of the future will all be planned and organized like Brasília.

Emilio, 57

Government official in Ministry of Health

I was 28 and living in Rio de Janeiro when President Kubischek officially opened Brasília. Like other government employees, I was very upset about moving to Brasília. I did not want to leave Rio. I enjoyed the beaches, the restaurants, the night life, and my apartment.

Over the years my family has adjusted to life in Brasília. Living here has been better than we expected. It is a very modern and comfortable city but it is not as interesting as Rio de Janeiro. We have very good schools and a university for our children. We also have the ballet, theaters, and lots of restaurants and shopping centers. I really like the blue skies and clean air here. There are no large industries in Brasília, so there is no air pollution.

I also like the convenience of having all the government offices together. In Rio the government departments were spread out in a hundred offices throughout the city. It was impossible to talk to people from other offices. They might be several kilometres away. Telephone service in Rio was terrible. The lines were always busy or they didn't work. Here in Brasília, the telephone lines are new and they always work. I can always get through.

For the government, the move to Brasília has produced some unexpected results. Forcing the workers and the poor to live outside Brasília has isolated the government officials from many of the real problems of the people. This is an artificial city. It is a city of people with good wages, nice apartments, and plenty of food. Outside the city, in the satellite towns, there is a different Brazil. The government makes the decisions about education, housing, and health care but it is too isolated from the everyday problems of most Brazilians.

The Effects

On Settlement Patterns

The Brazilian government moved nearly a million people into the interior.* This drastically changed the settlement patterns. The move focused attention on the sparsely-populated and potentially wealthy region in the interior of the country. The rain forest could be cleared for farms and cattle ranches. Gold and other minerals were located in the interior. The rain forests held a wealth of valuable timber. Highways were built to connect Brasília to the coast and other interior locations.They provided access to the interior for thousands of settlers, ranchers, loggers, and gold miners.

The construction of Brasília did not alter the problem of thousands of poor, landless farmers. Most of the landholdings in Goáis and Mato Grosso opened up by Brasília are large landholdings.They are held by corporations or wealthy individuals. There are few small family farms. Most of the movement of people to the interior has been to the new interior cities. These are Brasília, Cuiabá, Campo Grande, and Goiâna. Populations in these cities have increased substantially since 1960. For the newcomers, living conditions in the cities are poor. Many live in *favelas*, much like those in the large coastal cities. These people have not improved their living conditions much by moving to the interior.

On Native Indians

The development of the interior has seriously affected the population of native Indians. The largest populations of Indians are in the interior area. There are many Indian land reserves. They are in Mato Grosso, Pará, Amazonas, Ron-dônia, Acre, and Roraima. Conflict between the Brazilian Indians and the new settlers, cattle ranchers, and gold miners has increased greatly since the 1970s. The set-tlers, ranchers, and gold miners want access to Indian lands. They want to develop farms and ranches. They also want to look for gold. In recent years there have been several violent clashes between Indians and armed bands of gold miners or settlers. The Brazilian government has set aside large areas as protected Indian reserves. It has, however, also encouraged settlers, ranchers, and miners to settle and develop the lands of the interior. The number of Indians continues to decrease as the number of settlers to the interior continues to increase. This means that Brazilian Indians are finding it very difficult to preserve their lands. The government has established several departments to oversee Indian rights and lands. Since the building of Brasília and the roads into the interior, these departments have not been able to secure all Indian lands. Settlers, ranchers, logging companies, and gold miners all want the land.

On the Land

The construction of Brasília encouraged the development and settlement of the interior states. Over the past 30 years this development and settlement has altered the natural vegetation of the interior. Environmentalists are concerned about the development. They say it has damaged the natural environment of the region.

Clearing thousands of hectares of *cerrado* vegetation and rain forest is one concern. This land is used to make farms and pasture for cattle ranching. The removal of the natural vegetation has resulted in the erosion of many areas. The effect of the heavy rains on the exposed soil is also reducing soil fertility.

Chemical pollution is another problem. The soil of the Center West region is not very fertile. It needs heavy use of fertilizer to maintain high crop yields. During the rainy season, the chemicals from these fertilizers flood into the river systems. Many of the rivers in the region now contain high concentrations of chemicals. These are harmful to wildlife and humans. Gold miners have also added their own contamination. The **silt** washed away from the mining operations is beginning to clog the rivers and ruin fish breeding grounds. Several rivers can no longer be used for transportation. They have become too shallow. The mercury used to extract gold is also washed away with the silt. It has contaminated many of the rivers and streams. The mercury is particularly deadly to fish, wildlife, and humans who use the rivers for drinking water.

Development and settlement of the Center West region has seriously damaged the natural environment.

---

*In the 1960s, the term interior meant the Center West region: Brasília, Goiás, Mato Grosso, and Mato Grosso do Sul. By the 1970s, the term interior included Rondônia, Acre, Amazonas, Roraima, and Pará.

Silt—earth washed down by a river

CASE STUDY: Life in Brasília

Discussion

1. What would you consider the main differences between Brasília and most cities in North America?
2. Brasília has been carefully planned to separate people from traffic. How was this done?

Activities

1. Evaluate the arguments for and against living in a planned city. Then complete the following statements:

   a. In my opinion, the most important argument for planned cities is.......

   b. In my opinion, the most important argument against planned cities........

   c. I would like living in a planned city because ....

   d. I would not like living in a planned city because.....

   e. If I were planning a city, these are five considerations I think are most important:

2. Do you think that a planned city is an improvement? Go back to the beginning of the case study and complete the chart you started on page 108. What are the advantages and disadvantages of living in a planned city such as Brasília?

3. Choose new capitals for Canada and the United States. Consider location, climate, topography, and transportation when you choose a site.

> ## ?
> ### New Capital Cities

4. Luis Costa designed Brasília like a bow and arrow pointing into the interior. The residential and business areas are along the curve of the bow. The government buildings are along the arrow. Use the map of Brasília on the right to help you plan new capital cities for Canada and the United States. What features would you incorporate into your design?

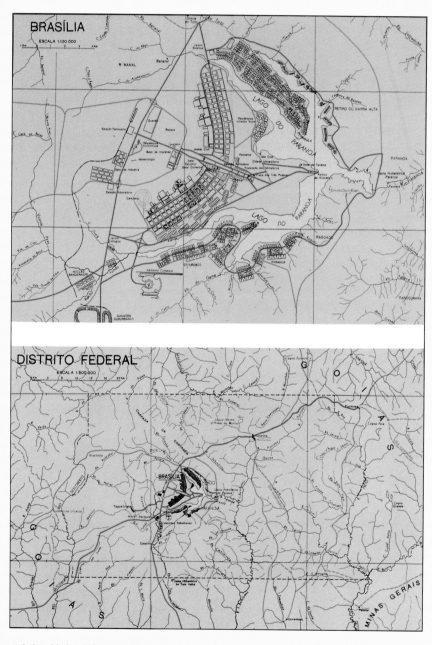

114

? **Problem Solving**

Use the Problem Solving Strategy introduced earlier in the text to work through the problem. Use the retrieval chart shown on this page to record information.

Development activities such as mining, cattle ranching, farming, logging, and hydro-electric dams have affected the natural environment. This case study shows how development activities in one area can affect areas hundreds of kilometres away.

As you read through the case study consider the following problem:

Why is the Pantanal endangered?

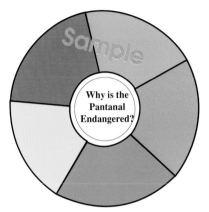

Sample

Why is the Pantanal Endangered?

Retrieval Chart

The Pantanal

Location

The Pantanal is an area of flat, low-lying land in the Center West region. The Pantanal stretches in a triangle between Cuiabá in Mato Grosso, Campo Grande in Mato Grosso do Sul, and Brazil's border with Bolivia and Paraguay.

Topography

The diagram on the lower right shows the elevation of the Pantanal. It is much lower than the surrounding plateaus in Mato Grosso and Mato Grosso do Sul. During the rainy season (November to March), water from the heavy rains flows down into the low-lying Pantanal. The rivers overflow their banks and flood the Pantanal. The Pantanal is often called a swamp, but this is not an accurate description. A swamp is flooded all year. The Pantanal is only flooded for part of the year. During the dry season (July to the beginning of October), the flood waters dry up. Then the Pantanal is dry grasslands and forests.

Cuiaba

Campo Grande

The Pantanal

115

CASE STUDY: **Endangered Pantanal**

The wildlife of the Pantanal has been seriously affected by recent developments in the Center West. Development of logging, mining, cattle ranching, farming, and industries has produced some devastating results. Many Brazilian ecologists are worried that human activities will eventually destroy the wildlife of the Pantanal.

The Brazilian alligator is called the JACARÉ. During the dry season, *jacarés* can be seen basking in the sun on the sandy beaches.

The *tuyuyú* stork is nearly two metres tall. It builds nests large enough to hold a human.

Hunting

World demand for alligator skin and ocelot and jaguar fur clothing has attracted hunters to the Pantanal. This has become a problem in the last ten years. Hunters have seriously reduced the alligator, ocelot, puma, and jaguar populations in the Pantanal.

Clearing the Natural Vegetation

Large areas of natural vegetation in the Center West region have been cleared for pasture, farmlands, and logging. Since building Brasília and constructing the BR-364 Highway across the interior, the Center West has become one of Brazil's most rapidly growing agricultural areas. The development of farms and ranches, however, has had a damaging effect on the Pantanal. As the natural vegetation is removed, the land is exposed to erosion from the winds and rains. During the rainy season, the heavy rains wash the exposed surface soil away. This silt is carried by the rivers into the Pantanal. It is deposited in the river beds and over the land. Vast quantities of silt are filling up lakes, rivers, and marshes. It is also destroying fish breeding areas, and damaging bird nesting and feeding areas.

The piranha is probably the most widely known Brazilian river fish.

116

Increased Access

Building the Trans-Pantanal Highway increased access to the Pantanal. It also contributed to the destruction of the land and wildlife. The highway is a single-lane dirt road with over 150 wooden bridges. Sections of the highway are washed away or under water during the rainy season. As a result, rivers continue to provide the main year-round transportation through the Pantanal. However, the highway has brought more people and development activities to the areas farthest away from the rivers. During the dry season, the highway provides a fast and convenient route for trucks and machinery to travel into the Pantanal.

A small wooden bridge over an area of flooded marshland is a common sight along the Trans-Pantanal Highway.

Chemical Contamination

Chemicals used on the farms and ranches in the Center West region have **contaminated** the Pantanal. The soil in the Center West region is low in nutrients. It must be heavily fertilized to produce good crop yields year after year. Farms also use chemicals to kill weeds and insects that damage crops. Cattle ranchers have used chemical **defoliants.** These clear the natural vegetation quickly to make cattle pastures. During the rainy season, these chemicals are washed away and flood into the Pantanal. Many of these chemicals can seriously affect the plants, insects, and animals in the Pantanal. Some chemicals affect how many eggs the birds lay each year.They also affect how many eggs develop and hatch. Some of the chemicals interfere with an animal's ability to digest food. The newly constructed industries and factories in the Center West region have resulted in an increase in **toxic** chemicals. These and other waste products flow into the rivers in the Pantanal.

The Pantanal is flooded for several months of the year. Environmentalists fear these flood waters carry dangerous chemicals that pose a danger to the thousands of birds that come to the Pantanal to breed.

Contaminated—polluted
Defoliant—chemical that causes leaves to fall from plants and trees

Toxic—harmful, dangerous

117

Mining

Gold prospectors are also contributing to the damage in the Pantanal. Many of the miners use mercury to extract gold from the earth. This chemical is easily washed away in the gold mining process. The mercury is deadly to fish and birds. It is also poisonous to the humans who use the rivers for drinking water or rely on the river fish for food. Recent testing indicates that there are high concentrations of mercury in several areas of the Pantanal. Scientists are concerned about the mercury poisoning. They think it may be responsible for the declining populations of a number of bird species in the Pantanal.

Small gold mining pits like this are adding dangerous chemicals to the rivers in the Pantanal.

Cattle Ranching

To raise more cattle, ranchers have drained large areas of the Pantanal. They have also cleared forest areas to make new pasture lands. Creating new pasture lands has destroyed many of the bird nesting and food gathering sites. Clearing large forest areas has also destroyed the habitats of numerous other animals.

Large herds of **zebu** cattle are raised on newly cleared Pantanal land.

Endangered Pantanal: Several Viewpoints

Benjamin Garcia

Cattle Rancher and Soya Bean Farmer

The Center West, including the Pantanal, is a land of great opportunity. The interior is the future of Brazil. In the Center West region we are developing some of the best farming and ranching in Brazil. We must develop Brazil. We must make jobs for people. We must feed people. To do this, we must develop all of Brazil's resources. The land of the Center West is one of Brazil's resources.

Before we can use the land, however, it must be cleared. Farmers and ranchers have been criticized for clearing and burning the forest and the savanna. But those are only trees and bushes! When it is cleared, I can plant **soya beans** or rice. I can graze large herds of cattle. These are the things that will make Brazil wealthy.

Trees and bushes will do nothing.

The soya bean farms are a good example of the potential of the Center West. Twenty years ago there was not one soya bean farm in Mato Grosso State. In 1988 Mato Grosso was one of the world's leading producers of soya beans. Cuiabá is the capital of Mato Grosso State. It has grown from a small interior town to a major city. Cuiabá is the center of the rice and soya bean industry. Banks, trading

Soya beans—beans rich in protein   **Zebu**—a mixed breed of Brazilian and Indian cattle

118

companies, and industries are moving here because of the soya beans and rice. This means jobs for the people and money for the country. What is the loss of some trees and bushes compared to this development? Trees and bushes do not feed people or provide jobs for anyone. My soya bean and rice farm employs many people. My crops will help make Brazil wealthy.

We need much more development here in the interior. I can see that one day we will have many industries here. They will employ thousands of people. Brazil needs ways to make money in order to solve its financial and social problems. To make money, we need to develop all of our country's resources. The land of the Center West must be developed. Some of the natural environment will be destroyed, but it will be replaced with something more valuable to Brazilians. Development may mean that we lose some trees and animals, but we will be gaining farms, industries, and jobs.

Luis

Pantanal Park Ranger

I have been a ranger in the Cara Cara National Park in the Pantanal for five years. There are many problems in the Pantanal. The hunters are one of the major problems. They come to the Pantanal to kill the Brazilian alligators we call *jacaré*. They use power boats, high-powered rifles and radios. A group of five hunters can kill up to a thousand alligators in three nights. The hunters only get about $1.00 US for each alligator skin. Consequently, they must kill many alligators to make money. They sell the skins to the skin dealers across the border in Bolivia.

A few years ago there were often groups of a hundred *jacaré* on the large sandbars. Today, a large group is twenty or thirty. In some areas of the river there are no alligators.

Two years ago the government promised a special Pantanal army to patrol this area and protect it from hunters. But nothing has changed. The Pantanal is protected by only a handful of poorly equipped rangers. I have one small motor boat, a pair of handcuffs, and a rifle. We have only a few rangers and a couple of old power boats. Still, we have to patrol an area that is nearly as large as some countries.

It is not just the hunters that are hurting the Pantanal. Even the Pantanal residents do not worry about protecting the wildlife. If they are out working with their cattle and spot a jaguar, they shoot it. The skin is worth much money to them. They do not worry that the jaguars are almost **extinct.**

The chemicals washing into the rivers from the farms, cattle ranches, and mines are also a danger. There are fewer birds here than a few years ago. Biologists think chemicals in the rivers are slowly poisoning the birds. Some of the birds are not able to reproduce. Some of the young birds are too weak and do not survive.

We need to find ways to protect the Pantanal before it disappears completely. We need to educate the people of Brazil so they will recognize the importance of protecting the land and the wildlife.

Our schools do not teach children to protect the wildlife. We need to protect the Pantanal from hunters. We must educate the people of Brazil so they will recognize the importance of protecting the wildlife.

Preservacão Da Natureza*

1. Evaluate the information gathered from this chapter and case study. Develop a concluding statement to answer the problem:
   Why is the Pantanal endangered?

2. Use the Problem Solving Strategy introduced earlier in the text and the retrieval model shown at the beginning of this case study to work through the following problem:
   How might the Brazilian government protect the Pantanal?

Work in small groups to brainstorm solutions. Are there ways for the Brazilian government to minimize damage to the Pantanal while continuing to encourage development activities? Consider the feasibility of any action plans that might be needed to carry out a suggested solution. Evaluate the solutions suggested. As a group, develop a concluding statement to answer the question.

Jacaré—pronounced ja-car-ay

Extinct—no longer existing
*Save nature

CHAPTER 5
Millions on the Move

Since 1890 many Brazilians have moved from one region of Brazil to another. Millions of Brazilians have moved from the Northeast to the Southeast. Millions have moved from the countryside to the cities, and from the coastal areas to the interior wilderness. This chapter examines the factors that influenced these population shifts. It looks at how Brazil's settlement patterns have changed since 1890.

1. Why have millions of Brazilians moved from one part of Brazil to another?
2. What regions have experienced most of the population changes?
3. Why have millions of Brazilians moved to the cities?
4. How has the growth of urban populations affected life in Brazil?
5. Why have so many people from the Northeast region moved to the Southeast?
6. Why have millions of Brazilians moved to the interior regions of Brazil in the last twenty years?
7. How have these population shifts affected regional differences in population?
8. How have these population shifts changed the settlement patterns in Brazil?

Problem Solving

1. Explore possible answers to the question:

   How have recent population shifts changed the settlement patterns in Brazil?

2. Develop hypotheses about how the population shifts described in the chapter introduction could change settlement patterns. Copy and use the recording chart shown on this page to help you solve the problem.* Record your hypotheses on how the population shifts changed settlement patterns under the three headings: To the Cities, To the Southeast, and To the Frontier.

3. As you read through the chapter on population movement, add new information to the chart. You may need to revise and change your original hypotheses as you gather more information.

4. At the end of the chapter you will be asked to evaluate the information and develop a concluding statement to the problem of how population shifts changed the settlement patterns in Brazil.

Millions on the Move

Problem: How have recent population shifts changed the settlement patterns in Brazil?

To the Cities	To the Southeast	To the Frontier
• _____	• _____	• _____
• _____	• _____	• _____
• _____	• _____	• _____
• _____	• _____	• _____
• _____	• _____	• _____
• _____	• _____	• _____
• _____	• _____	• _____

Sample

| Concluding Statement | Concluding Statement | Concluding Statement |

* Recording Chart is available as black-line master in the Teacher Resource Package.

MILLIONS ON THE MOVE

REVIEW OF CHAPTERS 3 AND 4

For most of its history, the population of Brazil has been concentrated along a narrow coastal strip 500 kilometres wide.

Immigration in the 1890–1930 period accounted for a large part of the population increase in the South and Southeastern regions. The families of European immigrants eventually moved from the coffee plantations to the cities or they moved farther inland into São Paulo and Paraná states. This movement of immigrants helped shift the frontier farther westward and farther inland from the coast.

The large population increases and the government plans to open up the interior areas of the country for settlement, resulted in movement of people into the sparsely populated Center West region.

ADVANCE ORGANIZER

Population Movements

Since the 1940s there has been a tremendous increase in INTERNAL MIGRATION. Millions of people have left parts of the country and moved to other parts. By the early 1980s nearly 40% of all Brazilians were living in places other than their birthplaces. They were searching for jobs, land and better living conditions. There are three significant patterns to the internal migration: movement to the cities, movement to the Southeast, and movement to the frontier.

1. Movement to the Cities

Many Brazilians have moved from the countryside to the cities in Brazil since 1940. Brazil's population grew substantially from 1940 to 1989. The cities absorbed most of this population increase. Cities along the coast and in the interior have shown a substantial increase in population in the last 50 years.

2. Movement to the Southeast

Since the 1860s gold rush there has been a continual movement of people. They have gone from the Northeast to the South and Southeast regions. The many droughts in the Northeast have forced many rural families to move. The South has attracted people from the Northeast. The South has more factory jobs, higher wages, increased agricultural production, and large, exciting cities.

3. Movement to the Frontier

The government built Brasília and the new interior highways. Since then, hundreds of thousands of Brazilians have migrated into the vast frontier of the Center West and North regions. This has affected Goiás, Mato Grosso, Rondônia, and Acre. Their populations have increase dramatically in the last twenty years.

The states of Mato Grosso, Rondônia, Acre, Amazonas, Pará and the territories of Roraima and Amapa are often called Brazil's frontier states.

Internal Migration in Brazil

MIGRATION is people moving from one place to settle in another. Since the 1960s millions of Brazilians have migrated from one part to another part of Brazil.

123

Movement to the Cities

Another change in Brazil's settlement patterns during the second half of the 1900s has been the shift from rural areas to cities. Since the 1940s a large part of the population in the rural areas of Brazil has moved to cities. This population movement is called URBANIZATION.

Even during the early settlement of Brazil, towns were more popular places to live than the countryside. Brazilians have always loved the excitement, activity, and cultural life of the city. The jobs, however, were always in the countryside. People worked on sugar or coffee plantations, small farms, or cattle ranches. Until the 1940s, the cities and towns in Brazil were small and the populations grew slowly. Most Brazilians lived in the rural areas. After 1940, the population began to shift to the cities. Look at the graph above and the chart on page 125.

They illustrate the percentage of the population living in rural and urban areas in 1989.* Figures are also given for Canada and the United States. You can make comparisons with Brazil.

The move to the cities did not just affect the settled areas along the coast. All regions showed a population shift from rural to urban. Thousands of people migrated to the Center West and North regions along the new highways. Many settled in the interior cities and towns rather than the countryside.

---

* Small towns (less than 1 000 inhabitants) are included as "urban" for census purposes.

124

Growth of Cities

The large cities along the northeast and southern coast have shown a dramatic increase in population since 1940. São Paulo and Rio de Janeiro, in particular, have shown spectacular growth in the last fifty years.

Rio de Janeiro and São Paulo were the first cities in Brazil to reach populations of one million.

The population growth is not just confined to the city boundaries. The areas several kilometres outside these major cities have also shown a large increase in population. Fifteen kilometres outside São Paulo, for example, hundreds of thousands of migrants have built shelters and set up small settlements.

No part of Brazil appears to have escaped the recent urbanization. Even the new interior cities have shown enormous population growth. Porto Velho in Rondônia had a population of only 27 000 in 1950. In 1989 it had a population of 700 000. Rio Branco in Acre had only a scattered population before 1970. Now it has over 100 000 inhabitants. Goiânia was a new city in 1937. It had a population of less than 20 000. By 1970 its population was 400 000. By 1989 it had a population of 700 000. Refer to the map on page 123 for the locations of the above mentioned cities.

The chart below shows the locations and populations of the cities in Brazil with populations over one million. The chart includes for comparison some large cities in Canada and the United States.

Cities with Populations of Over One Million in Brazil, Canada, and the United States

CITY	POPULATION*
SÃO PAULO	12 000 000
RIO DE JANEIRO	9 000 000
BELO HORIZONTE	2 500 000
RECIFE	2 389 000
PORTO ALEGRE	2 275 000
SALVADOR	1 800 000
BRASÍLIA	1 500 000
FORTALEZA	1 300 000
BELÉM	1 000 000
CURITIBA	1 000 000
TORONTO	3 500 000
MONTREAL	2 900 000
VANCOUVER	1 400 000
NEW YORK	14 598 000
HOUSTON	3 000 000
CHICAGO	6 511 000
SEATTLE	2 341 000
LOS ANGELES	9 638 000
SAN DIEGO	2 286 000

*Population of metropolitan area 1989

Why the Move to the Cities?

The main reasons for increased urbanization after 1940 were economic. However, there were also several social reasons for the population movement to the cities. *

- **Lack of Farmland:** The years from 1940 to 1989 had rapid population increases. The population in the rural areas increased. There were too many people to farm the available land. The lack of farmland forced many rural families to move to the cities in search of jobs.
- **Weather Conditions:** There were years of drought and floods in the Northeast. They contributed to the number of people forced to leave the land. Nearby cities offered the chance of jobs for some people. Others moved to the closest large-sized town.
- **Employment Opportunities:** Industries in the larger cities were growing. They offered the possibilities of a steady job and a monthly income.
- **Living Conditions:** Cities offered the chance of better living conditions. Cities often offered health care facilities, sanitation services (running water), and schools. These and other services were not readily available in the rural areas.
- **Transportation Systems:** Improved transportation permitted more people to move from rural areas to cities. Roads built after 1920 allowed people a walking route out of rural areas. After the introduction of bus transportation, even more people could leave the countryside.
- **Communication Systems:** Better communication systems increased the awareness of people in isolated rural areas. They learned what was happening in the cities and other parts of Brazil. The building of radio stations and the increased availability of electricity provided **residents** in rural areas with news of the cities. By the 1960s there were transistor radios. They were keeping rural areas informed of events elsewhere. Movies were also common in the rural areas after 1930. They showed what life was like in the cities. Postal services and newspapers increased. Rural people no longer thought of cities as places where they would never live.

---

* Economic reasons include such things as getting enough money to pay for food, clothing, and shelter. Social reasons include things relating to mental and emotional well-being, such as health, education, leisure activities, and religion.
Residents—people who live in a particular area

Problems of Urbanization

The rapid population increases in the cities have produced serious problems. The demand for housing, sanitation services, education, electricity, transportation, and jobs has grown faster than the cities can provide them. Many of the migrants who move to large cities are forced to live in very poor conditions. Most migrants find themselves living in *favelas*. The photograph on the right shows a *favela*.

A Morning in Fortaleza
(Factual Narrative)

Carla drank her cup of coffee quickly.* If she didn't hurry she would miss the bus to the city. Her younger sister, Sandra, had been ill for two days. She had a fever and pains in her stomach. She'd been awake all night tossing with fever. Carla didn't want to leave until Sandra was settled and asleep. Their mother had died three years ago. Since then, thirteen-year-old Carla had taken care of four-year-old Sandra and her two younger brothers.

Looking at Sandra's pale face, Carla tried to push aside her worry. Her family had moved to the city two years ago. She had hoped they had left sickness behind them.

Carla's family was like thousands of other families from the *sertão*. The long drought and conditions in the countryside had forced them to leave the countryside. Carla's father had rented land from the landowner. In exchange for the use of the land, Carla's family gave the landowner 50 per cent of their cotton and 30 per cent of their manioc. Carla's father was also forced to work two days a week for the landowner. So was her older brother. The drought continued into the second year. There was no water for cultivating crops. There wasn't even enough water for drinking. They had to rely on the arrival of a government water truck twice a week for drinking water. Many people died of starvation and disease. Carla's mother and tiny baby sister had been two victims of the drought. The landowner finally **evicted** Carla's family and the other farmers. They couldn't pay any rent. There was nothing else for them to do but move to the city. They hoped that things would be better there.

At least here in the city we're free from the landowner, thought Carla. We don't pay any rent. The water is free. Carla's family lived in one of the two hundred crowded *favelas* in Fortaleza. Nearly half a million people, mostly migrants from the *sertão*, lived in *favelas*. Most lived in conditions far worse than Carla's family.

Carla's family had been very lucky. Carla's uncle had come to Fortaleza a year before they did. He was able to help Carla's family find a place in the *favela* to build a small shelter. The house was one room with a lean-to cooking area at the back. They'd built it from a collection of old boards, flattened oil drums, and a few bricks and mud. The roof was a sheet of plastic held down by several boards and a few scattered bricks.

There was no running water. Every morning Carla's youngest brother, Antônio, walked down to the public tap. It was near the road. He brought back a kerosene can full of water for drinking and washing. They did have electricity. Someone in the *favela* had found a way to attach a wire to the city power line. Other families had connected lines to that one. Electricity was shared this way from one house to another. One bare light bulb hung from a nail in the wall over the bed Carla shared with her sister.

Carla quietly reached over the bed. She switched off the light and tucked the blanket around Sandra. Carla did not want to leave Sandra alone. However, she had no choice. There was no one to look after her. Everyone else in the family had left an hour ago to get to

---

* Coffee is a common breakfast for children and adults in Brazil.

Evict—expel or put out by a legal process from land or a building

127

their jobs. If Carla missed a day from her job she would be fired. The family needed all the money from their jobs just to buy food. Carla also didn't want to lose her job. The family she worked for had given Carla several pieces of used clothing. For the first time in her life, Carla owned two T-shirts, a skirt, and a dress.

After changing into a T-shirt and her skirt, Carla left the house. She hurried along the narrow dirt lanes between the *favela* homes. Chickens pecked at the piles of garbage. Laundry hung on lines strung between the houses. Barefoot toddlers played with pieces of plastic. They poked sticks at the rubbish floating in the open ditches. Mothers washed their clothing and babies in tubs which they set out in the lane.

Carla saw none of this. She was still thinking about Sandra. If Sandra was not feeling better by tomorrow, Carla decided she would take her to the *favela* health clinic. There had been no health clinics in the countryside. No one in Carla's family had ever been to a doctor. There had never been enough money. In the *favela*, the church had a women's health clinic. It was for mothers and children. A doctor came once a month to give shots to the children. Sometimes the doctor looked at sick children.

Carla reached the main road just as the bus to the city pulled up. It was already jammed with people. The crowd at the bus stop pushed and shoved their way onto the bus. Carla squeezed onto the back step of the bus. She handed her money up to the ticket vendor sitting at the back. Carla spent nearly one-quarter of her wages on bus fare. But at least she had a job!

On the farms and in the villages there were few paying jobs for women. Here in the city Carla had more chances to find work. There were often more jobs for women and girls than for men in the city. Carla's aunt worked as a maid in an apartment in the city. She had been able to get Carla a job. It was for three days a week as a kitchen maid for a family in the same apartment building. Carla worked from 8 AM until 8 PM helping the cook. She also cleaned the kitchen.

Almost all the teenagers and children in the *favela* did some sort of work. This added to their family incomes. In the city there were very few full-time jobs. There were small jobs for children and teenagers.

Carla's older brother worked for a scrap dealer at the city dump. He separated paper, plastic, wood, and metal from the garbage. Carla's father and uncle helped people find a parking space on the crowded downtown streets. Then they washed their cars while the owners shopped or went to work. Antônio and Vincente, eight and ten, sold newspapers and chewing gum to people stopped at the traffic lights by the big intersection. Altogether their incomes were enough to provide the family with coffee for breakfast and a meal of rice and beans twice a day. When they were on the farm they often had no coffee. There was only one meal a day.

By the time the bus reached the city, the streets were filled with rush-hour traffic. Well-dressed office workers filled the sidewalks. Vendors were selling belts, purses, jewelry, magazines, T-shirts, shoes, and candies. Their portable stalls were set up on the sidewalks. There were bright lights, traffic, stores, high-rise offices, movie theaters, and restaurants. They made the city far more exciting than the countryside. Carla loved to imagine that one day she could have a job in one of the shops. To get a job there Carla needed to be able to read and do sums. The church and the *favela* association were trying to get a school set up for the younger children. Carla hoped they would have a class for teenagers too. At least in the city Carla could hope that one day she would be able to learn how to read.

Carla's father and older brother wanted to move back to the farm when the drought was over. Carla wanted to stay in the city. There were more opportunities for her in the city. Her family would always have to worry about getting enough money for food. If they worked really hard Carla was sure things would improve for her family.

Carla was like the thousands of people who came to the city each month. She clung desperately to the hope that her life would improve. Maybe one day her family would be able to share in some of the wonderful things she saw in the city.

128

Movement to the Southeast

There was a gold rush in Minas Gerais in the 1690s. Since then there has been a steady movement of people from the Northeast to the Southeast. This population movement from the Northeast to the Southeast increased during the second half of the 1900s. The 1970s were years of significant population movement. People went from the Northeast to the cities in the Southeast. During the 1970s, for example, nearly 200 000 people a year migrated to Rio de Janeiro. At the same time, nearly 600 000 people a year were moving to São Paulo. This movement to the Southeast continued into the 1980s. In 1980 São Paulo State recorded one of its largest population increases. In that year nearly a million migrants moved to the state. Most of the people migrating to the Southeast are the poor trying to improve their lives.

There were several reasons for this increased population movement to the Southeast:

- Improved transportation in Brazil allowed more people from the Northeast to travel to the Southeast. Roads were built. The introduction of long-distance bus transportation made it possible for rural Brazilians to travel in greater numbers.
- Industries were developed in Rio de Janeiro and São Paulo. This offered the possibility of steady jobs and a monthly income.
- General economic conditions appeared better in the southern states. As a result, social conditions were better. Wages were higher.

There were more education, health care, and sanitation services in these modern cities.
- Communications (radio and television) improved. This made the people in the Northeast more aware of life in the large southern cities.
- The attraction of living in one of the largest and most important cities in the country offered excitement. There was a wide variety of public social activities such as shopping, festivals, markets, and soccer games.

The Cities of the Southeast

Most of the migrants leaving the Northeast and moving to the Southeast head for Rio de Janeiro or São Paulo. They have good reasons for their choice of cities. Rio de Janeiro and São Paulo are impressive cities.

Rio de Janeiro has the reputation of being one of the world's most beautiful cities. Nestled between the green mountains and rock outcroppings of the Brazilian Highlands, Rio de Janeiro stretches twenty kilometres along the Atlantic Ocean. It contains sixteen white sand, palm-fringed beaches bordered by luxurious hotels and apartments.

"Movimento"

São Paulo is the largest, wealthiest, and fastest growing city in South America. São Paulo is the financial and cultural center of Brazil. Everything of importance in Brazil happens first in São Paulo. Brazilians point proudly to São Paulo as an indication of the great wealth and potential of their country.

Shady trees along the streets of residential and shopping areas provide shade from the hot summer su and shelter from the winter rains. Rio de Janeiro is a city of freeways, skyscrapers, office towers, tree-lined residential areas, and elegant shopping centers.

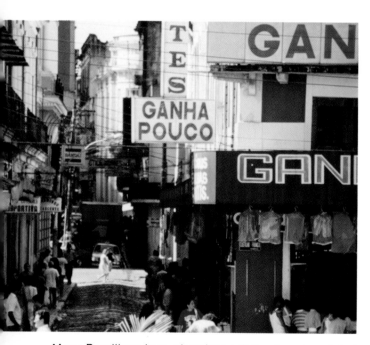

For many people the move to the cities of the Southeast resulted in improvements in living conditions. The cities offered services, transportation, employment opportunities, and entertainment that were not readily available in the villages of the Northeast countryside.

Many Brazilians love what they call the *"movimento"* of the cities. This term refers to the crowds, the noise, the bright lights, the activity, and the general excitement of living in one of the world's most impressive cities.

Not all the recent migrants to the Southeast have been able to share in the good life the cities have to offer. Very few migrants, however, would consider returning to their home states once they have experienced living in the cities of the Southeast.

A Winter Day in São Paulo   *(Factual Narrative)*

The cold wind blew down the street. It rattled the folding tables set up along the sidewalk. Luckily Everton's table was loaded with heavy gas stove parts, light bulbs, electric cords, and sockets. His table shook briefly in the wind. Many of the tables had to be held in place by the vendors to keep them from toppling onto the sidewalk.

Everton pulled his scarf tighter around his neck. He tugged his wool cap down farther on his head and blew on his hands as he rubbed them together for a little extra warmth. His light jacket and T-shirt were little protection against the cold winter wind gusting through the downtown streets. The weather report on the radio this morning said it was only 5°C. This was the coldest winter they'd had in São Paulo since he had come south eight years ago. If there had been a little sun it would feel warmer. But a thick blanket of gray smog hung over the city. It blocked out the sun and the tops of the high-rise apartments and office buildings. The city's chemical factories, industries, and millions of cars, trucks, and buses regularly produced smog blankets. They seemed even worse in the dry winter air.

No one in São Paulo liked the cold weather. In the winter the residents of São Paulo hurried quickly along the streets. They were trying to avoid the polluted air and the cold winds. This was terrible weather for the dozen vendors huddled along the edge of the sidewalk. Hardly anyone stopped to look at the merchandise. This was the only time that Everton longed for the warm sun of his hometown in **Bahia**.

It had been eight years since he and his family had traveled the 2 000 kilometres to São Paulo. Life had improved so much for Everton and his family since they moved to São Paulo. Now he rarely thought of Bahia.

Soon after they arrived in São Paulo, his father found work as a carpenter. His mother got a job as a maid for a well-off family. There were always a few odd jobs for eight-year-old Everton and his three brothers. They had worked as delivery boys and shoe shiners. They had sold newspapers and stamps on the street corners. Wages in the Southeast were so much higher than in Bahia! Suddenly the family found they could afford things they never dreamed of owning. They built a small house in a *favela* on the outskirts of the city. In the last eight years the *favela* association had convinced the city government to install water lines, a sewer, and electricity. They had even organized a school for children between the ages of six and eight. These were services that were not available in Everton's hometown.

Everton had hoped that when he was 16 he'd be able to find a full-time job. He wanted to work in one of São Paulo's factories. In the last three years, though, most of the factories had laid off workers. Thousands of factory workers were unemployed. At least in the city there were always odd jobs to do. There were many ways to make a little money. For the last six months Everton had sold stove parts from a sidewalk stall in downtown São Paulo. There weren't factory jobs now. Yet Everton knew that the best chance for a better-paying job in the future would be here in São Paulo. Most of the industries were located here. All he had to do was wait and hope. Things had to get better in the next year. Surely the factories would start needing more workers.

This possibility of jobs attracted thousands of people from the Northeast to the southern cities each month. Any vacant piece of land would suddenly be filled with the tents and cardboard huts of new arrivals.

Another icy blast whistled down the street. Everton shivered. He tried to think of the warm summer weather. He and his friends could go to soccer games or just wander the streets. They would listen to music blaring from the record shops. Sometimes there were street dances at the *favela* or a group of musicians playing. There was always something happening in the city. For Everton it was exciting living in the largest and most important city in Brazil. He just wished the winters were a little warmer.

Everton hoped that when the office workers quit work in an hour and hurried off to the bus stops and subway stations that at least one of them would buy something. He'd sold two light bulbs and a stove part in the morning. This meant he had busfare home. But it would be nice to make a little money after spending all day standing out in the cold.

Bahia—a state in the Northeast; pronounced beye-ay-yah

Movement to the Frontier

In the 1960s the Brazilian government encouraged the opening up and settlement of the interior regions. During the early 1960s and 1970s the movement of people to the Center West region increased substantially. In the late 1970s the government began to encourage the settlement of what Brazilians called Brazil's "last frontier." The frontier area receiving the most attention was Rondônia. The government offered free land and tax incentives for cattle ranches and logging operations to encourage settlement of the state. The government even attempted to resettle families from the Northeast in government-organized farming communities along the BR-364 Highway in Rondônia.

The free land attracted thousands of settlers. But it was the discovery of large gold deposits and the paving of the BR-364 to Porto Velho in 1984 that rapidly accelerated the movement of people to Rondônia. When farm machinery was introduced to southern Brazil, large numbers of workers were no longer needed. As a result, thousands of families came to Rondônia for the opportunity of owning their own land. The shortage of farm land in the Northeast combined with several years of drought forced many families to try their luck in Rondônia. Hundreds of thousands of settlers flooded along the newly paved BR-364. Many came by bus. Others came piled into the back of trucks. Many migrants merely followed the BR-364 and settled when they ran out of money for the bus fares.

Gold was discovered in Amazonas and Roraima. New logging and mining operations and the construction of several huge hydroelectric projects also attracted thousands of migrants to the frontier areas.

Urban Settlement in the Frontier

Much of the population shift to the frontier has been to the cities and towns. Some of these cities are Porto Velho, Rio Branco, and Boa Vista. They have had tremendous population increases in the last ten years. Living conditions in these interior towns and cities are similar to those found in the crowded cities along the coast. Those without steady incomes live in very poor conditions. Health care facilities, schools, proper housing, running water, and electricity are not readily available. The photograph below shows a *favela* on the outskirts of Porto Velho.

The Last Frontier

(Factual Narrative)

In August 1986 a TV news team toured Rondônia. They were preparing a news report on the movement of thousands of settlers to Rondônia. Reporter Izabel Andrade and photographer Alvaro Rodrigo spent two weeks interviewing some of these new settlers.

The car sped along the dusty dirt road, kicking up thick clouds of dust. The dust billowed in the dry air for a few minutes before gradually drifting down to cover the black tree stumps lining the road. The dust seeped into the car. It covered everything inside. Alvaro was kept busy wiping the dust from his video camera equipment.

"I got some great footage this afternoon, especially the Beckman family," Alvaro shouted to Izabel over the noise of the car. "If this dust hasn't ruined my equipment, I think I've just about got all the shots we'll need. Did you get some good material?"

Izabel had been lost in thought, watching the clearings flashing past the car. Since she had interviewed more than thirty settlers, the forest clearings had started to look the same. Each had a cleared patch of burned and charred trees. The house was built from rough timber. Patches of corn, beans, and manioc were scattered among the burned tree stumps. In the background loomed the dark wall of forest. No electricity. No running water. Only loneliness. And there was **malaria** to worry about. To Izabel it seemed these settlers were taking on a difficult life. But the people she had interviewed had been confident and enthusiastic about moving to Rondônia. All the newcomers felt that with hard work they could turn this rain forest wilderness into successful farms.

"Yes, I got some good material," replied Izabel. "I think I'll use the interview with the Beckman family at the opening of the report. Here, listen to this," she said to Alvaro, as she clicked on her tape recorder.

Roberto Beckman's confident voice filled the car.

"I came to Rondônia with my wife, Angelica, and my three sons and two daughters just over a year ago. We came soon after they finished paving the highway. We saw the government ads on television. The ads said we could get free land if we came to Rondônia to help settle the new frontier.

"My wife and I have worked since we were children on coffee plantations in Paraná. But the frosts killed the coffee plants several years ago.

The landowner decided to use the land for cattle. There were no jobs in the countryside so we moved to Londrina. I was very lucky and got a job in a factory there. But always my wife and I wanted our own land. We wanted something better for our children. Coming to Rondônia was a chance for us to own land. This was something we could not hope to do in Paraná. We decided Rondônia was our chance for a better life for our family.

"My children liked the city. They didn't want to come. They miss their friends. Here there are no movies, no electricity and no bright lights. The only jobs are clearing and planting. They don't want to stay. They think the work is too hard."

"It is hard work to clear the land. I've cut 40 trees a day with my chainsaw. I am luckier than most settlers. I came with a little money for supplies and equipment. Most of the settlers come unprepared. They have no money to buy even an axe. I have seen them getting off the bus or climbing down from trucks along the highway. They have only their bundles of clothes and a little food with them. That is not good. It is a difficult life here. That is why many of the settlers get discouraged and move to the towns along the highway. They don't have the equipment or the strength to farm this wilderness.*

"There are dangers too. Malaria and yellow fever are problems. But we are strong. You must be strong to survive here.

"At first we cleared just enough of the forest to plant food crops for the first year. Now we have enough land cleared to plant coffee, **cacão**, and rice. My wife and I have great hopes. Today we are struggling frontier settlers. In a few years we will be successful Rondônian farmers. That is the dream of our family."

Izabel clicked off the tape recorder. "Well, what do you think?" she asked Alvaro. "Do the Beckmans stand a chance out here? If we came back in five years, do you think the Beckmans would still be here? Do you think they really can turn this wilderness into coffee and cacão plantations?"

Malaria—a disease with chills and fever; spread by a parasite through mosquito bites
Cacão—plant whose seed pods produce chocolate

---

* In May 1989 the government began issuing chainsaws to new settlers in areas of Rondônia, Acre, and Amazonas.

Fading Dreams in Rondônia

In the last few years Rondônia has lost much of its attraction. Stories of infertile soil, diseases, and conflict between cattle ranchers and Indians eventually drifted back to the coastal areas. By 1988 there was little unoccupied or uncleared land in Rondônia. Settlers were being forced to move farther into the rain forests of Acre. In 1981 the governor of Rondônia had issued an invitation to the poor of Brazil to come and settle in Rondônia. By 1988 the governor was telling Brazilians to stay home. Rondônia could no longer handle the flood of migrants.

For most of the new settlers in Rondônia and Acre, life continues to be a struggle for survival. The following narrative describes the problems of the da Suza family in Ouro Prêto do Oeste. They are typical of thousands of families in Rondônia.

(Factual Narrative)

Alberto watched his father. He walked slowly between the stunted rows of corn. Occasionally his father's hoe struck out at a weed. Even weeds were having a difficult time growing here. The stalks of spindly corn fluttered in the hot afternoon breeze. The corn stalks were short, not even as tall as Alberto. The leaves were yellowish and dry. It was obviously a sickly crop—even worse than last year.

Alberto and his father had spent the morning working in their fields of manioc and beans. The bean and manioc crops were growing better than the corn. Yet it would still be a poor harvest next month. The poor crops meant they would have to clear more of the forest. Soon they would run out of forest to clear. Eventually they'd have to move and start again somewhere else.

They could not get another piece of land in this area. Alberto had heard that there were 20 000 people waiting for land in this district. It was the same throughout Rondônia. Two years ago, the government had stopped giving away land.

A dozen huge bumblebees were momentarily distracted from the bush of bright purple flowers. They swarmed around Alberto. Alberto swatted at them and leaped away. He hated the insects. That was one of the many things he had to get used to in Rondônia. When he and his family first arrived by bus in Ouro Prêto do Oeste, they had no idea what the rain forest would be like. They were used to plains and open areas. They all found the dark, shadowy rain forest very frightening. There were so many things to worry about.

"Alberto," called his father. "There is nothing more to do here today. We'll go back to the house. I want to rest."

Alberto looked sharply at his father. His father never quit working this early in the afternoon. Huge beads of sweat covered his father's face and bare arms. His skin was pale. Even his blue eyes looked faded. Alberto felt a band of fear tighten around his heart. Alberto tried to convince himself there was nothing wrong. It was only the poor crops and the heat. There was nothing wrong. Father is not sick. He couldn't be!

Alberto followed his father's slow steps along the narrow dirt path through a small area of forest they had not cleared. After a few minutes, Alberto's father stopped at the two crosses marking a small clearing beside the path. Each day on their way back from the fields, Alberto and his father stopped for a few moments. It had been two years since they'd buried Alberto's baby sister. Only six months ago Alberto's older brother, Claudio, had died of malaria.

His father usually stopped at the graves to say a short prayer. Today his father did not stay more than a minute. He turned quickly away. He headed along the path toward the house. Alberto followed his father's plodding footsteps along the path. His mind was years away.

Claudio and his father had planned the move to Rondônia together. In Paraná, the plantation they worked for started buying more machinery. Soon the farm didn't need all the farm workers. They had no land of their own. There was no chance to buy any. Nearly all the farming land in Paraná was owned by wealthy plantations. All Claudio and his father hoped for was a piece of land by the road. They needed a piece of good land to grow food and raise their families. Claudio had been eighteen that year and married only a year. He hoped that in Rondônia he could have his own piece of land. This was something he couldn't even hope for in Paraná.

That first year in Ouro Prêto do Oeste had been very difficult. They'd hung a tarp between the trees for a shelter. They slept in hammocks outdoors. The rains during their first rainy season had been miserable. It seemed to rain steadily for months. Everything they owned was wet. The rivers and streams overflowed. The dirt roads became deep mud pits. It was difficult to find dry wood for their fire.

Clearing the trees had been more difficult than they expected. The trees had very shallow roots but very hard trunks. It took a long time to chop them down. Then they had to wait for the dry season to burn them. When the burning season came, the heavy black smoke from all the fires in the district made breathing difficult. Everyone in the family developed a cough. Sometimes the sky was so black with smoke it looked like night even at noon.

Malaria was another thing to worry about. All of the settlers were terrified of malaria. Every family in the area had lost someone to disease. There were no medical clinics in the area. Families relied on home remedies if anyone came down with the fevers and chills.

Despite all the problems, their first crop of beans, corn, and manioc had been very good. Even Alberto's mother seemed happier once they'd built a house near the road. The house was small with wooden walls, dirt floor, and a palm-thatch roof. Yet it was so much better than the tarp. The house had only one room. It had the cooking stove, the table, and places for them to hang their hammocks.

Food from the store in Ouro Prêto do Oeste was very expensive. They could only afford a little coffee, sugar, and salt once in a while. The family ate only a little better than they had in Paraná. A little coffee for breakfast, beans and *farinha* for lunch and dinner. The only extras were the fruits and nuts his sisters collected in the forest. It was Alberto's two sisters' job to collect firewood for the stove. They also made the two-kilometre walk to the stream twice a day for water. There were no schools in this area so all the children helped with the farm.

Even with all the difficulties and hardships, that first year had been promising. It seemed that their dreams for a better life would actually happen.

The second year, however, the crops were not as good. They had to clear another area of forest. Then, last year, there was barely enough after the harvest to last them for six months. This year the crops were worse. It was the same with other families. Several of the neighboring families had already left. They'd sold their land to a rancher. He had burned off the trees and scrub to make a pasture for his cattle. His father said some of the settlers made more money selling their land than they did trying to grow crops on it.

As Alberto and his father emerged from the forest shade into the clearing by the house, he saw his mother washing in the yard. She turned toward them, surprised to see them back so early. Alberto's mother started to say something to her husband. She stopped quickly when she saw his pale, sweat-covered face and his shivering body. Wiping the soap from her hands, she silently followed her husband into the house.

At the doorway she glanced back toward Alberto but he had turned away. Alberto did not want to see the cold fear in his mother's eyes.

Farinha—flour made from ground manioc roots

SUMMARY: MILLIONS ON THE MOVE

Mass internal migration has been an important factor in Brazil's settlement patterns since 1940. Millions of Brazilians have moved from one part of the country to another. There were three trends in migration. They were movement to the cities, movement to the Southeast, and movement to the interior.

The one dramatic change in settlement patterns has been the population increase in the cities. Urbanization changed Brazil. Most of the population used to live in the countryside. Now nearly 75% of the population lives in towns and cities. Poor economic conditions in the rural areas; the possibility of steady jobs, education, and health services in the cities; and better transportation and communication services contributed to the movement of people to the cities.

Since 1940 the Southeast has dramatically increased in population. People from the Northeast have moved in large numbers to the cities in the Southeast. São Paulo and Rio de Janeiro have been the main destinations. There are poor economic conditions and lack of farmland in the Northeast. The Southeast has the chance for jobs and better wages. Education, health services, and better transportation and communication services are also present.

In the 1960s the Brazilian government encouraged settlement of the interior. By the 1970s and 1980s the government was encouraging settlement of what Brazilians called the "last frontier." The last frontier were the remote areas of Mato Grosso, Rondônia, Acre, Amazonas, Pará, and the territories of Amapa and Roraima. Rondônia was one area that experienced a dramatic increase in population over a very short period of time. The government offer of free land, tax incentives for cattle ranchers, the discovery of gold, and the paving of BR-364 all contributed to the movement of hundreds of thousands of people to Rondônia. By 1986, Rondônia had more people than the state could handle. There were no more offers of free land. Settlers were gradually moving into the even more remote areas of Acre and Amazonas.

Regional Differences in Population

The internal migration of large numbers of people to the cities, to the Southeast, and to the frontier areas increased the regional differences in population. Some regions are heavily populated. Others are sparsely populated by comparison. The Population Density map below illustrates how the population of Brazil is spread throughout the country. The population graph shows what percentage of Brazil's population lives in each of the five regions.

Population Distribution in Brazil

Population Density Maps

Population density maps show the average number of people living on each square kilometre.

The population density map on the right shows the different population densities throughout Brazil. In many areas of Brazil the population density is less than one person for every square kilometre. In some places the population density is greater than 200 for every square kilometre.

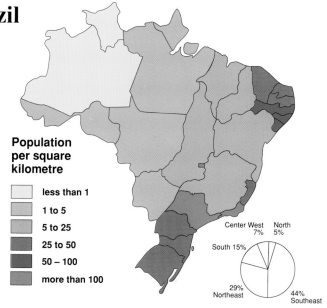

Population per square kilometre

- less than 1
- 1 to 5
- 5 to 25
- 25 to 50
- 50 – 100
- more than 100

Center West 7%
North 5%
South 15%
29% Northeast
44% Southeast

CHAPTER REVIEW

For Your Notebook

1. Predict what problems rapid urbanization might produce.
2. What cities in North America would be comparable in size and importance to Rio de Janeiro and São Paulo?
3. What problems might regional differences in population present for Brazil?
4. Page 97 of the text presents the viewpoints of several Brazilians about the settlement and development of the interior in the 1950s. Predict what additional viewpoints might be expressed in the 1990s.
5. Using your knowledge of Brazil's physical geography, list the physical features of Brazil that might make settlement of the frontier areas difficult. What features might assist settlement?
6. Using the Natural Resources Maps on pages 37 and 38, list the natural resources in the frontier areas that will likely influence settlement patterns in the next decade.
7. Predict how population movements may affect resource development in Brazil.
8. In your notebook copy the following headings: Economic and Social. List the reasons for the movement to the cities, to the Southeast, and to the fron-tier areas under one of the headings. Have social or economic reasons been more influ-ential in producing the massive internal migration of people in Brazil?

Economic	Social
• higher pay	• excitement of the cities
• _____	• _____
• _____	• _____
• _____	• _____

---

* Venn Diagram available as black-line master in the Teacher Resource Package.

Exploring Further

1.  Problem Solving Activity: (continued from page 121) Evaluate the information gathered on the recording sheet and develop a concluding statement to solve the problem: **How have recent population shifts changed the settlement patterns in Brazil?** Write the concluding statement in the spaces provided on the recording sheet.

2. Copy the Venn diagram shown below into your notebook. Compare the settlement patterns in Brazil in 1890 with the settlement patterns in 1989.* Under A and B list the settlement features that were unique for each time period. In C list the features that are common to both time periods.

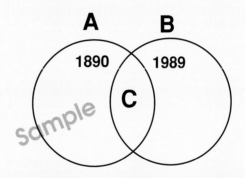

Evaluate the information. Have settlement patterns changed substantially in Brazil since 1890? What settlement pattern features have stayed the same?

3.  (Continued from Chapter Review on page 107) The Issue: Chapter 5 presented in-formation on the recent massive population movements in Brazil. Population movements will affect the natural environment of Brazil and resource development in Brazil. Use informa-tion gathered from this chapter to revise and add to the alternatives and consequences on your Decision Making Form.

4. Write a TV or newspaper advertisement en-couraging settlement in the interior. Include the features that would attract people and encourage them to move to the interior.

? Problem Solving

This case study looks at land reform in Brazil. Brazil is a large country, yet it has millions of landless farmers. Part of this problem is the result of LAND USE—what land is chosen for development and how it is developed. In Brazil, land shortages are closely linked to LAND DISTRIBUTION. This is the way that land ownership is shared among the people. Many people believe that too much land in Brazil is owned by large rich landowners. They want LAND REFORM. This would involve taking some land away from the rich and dividing it among the poor, landless farmers.

1. Many Brazilians believe that there could be enough land and food for everyone in Brazil. There are four important land use questions that need to be answered. Use the problem solving model introduced on page 3 to help provide answers to the following land use questions:

   • Are people making the land more or less productive?
   • Does the land feed people or animals?
   • Who eats what is grown on the land?
   • Is the land actually being cultivated at all?

2. Using a problem solving model, decide how the Brazilian government might solve the problems associated with land distribution.

Land Use

The need for more farmland has had an effect on Brazil's settlement patterns. The lack of farmland in the Northeast and the South, for example, has accounted for the movement of millions of poor, landless Brazilians. These people have moved to the crowded cities or the newly opened areas of the interior. Brazil needs to provide more agricultural land for these landless farmers. This need is often given as one of the reasons for clearing and developing Brazil's vast interior regions. However, many Brazilian **economists**, geographers, and **environmentalists** argue that Brazil already has enough cleared agricultural land for its population. They claim there is no need to clear the Amazon rain forest to provide more agricultural land.

The information at the top of the next page compares Brazil's land area (including and excluding the Amazonian rain forest) and population with the land areas and populations of several other countries in the world.

Agricultural Potential

How suitable the land is for agriculture is called AGRICULTURAL POTENTIAL. Agricultural potential affects a country in many ways. The cultivation of food crops is an essential part of a country's well-being. Countries with good agricultural potential can usually produce enough food to feed their people. Countries with poor agricultural potential must import food from other countries to feed their populations. The information on the next page illustrates some of the factors that influence a

country's agricultural potential.

Settlement Patterns

Agricultural potential can often affect settlement patterns. The location of good agricultural land can determine which areas of the country are settled. As a result, it can determine where most of the population lives. Settlement in areas of good agricultural land is easier than settlement in areas of poor agricultural land. The increasing need for more agricultural land can change settlement patterns and the natural environment. To make new farming areas, more areas of the country are settled and cleared of natural vegetation. New roads are built to service new farming communities. People from one region of the country often move to new areas of the country when farmland is made available.

Economist—a person who is trained in the science of economics, who studies the way wealth is produced, distributed, and used

Environmentalist—a person who believes in protecting the natural environment from pollution or destruction and is actively involved in keeping it healthy for future generations

Population Density

Geographers use population density to compare available land per person in different countries. POPULATION DENSITY is the average number of people per square kilometre in a country. It is calculated by dividing the population of a country by the land area. The chart below compares Brazil's population density with that of other countries.

Country	People per sq. km.
Brazil	
(excluding rain forest)	30
(including rain forest)	18
Canada	2.6
Argentina	11.8
USSR	12.8
United States	26

COMPARISON OF LAND AREAS AND POPULATIONS FOR SELECTED COUNTRIES (1989)

COUNTRY	LAND AREA (sq km)	POPULATION	DENSITY (people per sq km)
BRAZIL	8 511 965	153 000 000	18
CANADA	9 976 137	26 100 000	2.6
UNITED STATES	9 428 692	246 100 000	26
USSR	22 402 200	286 000 000	12.8
CHINA	9 327 600	1 087 000 000	111
WEST GERMANY	248 556	60 162 000	242
FRANCE	571 486	55 900 000	97.7
DENMARK	43 076	5 074 000	117.8
ARGENTINA	2 780 092	32 000 000	11.8
AUSTRALIA	7 682 300	16 090 000	2
JAPAN	377 738	122 000 000	326
ISRAEL	20 322	4 477 000	220
INDIA	3 287 590	816 800 000	254
INDONESIA	1 904 197	177 440 000	98.6
GREAT BRITAIN	244 026	56 648 000	232
ITALY	301 202	57 439 000	190.7
HONG KONG	1 063	5 608 000	5 265

Natural Factors that Determine Agricultural Potential

1. CLIMATE—An area must have sufficient precipitation to grow a particular crop and it must get the rain at the right times of the year. The temperature must be warm or cool enough for long enough periods of time to grow specific crops. Areas that have long, cold winters, for example, have shorter growing periods. These areas can support only a limited variety of crops. Most grain crops, for example, require at least 160 frost-free days for their growing seasons. Other crops require even longer growing seasons. Latitude is usually the main factor influencing climate. Areas that are farther north or south of the equator have cooler temperatures and shorter growing seasons. Areas nearer the equator have warm temperatures year-round. They have a year-long growing season and may grow a wider variety of crops.

2. SOIL—Crops need fertile soil to grow. The best soil is deep and rich in nutrients. Soils with only a thin layer of nutrients are usually not suitable for continuous farming. Many soils require heavy fertilization to maintain good crop yields year after year.

3. LANDFORMS—Flat land is best for growing crops. Plains and flat plateau areas are usually first choices for agriculture. Hills can grow specific crops if the land is terraced into flat shelves along the hillsides. Mountainous areas are not suited for farming.

4. NATURAL VEGETATION—Natural vegetation is often a good indicator of an area's agricultural potential. Sparse vegetation may indicate soil or climate conditions unsuitable for plant growth. Lush, varied vegetation often indicates soil and climate conditions suitable for agriculture. The natural vegetation is often an obstacle to agriculture. For example, forests need to be cleared before crops can be planted.

CASE STUDY: Land Reform

Land Distribution

Brazil has a large area of good agricultural land. Why then are there millions of farmers without land? Why is the Amazon rain forest being cleared to make more farmland?

Many Brazilians believe that Brazil is not lacking good agricultural land. Instead, they link the problem of large numbers of landless farmers to land distribution. Most of the good agricultural land in Brazil is owned by a small number of people. Each member of this small group of people owns large amounts of land.

In Brazil most of the land is divided into large landholdings owned by a few wealthy individuals. This pattern dates from almost the very beginning of the Brazilian colony four hundred years ago. In the early settlement period, huge land grants were given to friends of the Portuguese king. The development of large sugar cane plantations with a slave work force reinforced this pattern. Eventually, the African slaves were replaced by paid farm workers. However, the pattern of large landholdings owned by a few individuals continued to dominate rural Brazil. Today, the pattern continues with a few wealthy landowners controlling a great deal of Brazil's agricultural land. The major difference now is that wealthy families are not the only landowners. The owners of large landholdings are often companies or government corporations. The Volkswagen Corporation, for example, owns large areas of agricultural land and several cattle ranches. The Brazilian government also owns large areas of agricultural land.

Organization in the Countryside

Land use arrangements vary throughout Brazil. A small percentage of farming families live on small landholdings which they own. These landholdings are usually less than 10 hectares. Most are less than 5 hectares. Millions of farmers in the countryside, however, own no land at all. Many of these farmers rent small plots of land from large landholdings in order to grow food crops for their families. Other farmers make arrangements to cultivate an area of a large landholding and share the crops with the landowners. Many farm workers are forced to live in the small villages and towns in the countryside and hire themselves out to the large landholdings on a day-to-day basis. The list which follows provides general characteristics of the various landholders in Brazil. There are, of course, exceptions in each of these groups.

Large Landowner
- owns the best land in the area
- often near a water supply
- may live in a large house on the plantation
- may live in a city thousands of kilometres away
- hires managers to run the landholding
- can evict tenants, sharecroppers, squatters from land at any time
- a small but powerful group in Brazil

Squatter
- lives on a landowner's land without permission
- often people who have been evicted from tenant lands
- occupies land not used by the large landowners
- builds a small house
- plants food crops (beans, rice, manioc) on a small plot near the house
- sometimes works for a small wage on landowner's developed property
- faces eviction at any time by gunmen hired by the landowner
- a large group throughout Brazil

Small Landowner
- most farm small landholdings under 10 hectares; many are less than 5 hectares
- usually owns land that is poor
- often owns too little land to grow food for the family
- often become tenants of landowners to get enough land to grow food
- often become tenant farmers to feed their families

Tenant Farmer
- rents land from a landowner
- receives small plot of land from the landowner in exchange for working on the landowner's land
- sometimes receives a small house
- able to grow food for the family on a small plot near the house
- sometimes paid a small wage for cultivating the landowner's fields and caring for the landowner's animals
- does not own a plot of land and can be evicted at any time
- millions of tenant farmers are removed from the land each year

Sharecropper
- is a renter (tenant) who pays rent with 50% or more of crop
- grows beans, manioc, corn, rice, and cotton on large landowner's land
- must also work several days a week on the landowner's land
- builds own house
- responsible for seed, plows, equipment
- does not own the land and can be evicted at any time
- many own a tiny plot of land that is too small to cultivate crops
- a rapidly disappearing group

Landless Farm Worker
- usually people who have been forced from their tenant plots by the landowner
- must move to nearby towns or cities in order to live
- hire themselves out to landowners for a small daily wage
- do not have any land to grow food for themselves
- a rapidly increasing group in Brazil

A wide variety of land use agreements and land rental contracts are found throughout Brazil. The diagram on the next page shows how agricultural land is often organized in the Northeast. This pattern is typical of the Northeast and many other regions in Brazil.

140

An Example of Land Organization in the Northeast

Large Landowner

Tenant Farmer

Sharecropper

Squatter

Farm Worker

Small Landowner

141

CASE STUDY: Land Reform

Problems With Land Distribution

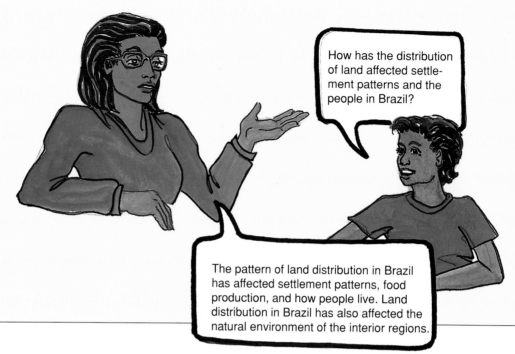

How has the distribution of land affected settlement patterns and the people in Brazil?

The pattern of land distribution in Brazil has affected settlement patterns, food production, and how people live. Land distribution in Brazil has also affected the natural environment of the interior regions.

1. Large landholdings occupy most of Brazil's good agricultural land. Small landholdings are usually on the lands with poor soils. The majority of Brazil's farmers live on small landholdings. They cultivate some of Brazil's poorest agricultural land.

Large Landholding

Small Landholding

2. Many large landholdings do not use the land well. It is estimated that nearly 40% of Brazil's government-owned agricultural land is not used for cultivation or animal pasture. Another estimate indicates that nearly 30% of Brazil's good farmland is not used for crops or pasture. Small landholdings, however, tend to use the land more productively. The diagram to the right shows the difference in land use between large and small landholdings in the Northeast.

House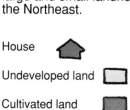

Undeveloped land

Cultivated land

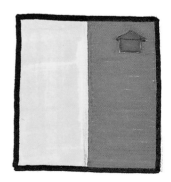

Large holdings usually have less than 15% of their land under cultivation or in use as pasture for animals.

Small holdings usually have at least 50% of their land under cultivation or in use as pasture for animals.

3. Much of the food eaten in Brazil is produced on small landholdings. In recent years many of these small landholdings have dropped below 10 hectares as land is divided among sons. These landholdings are often too small to produce enough food even for the family. As the supplies of Brazilian-grown food products have decreased, prices have risen. Many food products are also being imported at greatly increased prices. Even basic food products such as beans, rice, and manioc are often too expensive for many Brazilian families.

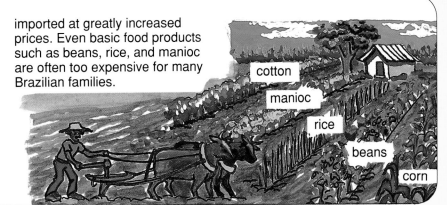

4. Most large landholdings do not cultivate food products for Brazilians. They are most often used to produce export crops such as soybeans, cotton, wheat, corn, rice, and oranges. These products can be sold to other countries for high prices. By 1985, for example, Brazil was one of the world's largest exporters of food products. Large landholdings are also being used to produce sugar cane to supply cane to the alcohol factories. These factories produce alcohol to run trucks and cars in Brazil. Many large landholdings are also used for cattle ranches. Cattle require large pasture areas to produce small quantities of meat. These meat products are usually exported rather than used to feed Brazilians.

5. Most of the farmers in Brazil do not own their own land. They can be made to leave the land they rent from the landowners at any time. Once landless, they are forced to move to the towns or cities to look for work. In many areas, the massive eviction of tenant farmers has resulted in angry demonstrations and violence. Violent clashes have occurred between tenants and gunmen hired by the landowners to remove them. In some places, large groups of evicted farmers have protested. They have occupied areas of large landholdings and refused to move. This has also resulted in violent conflicts between the farm workers, the landowners, and the local police.

6. The Brazilian government has attempted to provide farmland for the large number of landless farmers. It has opened new areas of the interior for agricultural development. Unfortunately, many of these areas are not suitable for the cultivation of important Brazilian food products. Beans, rice, potatoes, and manioc do not grow well in these areas. Widespread clearing of natural vegetation to make farmland has also been devastating for the natural environment of the interior.

CASE STUDY: **Land Reform**

Land Reform in Brazil

Many Brazilians talk about government land reform plans. What is land reform?

LAND REFORM is a government policy of land redistribution. Privately-owned large landholdings that are not being farmed would be bought by the government. The government would then divide the land into small parcels. It would either be given to landless farmers or sold to the farmers for a small price. The government expected that most of this land would come from many of the large estates. These estates presently cover nearly 80% of Brazil's agricultural lands.

Many of these large landholdings are owned by land speculators. LAND SPECULATORS buy land in the hope that it will increase in price. When land prices rise, they sell it to someone else for more money. Most land bought by speculators is left undeveloped. They do not cultivate the land or use the land for pasture.

Only a small amount of the large landowners' lands would be included in the land reform plans. How-ever, the landowners have strongly resisted these government land reform plans. The large landowners have continually **lobbied** the government to revise its plans. This has slowed the pace of land reform. At today's rate of land redistribution, many economists estimate that land reform will take nearly 100 years.

Not Everyone Agrees...

An Economist:

Brazil has enough agricultural land to provide farmland for all its farmers without clearing the rain forests. The problem is that most of the good agricultural land is owned by only a few landowners. Too much of this land is not being used to grow food crops for our people. If the government purchased much of this undeveloped land and divided it among the poor, landless farmers, there would be enough land for everyone in Brazil. There would be no need to further clear the Amazon rain forest to produce new farmlands.

Land reform would have a positive effect on many problem areas:

- land reform could increase productivity 15%-25% as unused land was cultivated or used for pasture.

- land reform could absorb a large part of the rural labor force. This would stop the flow of people to the already overcrowded cities.

- the increased production of food products would lower prices for food in the markets and cities. More people would be able to buy food. The number of families able to afford a minimal diet would increase.

A Government Official:

The Brazilian government has not been unaware of the country's land ownership problems. So much of the ownership of agricultural land is concentrated in a few large landholdings. Attempts to build a rural middle class of small farm owners actually began in the late 1800s. The early attempts at land reform, however, met with strong resistance from the large landowners. They did not want to give up any of their land or lose their farm workers. Some poor agricultural lands in the South and Southeast were given away to encourage European immigration. However, land reform made little progress in the Northeast.

In recent times, INCRA* successfully settled nearly 7 000 families on 100 hectare plots in Rondônia. INCRA's settlement plans began to fall apart, however, when the flood of settlers began arriving in Rondônia. There were just too many settlers for INCRA to handle. There was conflict over land titles. Settlers, Indians, and squatters clashed over ownership of the land.

Recently, the government has recognized the serious need for land reform. In 1981, the government reduced the length of time a squatter had to occupy land to establish ownership rights. A squatter had to be on the land for only 5 years instead of the previous 10 years. In 1985, the National Agrarian Reform Plan set out goals to buy large areas of undeveloped land in the Northeast for redistribution to landless farmers. The 1988 constitution also confirmed the government's commitment to land reform.

The resistance from the wealthy landowners and corporations is very strong. They are fighting land reform in the law courts. These legal battles could delay land reform for years. Without cooperation from the landowners, the government cannot resettle the millions of landless farmers. These landless poor will continue to flood into the cities from the countryside. This will create more problems for the already overcrowded cities.

Without land reform, the only alternative to providing land is opening new agricultural areas in the Amazon rain forest. This is not a welcome choice for many members of the government.

Lobby—a person or group that tries to influence decision-makers
*INCRA—(translated from Portuguese) the National Institute for Colonization and Agrarian Reform

144

A Large Landowner:

I am very angry with the land reform proposed by the government. This land has belonged to my family for well over two hundred years. Now the government wants to take away part of it and divide it among the poor. The Church has sided with the poor people, and told them that they have a right to move onto my land. This is a criminal act, but the courts do nothing. Part of my land is occupied by squatters. Now the government tells me that I must sell that part. The government is offering to buy the land. However, their price is far less than the land is worth. Why take my land? This is a huge country. There is plenty of land in the Amazon and the Center West. The government could open up more of these areas for settlement. That is a better solution to the problem of the landless poor in Brazil. Landowners have supported the government for years. We developed the land and made Brazil a great agricultural country. Now we are being betrayed by our own government.

Landowners in Brazil are determined to fight land reform. We will defend our land. We have formed our own national organization called the Rural Democratic Union to resist government land reform. If necessary, we will hire people to guard our land from squatters. This is our land!

A Tenant Farmer:

Fences! Fences! Fences! There are fences everywhere. They are the symbol of the land problems in Brazil. Millions of poor rural farmers are fenced off from the land. In the last ten years, millions of rural farm workers have been pushed off the land. The landowners want to use every bit of their land. They want to grow new crops such as soya beans. Now more of the farm land is owned by large corporations or banks. Sometimes these companies do not use the land, but we are told that we cannot live on it. Often the landowners buy expensive new machinery to use on the farms. Then they need fewer workers. As a result, some of us are forced to the far edges of the property. Many others are forced off the land altogether. When this happens, we lose our houses and the garden plots that feed our families. We must live in the towns and work for a daily wage on the plantations. The wages are often not enough to feed our families. We want the government to share a small part of the undeveloped agricultural land with the landless. Convincing the government is a difficult fight. It is also a dangerous fight against the landowners. Sometimes we occupy undeveloped land on a large estate. Sometimes we march in demonstrations. In Rio Grande do Sul last year, nearly 50 000 protesters marched in support of land reform. Many squatters and organizers have been killed. Despite the fear for our lives, we are continuing to organize and fight for land.

A Roman Catholic Church Worker:

In Brazil nearly 12 million rural families are landless. Each year nearly one million more are forced from the land. Without land these people cannot grow food to feed themselves. Nearly 40% of the good agricultural land owned by the wealthy landowners or the government is undeveloped. If even a small percentage of this undeveloped land was distributed among Brazil's landless farmers, everyone would have plenty of land and food. The Roman Catholic Church in Brazil is helping the landless organize and fight for land reform. This support has been dangerous. Several priests and nuns active in the land reform movement have been killed.

A Union Worker:

In the last decade landless farmers have united to form organizations to help speed up land reform. Tens of thousands are members of the nation's Movement of the Landless (*Movimento dos Sem Terra*). The government has been very slow to introduce many land reform plans. The problem is that many members of the government are themselves large landowners. Even the government owns many large estates that are not being cultivated. In some areas hundreds of landless people have occupied small areas of undeveloped land on a large estate. They hope this will convince the government to move faster with land reform. This is very dangerous. These people are open to attack from the gunmen hired by the landowners. In the last four years nearly 500 people in Brazil have been killed in land conflicts. We will not be frightened by guns or threats from the landowners. We must fight for a small piece of land for our families.

145

CHAPTER 6
The Threatened Rain Forest

Until the 1960s the Amazon rain forest in Brazil's North region was largely undisturbed. In the 1960s the Brazilian government began an intensive program to open up the interior areas for settlement. They wanted to develop the land and natural resources. This settlement and development has had a disastrous effect on the Amazon rain forests. This chapter examines the factors that have contributed to the rapid **deforestation** of Brazil's rain forest, the effect of deforestation on the earth's climate, and the possible solutions to save what is left of the Amazon rain forest.

1. What is a rain forest?
2. Where are the world's rain forests located?
3. Why are the rain forests considered valuable?
4. Why are the world's rain forests disappearing so rapidly?
5. What factors have contributed to the deforestation of the Amazon rain forest?
6. What effect do scientists think the burning of the rain forest is having on the world's climate?
7. What is a mega-project? How have these projects affected the Amazon rain forest?
8. Why are the natural resources in the rain forest being developed?
9. How have loans from other countries affected the deforestation of the Amazon rain forest?
10. What can be done to save the Amazon rain forests?

Deforestation—the clearing of forests

 **Problem Solving**

1. Explore possible answers to the question:

   What has been the interaction between human and physical geography in the rain forest?

2. Human geography refers to the activities of people. Physical geography refers to the physical features of the rain forest (land, natural vegetation, soils, rivers, climate). Use your knowledge of the rain forest and what you know about how human activities can affect the physical geography of a country, to form your hypothesis. Predict what effect human activities such as settlement and development will have on the rain forest. Copy the recording chart shown on this page into your notebook and use it to record your hypothesis.*

3. As you read through this chapter doing research on the problem, add more information or revise your hypothesis. On page 159 you will be asked to evaluate the information you have collected and develop a concluding statement to the problem.

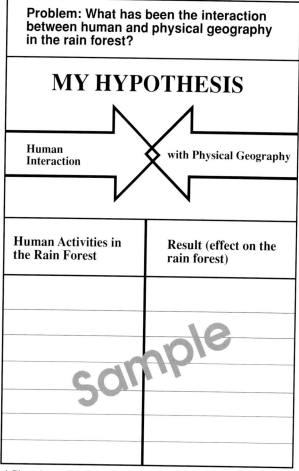

Problem: What has been the interaction between human and physical geography in the rain forest?

MY HYPOTHESIS

Human Interaction	with Physical Geography

Human Activities in the Rain Forest	Result (effect on the rain forest)

*Chart is available as black-line master in the Teacher Resource Package.

The Threatened Rain Forest

While rain forests throughout the world are rapidly disappearing, it is the destruction of Brazil's Amazon rain forest that has captured the attention of the world. This chapter will investigate the destruction of the Amazon rain forest and the groups who are competing for a share of this vast forest resource.

Location of World's Rain Forests

Rain forests occur in a wide band north and south of the Equator. The largest areas of rain forest vegetation are in Brazil, Southeast Asia, and West Africa. Brazil has nearly one third of the world's rain forests. The map below illustrates the locations of the world's rain forests.

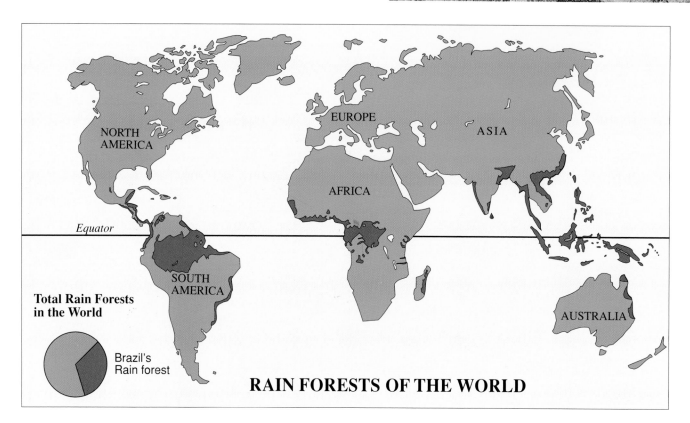

RAIN FORESTS OF THE WORLD

The Amazon Rain Forest

Amazon Rain Forest is the name given to the rain forest vegetation that covers the large area of lowlands in South America that are drained by the Amazon River and its many tributaries. Most of the Amazon rain forest is located in Brazil but the rain forest does extend into several South American countries. The Amazon rain forest is sometimes referred to as the Amazon. The map shows the location of the Amazon rain forest.

148

Disappearing Rain Forests

The world's rain forests are disappearing at an alarming rate. Rain forests are being destroyed faster than any other natural environment. It took hundreds of years to clear the forests of Europe, Asia, and North America. **Deforestation** in the Amazon rain forest is taking only **decades**. Each year millions of hectares of the rain forests are cleared to make way for roads, towns, hydro-electric dams, mines, timber operations, cattle ranches, and farms. At the present rate of destruction, scientists estimate that by the year 2000 the only remaining rain forests on earth will be in remote areas of Amazonia and Africa. Even these are expected to disappear by the year 2030. In the time it takes to read this page nearly 80 hectares of rain forest will be destroyed. The map at the bottom of the page illustrates the extent of the disappearing rain forests.

As rain forests disappear, the animals of the rain forests also disappear. Scientists estimate that one species a day becomes **extinct** because of deforestation. By 1990 this could rise to one species an hour disappearing from Earth. Within the next 15 years, deforestation of the rain forests may have destroyed up to 25% of all the world's wildlife.

Scientists believe the loss of the rain forests may drastically change the climate and weather patterns on Earth.

The destruction of the rain forests also has a human cost. Tribal peoples in the rain forest rely on the rain forests for all of their basic needs. When the rain forest disappears their way of life is also destroyed. The clearing of the world's rain forests is endangering thousands of different groups of tribal Indians throughout the world.

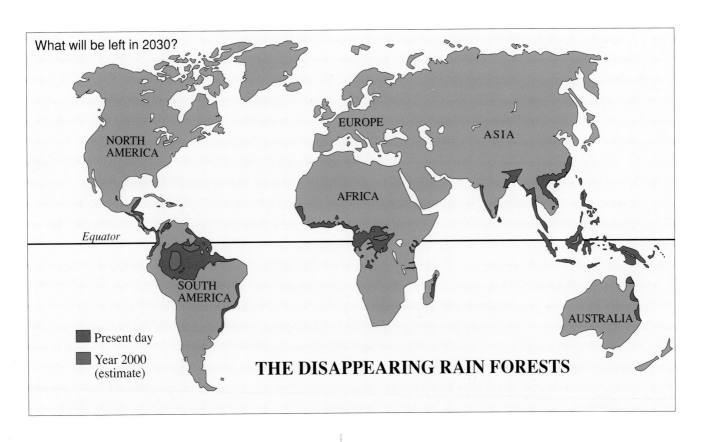

THE DISAPPEARING RAIN FORESTS

Deforestation—the clearing of forests
Decade—a 10 year period

Extinct—no longer living on earth

The Rain Forest on Fire

Settlers, cattle ranchers, and timber companies are moving into the interior of Brazil. They are clearing and burning extensive areas of the Amazon rain forest. Every day, huge plumes of grey smoke rise over the rain forest. Hundreds of hectares of Amazon rain forest are set on fire each day. Recent satellite photographs have been able to pinpoint up to 6 000 fires burning in the rain forest on a single day.

Effect of the Rain Forest Burnings on the Atmosphere

Scientists throughout the world are concerned that the burning of the rain forests is reducing the amount of oxygen in our atmosphere. Less rain forest means less carbon dioxide will be recycled into oxygen. The diagram on the right shows how the forest **ecosystem** works. Carbon dioxide in the atmosphere is absorbed by the forest. The trees and plants convert this carbon dioxide to oxygen. This happens during **photosynthesis**. The oxygen is then released into the atmosphere. Some scientists predict that as the rain forests are reduced, the amount of oxygen available in the atmosphere may decline. Other scientists disagree that the rain forests return large amounts of oxygen to the atmosphere. They believe that most of the oxygen produced by the rain forest is used up in the forest as plant materials decay.

The burning of the rain forests is releasing huge amounts of carbon dioxide into the atmosphere. Scientists estimate that in 1987 nearly 1.8 billion tonnes of carbon dioxide were produced by the burning of rain forests. The burnings in the Amazon rain forest may be responsible for nearly 20% of all the carbon dioxide added to the atmosphere each year. The diagram on the right illustrates the effect of rain forest burnings on the forest ecosystem.

The increased carbon dioxide in the atmosphere could cause severe changes in the world's climate. Large amounts of carbon dioxide in the atmosphere might result in warmer temperatures on earth. This occurs because carbon dioxide increases the greenhouse effect.

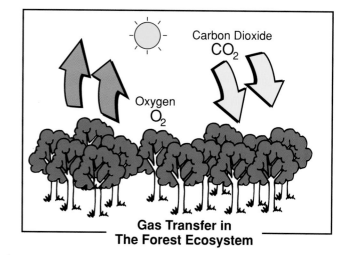

Gas Transfer in The Forest Ecosystem

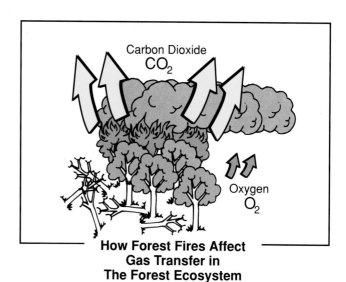

How Forest Fires Affect Gas Transfer in The Forest Ecosystem

Ecosystem—the system formed by the interaction between living things and their environment

Photosynthesis—process in which the energy from sunlight is used by green plants to produce food substances from carbon dioxide and water

150

The Greenhouse Effect

The earth's atmosphere allows most of the sunlight and heat from the sun to pass through it. The sunlight then heats the earth's surface. This heat from the sun is called SOLAR RADIATION. The earth then sends the heat back into the atmosphere. This heat is called THERMAL RADIATION. Normally some gases such as carbon dioxide, water vapor, and ozone absorb some of this thermal radiation as it passes through the atmosphere. These gases send the heat back toward the earth. This heat warms the earth's surface. The warming of the earth's surface by the gases in the atmosphere is called the GREENHOUSE EFFECT. The name was chosen because the gases in the earth's atmosphere act much like the glass roof of a greenhouse. Sunlight enters the greenhouse through the glass and warms the air inside. The glass also prevents heat from escaping quickly back outside. The glass keeps the air in the greenhouse warm. If there were no greenhouse effect, the temperature on earth would be around −10° Celsius. The oceans would be frozen. The greenhouse effect has made earth livable.

As the amount of carbon dioxide in the atmosphere increases, less heat escapes to the upper layers of the atmosphere. More heat is returned to the earth. This causes the temperatures on earth to increase. The increased carbon dioxide in the atmosphere could increase the temperatures on earth.

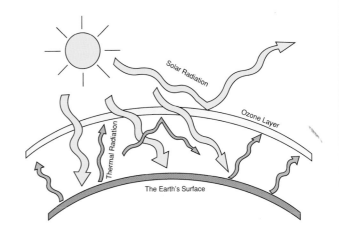

The Greenhouse Effect and the World

North Americans could feel the effects of the burning of the Amazon rain forest. The temperatures on earth may increase. Some scientists predict that as a result, the polar ice caps will slowly melt. This will raise the level of the oceans. The oceans could rise over one metre. This increase would flood all the low-lying land along the eastern coast of North America.

The winter ski industry in North America could be ruined. Warmer winter temperatures would cause a lack of snow. The warmer temperatures could also result in decreased rainfalls in the important grain-growing regions of North America. The Canadian and American prairies could experience more summer droughts. Droughts would seriously reduce wheat and corn production. Many scientists believe there is a strong connection between forests and climate. The forests put moisture back into the air. This helps to make sure that there will be more rain. Areas of rain forest that have been cleared often show a substantial reduction in rainfall. Some areas may become so dry that they cannot be used for agriculture. Over the last 20 years rain forests in Panama have been cleared. This has resulted in a decrease of 40 centimetres per year of rainfall.

Scientists believe that the loss of rain forests may affect the climate of the whole world. Areas farther away from the cleared rain forests may also experience warmer temperatures and less rainfall. Some scientists think the 1987-88 drought on the North American prairies may be a result of the loss of rain forests and an increased greenhouse effect.

The burning of the Amazon rain forest is not the only source of increased carbon dioxide in the atmosphere. The United States and Canada lead the world in the amount of carbon dioxide released into the atmosphere each year.* North Americans produce twice the amount of carbon dioxide produced by European countries. North American production of carbon dioxide is four times the world average. North Americans are not burning forests. However, we are using millions of motor vehicles. The exhaust from automobiles, buses, and trucks accounts for a large portion of the carbon dioxide released into the atmosphere each year.

*Canada averages 4.04 tonnes of carbon emissions per person compared to 1.03 tonnes per person for the world (including Canada).

The Amazon Rain Forest

Destruction of the Amazon Rain Forest

What Started the Destruction of the Rain Forest?

Until the 1960s the Amazon rain forest was largely undisturbed. The native Indians and the few settlers, rubber gatherers, and missionaries had little impact on the natural environment. The main means of communication and transportation were the rivers of the Amazon river system. Then in the 1960s things changed. The Brazilian government began a program to open up the vast interior of the country. You studied this in Chapters 4 and 5. The settlement and development activities that followed have contributed to the rapid destruction of the Amazon rain forest in the last three decades.

Roads

Since 1960 the Brazilian government has built an extensive highway system through the interior rain forest. These roadbuilding projects were financed largely by loans from the **World Bank**.

The government hoped these roads would open up the interior. The government wanted to encourage settlement and development of the interior. The government believed the interior rain forest would provide agricultural land for the millions of landless Brazilians. They believed that the resources of the interior would produce a new prosperity for Brazil.

Scientists and environmentalists argue that the highways built through the Amazon rain forest have destroyed much of the rain forest. Yet they have not produced a new prosperity for Brazilians. The new roads have allowed settlers, cattle ranchers, gold miners, and timber companies access to the resources of millions of hectares of rain forest. Development of these resources has not improved the living conditions for many Brazilians.

In 1986 the government arranged a 70 million dollar loan from the Inter-American Development Bank. This was to cover the cost of paving a 600-kilometre section of the BR-364 Highway through Acre. The government claimed the paving of this road would create jobs and new wealth.

Environmentalists worried that the paved road would only increase rain forest deforestation. A largely untouched rain forest in Acre would be opened to a flood of settlers, gold miners, loggers, and cattle ranchers. This is just what happened. As fast as the highway crews paved sections of the road, cattle ranchers and loggers moved in. They cleared the rain forest on either side of the highway. Environmental groups finally convinced the Inter-American Bank to stop payment on the loan. This forced the Brazilian government to take some action to protect the forest.

The government responded by creating several forest reserves. The problem is the lack of people to patrol the forest reserves. No one ensures that the reserves are not cleared. Many people blame the international banks that funded these road-building projects. They did not consider the effect of the roads on the natural environment and the people of the rain forest.

World Bank—Officially called the International Bank for Reconstruction and Development, it is loosely attached to the United Nations. The World Bank provides loans and technical assistance for economic development projects in developing countries.

Cattle Ranching

Cattle ranching has been responsible for the largest amount of deforestation in the Amazon rain forest. Some scientists estimate nearly 80 per cent of rain forest clearing has been caused by cattle ranching. Cattle ranches need large areas of pasture for their herds. The cattle ranchers saw the opening of the interior rain forest as an opportunity to buy cheap land to clear for pastures. The Brazilian government wanted to encourage development. They sold many areas of the interior rain forest for 25 cents a hectare. The owners of Brazilian cattle ranches are usually large companies, wealthy business people, or wealthy farmers. They were able to buy vast areas of the rain forest for their ranches.

The first area of extensive rain forest cattle ranching was in Pará State. There the Trans-Amazon Highway provided cattle ranchers with access to the interior. The BR-364 Highway is now completed. This has made Mato Grosso, Rondônia, and Acre the new center of cattle ranching operations in the rain forest.

Unfortunately there are problems trying to grow food crops on the rain forest soil. There are also problems trying to maintain pasture land in the rain forest. The rain forest produces thousands of species of plants. But there is nothing in the rain forest a cow will eat! Before cattle can be raised in the rain forest, the trees and vegetation must be removed. Just like settlers, cattle ranchers use the slash-and-burn method to clear the rain forest. This creates open pasture lands for their cattle. The photograph above shows an area in Rondônia cleared for cattle pastures.

For the first year the pasture is very good. Each year after that the grasses become thinner. A mixture of woody bushes and shrubs called SCRUB starts growing back in the cleared areas. Cows won't eat scrub so it must be cleared off. Sometimes the scrub is scraped off using a bulldozer. Chemical **defoliants** are sometimes used. The most common and cheapest method of removing the scrub is to burn it off. This yearly burning destroys what little nutrients are left in the soil.

In less than six years, most of the cleared rain forest is useless as cattle pasture. Rain forest lands are inexpensive. They are usually abandoned once the soils will no longer produce good pasture grasses. Cattle ranchers are continually clearing the forest. This provides new pastures for their cattle.

It has been difficult to maintain cattle ranching in the rain forest areas. **Agronomists** estimated that almost all the cattle ranches established in the Amazon rain forest before 1978 would be abandoned within twenty years.

Hamburger Connection???

Many of the large cattle ranches in the Amazon rain forest are owned by large corporations in São Paulo and Rio de Janeiro. Brazilian beef is sold to many countries. It produces large profits for Brazilian meat companies. Millions of dollars worth of frozen and canned Brazilian beef is sold to Iraq, England, the United States, Canada, and Germany each year. Many environmentalists claim Amazonia is being deforested to provide inexpensive hamburgers for the rest of the world.

Defoliant—chemical that kills plants by destroying their leaves
Agronomist—someone who specializes in the management of soils and crop production

155

Settlement

In 1973 the rain forest areas of Rondônia and Acre were still largely undisturbed. The BR-364 was a dirt road that was extremely difficult to travel during the rainy season. The trip across the length of Rondônia alone could take from four to seven weeks. This depended on the condition of the road. Since the completion of paving the BR-364 in 1984, hundreds of thousands of people have come to Mato Grosso, Rondônia, and Acre. They came to look for land. Many of these settlers were the landless poor from other regions of the country. Some towns in Rondônia reported 30 busloads of people a day. They came from southern Brazil and the Northeast. For a time, nearly 10 000 new settlers arrived in Rondônia each month. Porto Velho is the capital of Rondônia. Its population grew from a few thousand to 300 000 in less than five years.

Farming in the rain forest has proved to be more difficult than many settlers anticipated. There is a rich growth of trees. However, the soils of the rain forest are very low in nutrients. Rain forest vegetation gets most of its nutrients from the thin top layer of soil. Other nutrients are in the decaying leaves and plants on the forest floor. Settlers clear and burn the natural vegetation. Then the soil is exposed to hot sun and heavy rains. The heavy rains wash away many of the nutrients in the soil. When rain forest soil is exposed to the constant heat of the sun, it often becomes as hard as baked bricks. Most cleared areas of the rain forest can support plant growth for only a few years. After three or four years there are no nutrients left in the soil. Crops fail to grow. Settlers are unable to grow enough food to feed themselves. They are forced to continually clear new areas. The settlers know that the clearing and burning of the trees destroys the soil but they have no choice. It is the only way they can grow food for their families.

Many of the settlers eventually give up. Some sell their land to cattle ranchers. Others simply pack up and set off for a new place farther into the rain forest. There they begin the process of clearing and burning over again.

156

Logging

The Amazon rain forest is one of the largest forests on earth. It contains an abundance of valuable timber. Before 1960 these resources could not be logged. There was only river access to the rain forest. Transportation to sawmills was too difficult. Now new highways stretch into the rain forest. Logging companies have started to harvest the timber in the rain forest.

These logging operations have usually had a disastrous effect on the rain forest. There are large profits to be made in the timber business. Logging companies are removing thousands of hectares of forest timber as quickly as possible.

Loggers are often looking for only a few valuable species of trees such as Brazilian mahogany. Trees of the same species do not grow closely together. Loggers often have to clear large areas of rain forest to secure a supply of any one type of tree. Some of the trees felled are not useful to the logging operation. Many trees are left on the ground. They are burned. Extensive areas of the rain forest are often destroyed. This secures only a small supply of valuable timber. This type of logging is called CLEAR-CUT LOGGING.*

Even the logging roads contribute to further destruction of the rain forest. Logging roads are used by cattle ranchers and settlers. Now they can get to more remote areas of the rain forest. Cattle ranchers followed the loggers. They took over the cleared land for cattle pastures.

Gold Rush

For thousands of Brazilians it is not land or the cattle that has attracted them to the Amazon rain forest. It is the sparkle of gold.

In the 1980s several large gold discoveries were made in the Amazon rain forest. These gold discoveries attracted thousands of gold prospectors called *garimpeiros*. They came to isolated gold fields in Mato Grosso, Roraima, Rondônia, Amazonas, and Acre. These gold rushes in Brazil are similar to the gold rushes that took place in British Columbia and California in the 1800s.

Gold prospectors are often poor. They have fled the *favelas* of the cities or the poverty of the Northeast countryside. Some are teachers, office workers, bus drivers, or farmers. They have dreams of making a rich find.

The gold rushes in Amazonia have had an effect on the rain forest. With the gold rushes have come further destruction of the rain forest. Pollution of the rivers and streams has followed. The rain forest is cleared and burned. This makes way for airfields, towns, and mining camps. Many of the gold mining operations use mercury to extract the gold flakes from the earth. Mercury is then washed into the streams and rivers. It is deadly to insects, birds, and fish. Humans also use the rivers for drinking water. They rely on river fish for food. High concentrations of mercury have been found in several of the smaller rivers and streams near gold mining operations. The mud washed away from these mining sites is also beginning to clog smaller rivers and streams. The heavy concentration of earth flowing into the streams can easily damage stream beds. This causes more extensive flooding during the rainy season.

The author is standing on a logging road in Rondônia. She is in front of a rain forest tree that is the sole survivor of a rain forest that once covered this area.

---

*Clear-cut logging is also used in North America. Some environmental protection groups have protested this type of logging for many years.
Garimpeiros—pronounced gar-im-pear-eeos

Large Mining Operations

The Amazon rain forest in Brazil has a wealth of minerals. They include gold, tin, copper, silver, manganese, iron ore, and bauxite (used for making aluminum). The map on page 38 illustrates the mineral resources found in the interior rain forests. Each year new mineral deposits are located. Many of these deposits are located using satellite photographs.* Aircraft-mounted radar can map soil and vegetation as well as topography. Information from these sources as well as ground samples have located many more potential mineral deposits in the Amazon rain forest.

In recent years several large mining operations have been established in the rain forest. One example of a mining mega-project is the iron ore development at **Carajás**, in northern Pará. Carajás contains the largest iron ore deposits on earth. It also has extensive deposits of manganese, copper, nickel, gold, and bauxite. The mineral wealth has attracted a flood of Brazilian and foreign companies. They are interested in extracting and refining the minerals. The government plans to develop at least 20 iron ore **smelters** and a dozen other mining and smelting operations in the Carajás area.

The development of mines and smelters at Carajás has also resulted in the destruction of thousands of hectares of rain forest. This mining development will require the cutting of millions of hardwood trees. They are needed to produce the charcoal fuel needed in the smelting and refining process. Already more than a thousand hectares of rain forest have been cleared. The space is needed for the mine pits, smelters, roads, railways, and towns for the workers.

The mining development is expanding. So is the destruction of the surrounding rain forest.

Hydro-Electric Dams

Since 1960 the Brazilian government has built several hydro-electric dams in the Amazon rain forest. Money to build these dams has been provided by loans from the World Bank.

These hydro-electric projects have generated a great deal of criticism. They have destroyed thousands of hectares of rain forest. Much of the flooded rain forest has been within Indian land reserves. Brazil has plans to build several more hydro-electric dams in the rain forest. These will provide electricity for the industries and large cities along the eastern coast. Loans for these hydro-electric projects will also come from the World Bank. International environmental protection groups, wildlife protection groups, and Brazilian Indian tribes have organized a strong opposition. In early 1989, several Kayapó Indian Chiefs organized an extraordinary meeting. Several hundred Indians from 37 Indian groups met in the small town of Altamira in the heart of the rain forest. The Indians met with government officials and representatives from the electric company. They met to protest the construction of more hydro-electric dams in the rain forest. This meeting marked the first time that so many different Amazon Indian groups had joined together in a united effort to protect their rain forest lands. They wanted to convince the members of the World Bank to vote against loans for dams in the Amazon rain forest.

---

*A Canadian company has developed Brazil's satellite systems.

Carajás—pronounced cair-a-jazz
Smelter—a plant where minerals are extracted from the ore dug from the ground

Development Loans

Since the early 1960s, the Brazilian government has borrowed billions of dollars. Some of the money comes from banks in North America, Europe, and Japan. More money comes from the World Bank and the Inter-American Development Fund. This money has financed road building, mining, logging, and hydro-electric projects. Many international environmental protection groups and scientists have criticized these banks. They are particularly angry at the World Bank for not considering the effect of these projects on the Amazon rain forest and the Brazilian Indians.

In recent years international banks and the World Bank have been under pressure. International environmental protection groups and groups of Brazilian Indians want them to stop loans for projects that threaten the rain forest environment and Indian land reserves. In 1989 environmentalists and Brazilian Indians protested a World Bank loan. The money was to build several hydro-electric dams on the Xingu River.

The World Bank and other banks have responded to the protests. They say that environmental considerations will not be ignored. Any new loans to the Brazilian government will include plans to avoid or minimize damage to the rain forest and Indian communities. The threat of losing these funds has forced the Brazilian government to develop new plans. Now the government must respect Indian land reserves and some areas of the Amazon rain forest.

For Your Notebook

1. **? Problem Solving** Problem Solving Activity (continued from page 147): Modification of the physical environment can have beneficial and **detrimental** effects.

   a) Copy and use the chart shown on this page.*

   b) Evaluate the information gathered on your Hypothesis Chart started on page 147. What human activities in the rain forest have produced beneficial results? What human activities have resulted in detrimental effects? In the + column list all the results that in your opinion were beneficial. In the – column list all the results that in your opinion were detrimental. Your list may differ considerably from other students' lists, depending on your own point-of-view.

   c) In your opinion, how would you evaluate the human interaction with the rain forest environment? Develop a concluding statement to answer the problem: **What has been the interaction between human and physical geography in the rain forest?**

   d) What action plans might be put into place that would change the negative consequences of human activity? What action plans might be put into place to continue the positive consequences of human interaction with the rain forest? List plans in the Action Plan column of the recording chart.

2. Based on the information gathered from this chapter, who appears to be benefiting from the development activities in the rain forest?

3. In your own words, describe the greenhouse effect.

4. Why do scientists think the world should be concerned about the destruction of the rain forests?

5. In what ways might the destruction of the Amazon rain forest affect people in North America?

RESULTS OF RAIN FOREST ACTIVITIES		
+ Beneficial Results	**–** Detrimental Results	**My Conclusion**
		My Action Plan

Sample

Detrimental—negative, harmful or causing loss

*Chart available as black-line master in the Teacher Resource Package.

159

Point-of-View Activities

The development of a country's land resources often involves conflict between groups with widely different opinions on how the land should be used. Each group believes that they have the right to use the land in a way they think best. Conflict between groups about the use of land is a common occurrence in Brazil as it is in North America. The following point-of-view activities allow you to experience problem solving and conflict resolution.

Point-of-View Activity #1

PROBLEM: **Who has an interest in the rain forest?**

The interviews on pages 161 to 166 present the points-of-view of various groups with an interest in the Amazon rain forest. Each group believes they have a right to say how the rain forest is used.

As you read through the interviews, make notes in the appropriate "Piece of the Pie" Recording Chart that you copy into your notebook.* List the arguments presented for each group to back-up their claims for control of the rain forest.

"Piece of the Pie" Chart

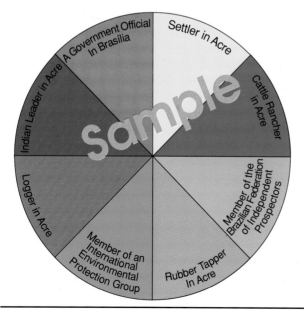

*Chart is available as black-line master in the Teacher Resource Package.

160

Point-of-View Activity #2

PROBLEM: **How can the interests of all the groups concerned about the rain forest be accommodated in the development plans for the state of Acre?**

a) Divide class into small groups of eight students.
b) Have one student in each group represent a Brazilian Indian, a cattle rancher, a settler, a rubber tapper, a logger, a gold miner, a Brazilian government official, and a member of an environmental protection group.
c) Take on the role of the interest group you represent. Your personal views are to be ignored. You are to argue the point-of-view of your interest group. For example, if you are assigned the role of the government official, you are to present his or her point-of-view, whether or not you agree. Each group must work together to try to formulate a **compromise plan** for the development of Acre State. The concerns of each interest group should be addressed.
d) Each group should present their development plan for the Acre state to the entire class.

Looking for Bias

Problem solvers do not believe everything they hear or read. They listen careful for what are opinions and what are facts in supporting arguments. Sometimes people state opinions as if they were facts. This is often called BIAS. Often the speaker has a predetermined goal and presents only arguments that support that goal. Sometimes facts are exaggerated or distorted. This is an attempt to influence the listener. As you read through the following interviews, look for opinions that are being presented as facts. Look for exaggeration and a one-sided point-of-view.

Acre—far western state in Brazil, pronounced awk-ray
Compromise Plan—a plan whereby each side gives up part of what they demand in order to settle the dispute.

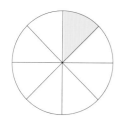

Settler in Acre

Between 1970 and 1985 over a million settlers came to the Amazon. Most were like my family. We were poor. We had no jobs, no land. We were encouraged by government television advertisements to come to the Amazon. We wanted to find land and to build a better life for our families.

We were forced to come to this wilderness for land. There was no land for us in Paraná. Too much of the good farm land in Brazil is owned by only a few large landowners. The government doesn't find ways to divide up the land held by the large landowners. Instead they encouraged us to move to the rain forest to find land.

All we wanted was a little land near the road. We want to grow food for our family. But we have found the same problems in the rain forest that we faced in Paraná.

For most poor farmers prosperity has been only a dream. The land looks so rich. But after a few years it gives out. Then we have to sell out to a rancher or just leave. We move farther into the forest to start again.

We do all the work to clear the land. We risk the malaria. Then we have to turn the land over to cattle ranchers. They make the profits.

Sometimes settlers do not even get a chance to farm their land. Wealthy cattle ranchers are able to get false deeds to the land. They force the settlers off the land. Many settlers have been evicted illegally from their plots. They cannot afford lawyers to fight their eviction in courts. The land agents, the police, and the courts are on the side of the wealthy landowners.

Soon our land would not grow crops anymore. We had to sell it to a cattle rancher. We moved farther into the rain forest. When we came to Acre we found that there was no land for us. All the land is owned by large cattle ranches, timber companies, and the Indian tribes. Where is the land for the poor farmers?

We must fight for a place to live. Many of us banded together to fight the cattle ranchers. We occupied some cleared land owned by a cattle rancher. The large landowners and the cattle ranchers failed to persuade us to leave. They used their hired *pistoleiros* to try to force us to leave. There have been several gunfights between the settlers and the ranch *pistoleiros*. Gunshot and knife wounds kill nearly as many settlers here as malaria.

If we do not fight the cattle ranchers and timber companies, we must fight the Indians for land. The government says we cannot have the land here. It is an Indian reserve. How can they do this to us? The Indians have lots of land. We have so little. Some of the Indian reserves are very large. One in Rondônia is nearly five million hectares. The Indian populations are so small! They have too much land and we are without any land.

We are Brazilians. This is our land! We have a right to live here and own a small piece of land for our families.

Pistoleiros —hired gunmen

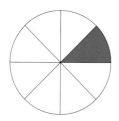

Cattle Rancher in Acre

The government has encouraged cattle ranchers to start ranches in Rondônia and Acre. They have sold us large areas of land. They have helped us develop a cattle and beef industry. I have paid the government a great deal of money for the land. I have a right to clear the land and raise cattle.

Cattle ranches will help develop the interior. They will provide new wealth for Brazil. Before this land was only wilderness and forest. The *seringueiros* made only a little money from the forest. The settlers have a difficult time making successful farms in the rain forest. Most are forced to leave the land after a few years. Cattle ranches are a good use of the land. There are many productive cattle ranches in the interior. They produce beef for **export**. The export of beef produces millions of dollars for Brazil. Last year more than 400 million dollars worth of beef was exported. We need this development. We need this industry. It will help push Brazil forward.

We have experienced many problems with the flood of settlers. They have come from Rondônia. In the last few years the Rondônia State government announced there was no more free land. Thousands of settlers have come to Acre. But there is no free land here either. Most of the land in Acre is owned by timber companies, cattle ranches, the Brazilian government, or the Indian tribes. Because the settlers can't find land for themselves, they try to take over our land. We have cleared it for our cattle. This has created quite a problem.

It costs me a lot of money to hire workers to clear the forest. Once it is clear, *posseiros* move onto the land. They keep my cattle and ranch hands away. It is much easier for the *posseiros* to take my land rather than try to find their own land to clear. Sometimes the *posseiros* have shot at my ranch hands. I had to hire armed workers just to keep the *posseiros* off my land and to protect my ranch hands. It is very dangerous here.

Sometimes the *posseiros* shoot at the ranch owner or the caretaker. I was shot last year. A group of posseiros attacked my car when I was heading into Rio Branco. I had three bullets in my stomach. I was in the hospital for two months. That is why I wear a gun now. I keep my family in Porto Velho. It is too dangerous on the ranch. Now I have armed men, *pistoleiros*, who patrol my land. They keep the settlers out. Cattle ranchers must use force to protect our investment.

Ranch owners have also had problems with the local *seringueiros*. I have 4 000 head of cattle. I need to clear at least 600 hectares of forest each year to provide new pasture. The grazing land is so poor I need to provide at least two hectares of pasture for every animal. I have to hire workers to cut, clear, and burn the forest. Then we can plant grass.

But the local rubber *seringueiros* come to interfere with the clearing operations. They try to convince my ranch workers to stop clearing the forest. Sometimes families, women and children, come and stand in front of my workers' chainsaws. A few have shot at my workers. I have had to hire armed gunmen to protect my workers. This is a terrible situation.

Seringueiros—rubber tappers. Pronounced sair-in-gair-ohs
Export—goods sold to other countries
Posseiros —squatters, landless homesteaders who illegally occupy land owned by other people

162

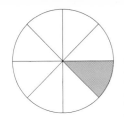

Member of the Brazilian Federation of Independent Prospectors

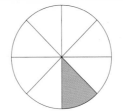

Rubber Tapper in Acre

Brazil's Amazon gold rush is ten years old. It is expanding rapidly as new gold deposits are discovered. Some newspapers call the Amazon gold rush the biggest gold rush in world history. Our federation estimates that there are 500 000 independent gold prospectors in the Amazon rain forest.

The Brazilian government has encouraged the gold rush in the Amazon. There is huge production of gold by independent prospectors. In 1988 large mining companies produced 12 tonnes of gold. Independent *garimpeiros* dug an estimated 63 tonnes of gold from the Amazon. This gold is worth almost 1 billion dollars to the Brazilian government.

In 1988 Brazil was the fifth largest gold producer in the world. If the Amazon gold rush continues Brazil could become the second or third largest producer of gold. The export of gold to the rest of the world is one way for Brazil to help pay off the huge amount of money it owes to world banks.

It is not only gold we are looking for in the rain forest. The Amazon has vast deposits of diamonds, nickel, tin, copper, and iron ore. The Brazilian government can sell all these minerals to other countries for high prices. These minerals can add to the wealth of the country. They can help improve living conditions for many poor Brazilians.

Garimpeiros must be allowed to continue searching the rain forest and digging for gold. But we are being denied access to much of the forest. The government tells us that large areas of the forest are set aside for Indian reserves. What will the Indians do with the land? The Indian populations are small. Their reserves are huge. They do not need all that land. The Indians want to let the forest stay untouched. They want to leave the mineral wealth untouched. These minerals don't belong just to them. They belong to all Brazilians. It is not right for the Indians and the government to tell us we cannot dig the minerals. We want to improve our lives. We want to add to the wealth of Brazil.

Rubber tappers and their families have been living successfully in the Amazon rain forest for many years. We make our living by collecting latex from rubber trees. We also collect Brazil nuts, medicinal plants, **chicle nuts**, and palm fibers from trees in the rain forest.

We do not make a great deal of money. Most rubber tappers make only about $1 200 a year. But our way of life uses the rain forest without destroying it. We can show others how to use the rain forest without destroying it. We do not clear large areas to grow food crops or raise cattle. We rely on trees to provide much of our food. For example, one Brazil nut tree can provide more protein than can be obtained from one cow grazing on three hectares of cleared forest.

Roads were built through the rain forest in the 1970s and 1980s. Before that, the only way to reach *seringueiro* communities was by boat along the rivers. Now our way of life is threatened by development. Road building, timber operations, farming, and cattle ranching have already destroyed large areas of the forest in Rondônia and Acre.

In Acre we are fighting the timber companies and the cattle ranchers. Deforestation by cattle ranchers in Acre has already forced 10 000 rubber tappers and their families to abandon their homes. They must give up rubber collecting. Many have been forced to move to the *favelas* in Rio Branco. Thousands more have fled across the border to Bolivia. If the rain forest is destroyed, our way of life is destroyed.

Many of the cattle ranches are owned by large corporations. They can afford to buy the land from the government. We do not own the forest. All we own is our hut and our small clearing. We have three or four trails in the forest leading to our rubber trees. We do not own the forest. We only use the forest. When the cattle ranchers come they clear the forest. They force out the *seringueiros*. We are driven out without any compensation.

The cattle ranchers want all the land. They want to clear and destroy all the forest in Acre. Soon everywhere will be fenced and full of cattle. But how will we live without the forest?

Garimpeiros—independent prospectors; pronounced gar-im-pear-eeos

Chicle nuts—nuts used to produce chewing gum

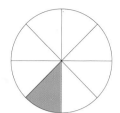

Member of an International Environmental Protection Group*

Rain forests are being destroyed around the world. The greatest and most rapid deforestation is taking place in the Amazon rain forest in Brazil. The Amazon rain forest is vanishing at an alarming rate. If the current pace of deforestation for land and timber goes unchecked, the Amazon forest will have vanished forever within a few decades. Deforestation of the Amazon rain forest is a great loss for all the people in the world.

Rain forests cover only 6% of the earth's surface. They contain 50% to 80% of all the living things on earth. Scientists estimate that as many as five million species of plants and animals may live in the rain forests of the world. The rain forest is a vast storehouse of plants and animals. They can be used for human benefit.

Rain forest plants can be used to make valuable medicines and to treat a variety of diseases. Nearly 25% of the ingredients for prescription drugs on the market today come from rain forest plants and animals. Curare is made from a rain forest plant. It is used by the Amazon Indians to make their arrowheads poisonous for hunting. It has been used to treat Parkinson's disease. Scientists estimate that there may be as many as 2 000 rain forest plants that could be used in the treatment of cancer.

Rain forest plants can also be used to improve world food production. One example is a strain of corn that was discovered in the Mexican rain forest. This corn is resistant to viruses that damage North American corn. Scientists are hoping to use the wild rain forest corn to improve North American corn crops. The Amazon rain forest is so vast that scientists have only just started to study all the plants and animals. Many plants have not yet been identified. Some of the plants of the Amazon rain forest exist nowhere else on earth. The destruction of the Amazon rain forest means all the plants and their potential benefits are lost to all the peoples of the world.

The loss of the rain forests poses dangers to people all over the world. Scientists believe the rain forests influence rainfall, regional climates, and world weather patterns. Destruction of the rain forests means serious changes to the world's climates and weather patterns. In Panama, for example, where the rain forest has been completely removed, the annual rainfall has dropped by 90 cm in the last 50 years. Some scientists believe that the disappearance of the world's rain forests have increased the spreading of the Sahara desert in northern Africa.

Elimination of the Amazon rain forest also causes immediate human hardships. The rain forest is home to a great many Indians. They rely on the rain forest for their way of life. Destroying the forest destroys the Indians. Other groups of people like the rubber tappers have also lived for many generations in the forest. Clearing the forest for cattle ranches and logging destroys their way of life.

North Americans and Europeans have learned that destroying the forests is a great loss. In North America we are learning to manage what forests we have left. We are trying to work for sustained development to utilize the benefits of the forest while still preserving the forest resource. We want to pass that knowledge on to Brazil. They do not need to make the same mistakes that were made in other countries. The Brazilian government can learn from our mistakes. They can keep their forest reserves intact and still benefit from the wealth of the forest. That is what we are trying to encourage the Brazilian government to consider.

---

*Note: This is not a Brazilian but represents a point-of-view of environmental protection groups throughout the world.

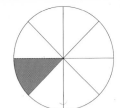

Logger in Acre

The rain forest has some of the world's largest timber resources. Many of the **hardwoods** found in the rain forest are very valuable. We can sell teak and mahogany to other countries for a great deal of money. We can use the timber to make paper products. We can use the lumber for building materials. With the rain forest resources, Brazil could become one of the world's leading exporters of valuable hardwood timber. This is very good for the country. Exports mean more money for the country and the government. Exports mean more jobs for people. Lumber mills mean more steady jobs for workers and good wages. This is very good for the people.

The large forest is a gift to Brazil to be used. There is plenty of forest for everyone here. We can harvest timber and there can still be land for the rubber tappers and the Indians. If timber companies do not cut the valuable timber it will just be burned off by the cattle ranchers and settlers. That would be a waste. Once we have taken out the valuable timber, the land can be used by cattle ranchers and settlers. This way the timber is not wasted. The land can still be used.

The rain forest is very wonderful to look at, but it does not generate wealth for the country or the people unless it is logged. We must use the resources of our country to better our lives.

Hardwoods—the terms "hard" and "soft" do not necessarily refer to the physical properties of the timber. The terms are derived from the ways in which the trees reproduce.

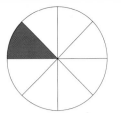

Indian Leader in Acre

We must fight for our land before it is too late. Already too many Indians have died. Too much of our forest has disappeared. The Brazilian government, the cattle ranchers, settlers, and gold miners want our forest. They do not understand. When they destroy our forest, they destroy us. We are part of the forest. The forest gives us food and all the things of our world. We must fight for the forest. It must be here for our children and grandchildren and their children.

We are the true Brazilians, not the whites who come to destroy the forest. It is our land. We have not given our land away. Our land has been taken away. Our forest has been taken away by lies and by force.

Everywhere the Brazilians have come in the forest, Indians have died. The gold miners and settlers bring diseases we have never known. The Brazilians hope that many Indians will die. Then there will be no one left to protest. Then they will take our lands.

The Brazilians who come from the government have lied to us. The Brazilians who come from the power companies have lied to us. They have promised to protect us and protect our lands. The government tells us we have a right to the land. But this right is not enforced. The government lets settlers and gold miners move onto our lands. They let the power company build dams that flood our forest. The Brazilian government tells us they want to protect us. But we can no longer trust the Brazilians. We must take up the fight ourselves and claim what is ours. Once they move onto our land the forest is destroyed. Then our culture disappears.

We must protect our way of life. We must feed our culture back into ourselves and into our children. We cannot let our children take on Brazilian ways. We must keep our lives as they have been since the days of our ancestors. We must keep ourselves separate in the forest. We must continue to follow our old ways.

Perhaps this is our last time to rise up to defend our forest and our way of life. We are disappearing. Soon there will be few Indians left to fight. We must fight for our forest now or we will vanish like the forest. We will be nothing but a memory.

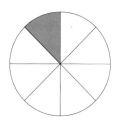

Government Official in Brasília

Brazilians are feeling pressured from international environmental groups and the World Bank to leave the Amazon rain forest alone. Yet we need to develop the resources of the Amazon.

Brazil needs to develop all of its natural resources. We must provide farm land for our people, expand industries, and pay our large **foreign debt**. We also need money to improve living conditions for our people. One way we can do all these things is to develop the vast resources of the rain forest.

There are millions of poor, hungry people in Brazil. We can settle these people in the interior. We can provide them with land to farm. If we can give people land they will be able to feed themselves. Large areas of the rain forest are being cleared by settlers but the cleared land is providing these people with food.

The rain forest will help us expand our industries. To build new industries requires raw materials and power. The rain forest has the raw materials (timber and minerals) and the rivers have the potential to produce electric power. In many places industries are still using oil for power. Brazil cannot afford to continue importing huge amounts of oil at high costs. We must develop the hydro-electric potential of our rivers. With dams we can supply industries with inexpensive electrical power. Cheap electrical power is vital to encourage new industries.

Developing the resources of the rain forest will help Brazil pay its foreign debt. Brazil owes many countries and international banks billions of dollars. To pay this debt, Brazil needs to sell more products to other countries. There are many resources in the rain forest that we can export. We need to greatly expand our timber, mineral, and agricultural exports. One example is the mineral resources of the rain forest. The government has encouraged Brazilian and foreign companies to develop the large mineral resources in the rain forest. The export of these valuable minerals will generate wealth for the country and help pay our foreign debt.

We must also consider the welfare of our people. The Brazilian government needs a great deal of money to provide more housing, schools, health clinics, and water and sewage facilities for all our people. Developing the resources of the rain forest will produce the necessary money to improve living conditions for our people.

Development means we will clear large areas of the rain forest. Some Indians will be displaced. There will be changes for some people already living in the rain forest. These are things we must consider. But we must continue with our plans to develop the resources of the rain forest.

Brazilians want the same chance to develop their resources that North Americans had to develop theirs. It is very disturbing to hear people in North America and Europe criticizing Brazil for developing the rain forest. This is our forest. It is our resource to use as we think best. It is for the benefit of Brazilians. Many of the people who criticize the way we are developing the rain forest live in developed countries. Their countries have logged their forests, built dams on their rivers, and developed mines and oil wells to take advantage of their resources. These people come from wealthy countries. They have used their resources to produce good living conditions for their people. Brazilians want the same chance to develop our resources.

Foreign Debt—the amount of money a country owes to international banks. Between 1960 and 1989 the Brazilian government borrowed large sums of money to build Brasília, to build the new highways, and to finance hydro-electric projects.

Conflict and Violence in the Rain Forest

Conflict and violence have become a feature of life in the Amazon rain forest. Much of the violence is the result of different groups fighting for a part of the forest.

Brazilian Indians

The Brazilian Indians are at the center of the fight for the rain forest. Brazilian Indians occupy large areas of the rain forest that gold miners, settlers, and cattle ranchers want to explore and develop. Many of the rivers the government would like to dam for hydro-electric projects flow through Indian lands. As development and settlement activities push farther into the Amazon rain forest, the Indians and their way of life are increasingly threatened.

In the last few years, many Indian groups have begun taking an aggressive stand against threats to their lands. In 1989 more than 500 Indians from 37 groups were at the Amazon city of Altamira. They met with government officials and officials from the Electronorte power company. The meeting was to protest plans to build dams on the Xingu River. The Indians claim that the dams will flood nearly 25 million hectares of Indian lands. This was the first time that Brazilian Indians had joined together to protest government plans for the Amazon.

The Brazilian Indians have support from international environmental groups. They have taken their protest to countries who fund Brazilian development projects. Chief Payakan, a Kayapó leader has toured North America. He attempted to convince the Canadian and American governments to vote against further World Bank funding of hydro-electric projects in the Amazon. Payakan also met with officials from Canadian and American banks to try to convince them to consider the rain forest and the Brazilian Indians. Then maybe they won't grant loans to Brazil for development projects in the rain forest.

The *Seringueiros* Fight for the Rain Forest

Rio Branco, Acre
December 27, 1988

ENVIRONMENTALIST KILLED—Francisco "Chico" Mendes, an internationally acclaimed ecologist and advocate of the preservation of the Amazon jungle, was shot and killed by unidentified gunmen last Thursday at his home in the remote Amazon jungle town of Xapuri. Mendes, 44, had told authorities he had received death threats from ranchers in the region.

The *seringueiros* and their families have also experienced conflict and violence in their fight for the rain forest. Their struggle to protect the rain forests has placed them in opposition to the wealthy cattle ranchers and timber companies. Some of the cattle ranchers have hired armed workers to discourage the *seringueiros*. In recent years several *seringueiros* active in the campaign to stop the clearing of the rain forest have been killed.

For more than ten years Francisco "Chico" Mendes led a successful fight in Acre to halt the deforestation of the rain forest and to protect the rights of Brazilian rubber tappers. His fight to save the rain forests began in the 1970s. The Brazilian government began cutting a road into Acre. Cattle ranchers and timber companies soon followed, clearing the rain forest and forcing out *seringeiros*. *Seringueiros* would often return at the end of a day in the forest to find their homes and all their possessions burned to the ground. Chico organized *seringueiros* to work together. They fought the ranchers' clearing operations. They tried to protect their way of life. Chico helped form the first Rural Workers Union in Acre. Eventually he became one of its most outspoken leaders.

Chico made speeches throughout Brazil and met with Brazilian politicians to explain the concerns of the rubber tappers. He traveled to England and the United States to persuade government leaders and bank officials to consider protection of the rain forest when they made loans to Brazil for development projects in the Amazon.

Chico Mendes soon became known world-wide for his fight to save the Amazon rain forest. In 1987 the United Nations Environment Program honored Chico Mendes. They said he was one of the world's top 500 environmentalists.

As a result of his work, the Brazilian government established twelve rain forest reserves. They totalled more than four million hectares in five Amazon states.

Chico fought to protect the rain forests and the *seringueiros's* way of life. This brought him into conflict with the timber companies and owners of cattle ranches. The cattle ranchers and timber companies strongly opposed the establishment of the forest reserves. In 1988 Chico began receiving death threats. He frequently told his friends that he had enemies with power and money. He knew that his life was in great danger.

What Can Be Done to Save the Rain Forests?

Many people in Brazil and in the rest of the world believe that the rain forests must be saved. There is no going back in time, however. We cannot bring back the Amazon rain forests as they were thirty years ago. The problem now is to find a way to ensure that the rain forests do not disappear completely.

What might the Brazilian government do to save the rain forests?

1. Establish Extractive Reserves

EXTRACTIVE RESERVES are one way to use the resources of the rain forest and still protect it from total destruction. An extractive reserve is an area of rain forest where burning and clearing are not allowed. Specific products such as medicinal plants, nuts, fruits, and rubber are carefully harvested from the forest.

Extractive harvesting is a long-term use of the rain forest. It allows the rain forest to be used for many years. Extractive harvesting can provide good incomes for workers. It produces valuable export goods. Many of the rain forest products, especially medicinal plants, are in great demand in Brazil and in other countries.

3. Restrict Cattle Ranching

Restricting how much land can be used for cattle ranching could save large areas of the rain forest. Cattle ranchers cut and burn vast areas of the rain forest and produce only small amounts of food. Cattle ranching is a very poor use of the rain forest. Cattle ranches produce less than 40 kilos of meat per hectare of land each year. In comparison, several brazil nut and banana trees growing on one hectare could produce three to four tonnes of food each year.

2. Establish Selective Logging Forest Reserves

The destruction of the rain forest might be reduced if the government set aside areas of the forest as logging reserves. Timber companies would be allowed to cut trees in these reserves only with government permission. Agents from the government forest service would supervise the cutting of timber in the reserves. This would ensure that the timber companies practiced SELECTIVE LOGGING. In selective logging, specific types of valuable trees are felled. Other trees are untouched. This allows other trees to grow in place of the logged trees. The area would not be completely cleared. The rain forest is maintained but the valuable timber is logged. This type of logging does not seriously damage the forest, the wildlife, or the Indians and settlers living in the forest.

169

4. Teach New Farming Skills

The rain forest needs permanent farmers. They must be able to support themselves on the same piece of land for many years. We need to stop the continued burning of new areas of the rain forest. We can help farmers grow food and **cash crops** on the cleared land. This will reduce the need to clear new areas. Besides food crops for their families, farmers could be taught how to grow coffee, black pepper, *cacão*, and tropical fruits and nuts on rain forest soils. These crops would provide farmers with higher incomes from one piece of land. The government could help by giving the settlers technical knowledge about growing long-term cash crops. It could also give settlers some financial help while their crops are being established. Then they would not need to clear more forest each year. Fertilizers, **crop rotation,** and other agricultural methods would make farmland more productive.

5. Enact Land Reform

Unused agricultural land in Brazil could be redistributed to the many landless farmers. This would reduce the need to clear the Amazon rain forest for farm land.

6. Reconsider Building More Hydro-Electric Dams

Many people believe that Brazil does not need to build new hydro-electric dams. They argue that many of the dams completed since 1960 are only working at half their capacity. Brazil may already have enough dams to provide all the power it needs. Environmental groups have suggested that the existing dams be made more efficient. They want the government to reconsider building any more new dams in the Amazon rain forest.

Nossa Natureza

The Brazilian government has received pressure from the World Bank and other international banks. They want Brazil to make an effort to preserve the remaining Amazon rain forest and to guarantee Indian lands. This pressure has yielded some results. In October 1988 Brazil's president announced a new plan to protect Brazil's rain forest from excessive deforestation. The new program is called *Nossa Natureza*, meaning "Our Nature." The chart on the right outlines the *Nossa Natureza* plan.

The New Plan

- The government would stop providing lower taxes and loans to encourage cattle ranching, farming, and logging in the rain forest.
- The export of valuable rain forest timber such as mahogany would be stopped for three months.
- Several forest reserves would be established in Acre.
- Cattle ranching in the Amazon rain forests would be strictly limited.
- The government guaranteed that it would provide Indian groups with their own lands in the Amazon.
- The government would set up several groups to develop an environmental plan. The plan would help determine Brazil's future development projects.

Cash crop—crops that are produced to be sold for money rather than as food for the farmer

Crop rotation—planting different crops in fields to ensure that the soil keeps its fertility

What might other countries do to save the rain forests?

1. Reduce Foreign Debt Payments
Banks might consider reducing Brazil's foreign debt or reducing the interest payments. Brazil is trying to pay its foreign debts with valuable exports from the rain forest. If Brazil's foreign debt were reduced the government would be under less pressure. It would not need to rapidly develop the valuable resources in the rain forest. Then the government would have time to consider how to best develop the resources. It could also decide how to preserve more of the environment. Countries in North America and Europe could help Brazil deal with its foreign debt problems. Then there might be more of a chance to preserve the rain forest from development.

2. Swap Debt for Nature
Several environmental groups in North America are experimenting with a debt-for-nature swap. With this plan an environmental group pays off part of a country's debt. In exchange, Brazil sets aside certain areas of rain forest as forest reserves. In order for this to work, both international banks and the government must agree to ensure the reserve is protected from clearing.

3. Ban the Import of Rain Forest Timber
Countries might consider banning teak and mahogany imports from countries that practiced clear cutting. This might help encourage countries to develop selective logging practices in the rain forest.

4. Support Environmental Groups
There are many world environmental groups who are working on various projects. They are trying to save as much as they can of the Amazon rain forest and other rain forests. These groups need volunteers and supporters.

5. Meet Environmental Concerns Before Granting Loans
At the World Bank, representatives from Canada and other countries vote on granting development loans to Brazil. The World Bank can require countries to meet environmental concerns before granting them new development loans.

Exploring Further

1. On pages 161 to 168 you read a variety of points-of-view by Brazilians and how they feel about the rain forest issue. Pages 169 and 170 presented several possible solutions from the Brazilian government. On this page, the author has presented some ideas on what the rest of the world could do about the rain forest issue.

   Have the ideas presented on this page taken into account the points-of-view of Brazilians and their government? Support your answer.

2. Give examples of local issues that could or do have an affect on the rest of the world.

CHAPTER SUMMARY

The rain forests of the world occupy only about 1/6 of the world's surface. They contain 50 to 80% of the world's plant and animal life. In the last thirty years the rain forests of the world have started to rapidly disappear. There is world-wide concern that the world's rain forests will completely disappear by the year 2030.

The rain forests are important for a variety of reasons. The rain forests contain thousands of animal and plant species that are unique to the rain forest environment. Many species have not yet been identified. Scientists believe that thousands of the rain forest plants have medicinal purposes. At least 25% of the ingredients in prescription drugs used in North America already come from rain forest plants. The rain forests are also home to thousands of tribal peoples who rely completely on the rain forest for their basic needs. As the rain forests of the world disappear, so will the plants, animals, and tribal peoples.

Scientists are also concerned that the burning of the rain forests will seriously affect the world's atmosphere. The burning of the trees is releasing huge amounts of carbon dioxide into the atmosphere. This may increase the greenhouse effect and raise world temperatures. Scientists also believe that the forests influence rainfall and weather patterns. The loss of the rain forests could affect rainfalls and weather patterns throughout the world. Already several droughts have been blamed on the loss of rain forests. The loss of the rain forests could also reduce the oxygen supplies in the atmosphere. The forest recycles carbon dioxide during photosynthesis and releases oxygen into the air.

All the rain forests on earth are endangered. World attention, however, has been focused on the Amazon rain forest because it is the world's largest remaining forest. Its rate of deforestion has been so rapid. Clearing of the Amazon rain forest did not really begin until the 1960s, when the government of Brazil began focusing attention on the interior. Building the new highways allowed road access for the first time to the interior rain forests. The land and mineral resources of the rain forest soon attracted cattle ranchers, settlers, gold miners, and logging companies. Large mining companies and government hydro-electric projects have also contributed to the destruction of the rain forest.

The development of the natural resources of the rain forest has created conflict among a number of groups of people. Settlers, cattle ranchers, loggers, gold prospectors, and rubber tappers have competed for land in the rain forest. The Brazilian Indians have tried to preserve their lands from invasion by these groups. Environmental groups and the Brazilian government also disagree on how the resources of the rain forest should or should not be developed. Each group believes they have a right to the land. Each group has a different opinion on how the land should be used.

Conflict and violence have become a feature of life in the rain forests. Settlers and cattle ranchers fight for occupation of land. The *seringueiros* battle logging companies to preserve the rain forest and their way of life. Gold miners fight Indians for access to Indian lands. Hydro-electric companies face opposition from international environmental groups and Brazilian Indians when they attempt to build new dams in the Amazon. The Brazilian Indians are waging a determined campaign to protect their lands from settlers, cattle ranchers, gold miners, and the hydro-electric companies. Individual groups will continue to fight for a share of this vast forest resource.

Saving the rain forest is a global concern and a global responsibility. The World Bank, international banks in North America, Europe, and Asia, and countries around the world all share a part in the destruction of the Amazon rain forest.

CHAPTER REVIEW

For Your Notebook

1. Why has conflict and violence become a part of the settlement and development of the Amazon rain forest?

2. Give an example of one group that believes it has a right to a share of the natural resources in the rain forest. Review their reasons.

3. Summarize the information gathered on your "Piece of the Pie" chart in a short paragraph. An opening sentence might be similar to the following:
   "Many groups are competing for a share of the natural resources of the Amazon rain forest."

4. Predict what issues are likely to influence the relationship between the people of Brazil and the physical environment of the rain forest.

5. In your opinion, which is most important to Brazil's future: the development of the rain forest or the preservation of the rain forest? Find evidence to support your position.

6. What economic reasons are often given for the need to develop all of the natural resources of the Amazon rain forest?

7. Why do some people consider the effort to save the world's rain forests a global responsibility?

8. What part do North Americans play in the destruction of the rain forests? What role might North Americans play in an effort to save the rain forests?

9. Forests in North America are also being cleared for logging, farming, highways, oil and gas pipelines, mines, and hydro-electric dams. What are the reasons for clearing North American forests? Copy and use the Venn diagram shown below to compare the reasons for clearing North American forests with the reasons for clearing Brazilian rain forests.* In A and B list the reasons that are unique for Brazil and North America. In C list the reasons that Brazil and North Americans have in common.

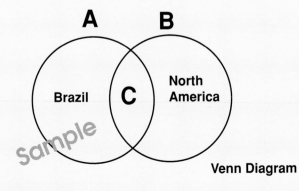

Venn Diagram

Exploring Further

1. Pretend you are meeting with World Bank officials to discuss development loans to Brazil. What arguments might you present in favor of granting loans for development projects in the Amazon rain forest? Consider paving and building highways, building hydro-electric dams, and building mines. What arguments might you present in favor of environmental safeguards to protect the Amazon rain forest?

2. Make a poster to display in your school with the title: Save the Rain Forests. Consider the school audience when planning the illustrations and wording on the poster. What might attract the attention of teenagers?

3. Plan a display for a local shopping mall on the topic of the world's disappearing rain forests.

4. Research the involvement of your country's government and banks in granting loans for projects in the Amazon rain forest.

5. Forests in North America are also rapidly disappearing because of development projects. What forest preservation concerns are there in your area?

6. It is difficult for textbook authors to remain neutral on controversial issues. In this book, the author has attempted to present a variety of points-of-view on the issue of rain forest destruction. The author also has definite feelings on the issue. What do you think they are? Provide examples from this chapter that reflect the author's point-of-view.

7. To what extent do you think Brazil considers its physical environment as it develops its natural resources?

Decision Making

(Continued from Chapter Review on page 137)

Use the information presented in this chapter to add to your Decision Making Form. Are there alternatives suggested in this chapter that can be added to your form? Are there positive or negative consequences that need to be added? Did the information in this chapter suggest new action plans that could be included on your form?

* Venn Diagram available as black-line master in the Teacher Resource Package.

PART IV:
Economic Geography

CHAPTER 7
Politics of
Development*

The goal of **economic development** is to improve living conditions by developing a country's natural resources and increasing a country's wealth.

Brazil's economic development in the last thirty years has been remarkable. Before 1960, Brazil was largely an agricultural country. Today, Brazil is ranked among the world's top industrialized countries. This chapter examines how the Brazilian government transformed Brazil into a modern, industrialized country. The chapter also examines the effects of economic development on settlement patterns, the natural environment, and living conditions.

1. Describe the government's plan to develop Brazil.
2. Why were the 1970s considered an "Economic Miracle" in Brazil?
3. Why does Brazil owe international banks billions of dollars? How has this huge debt affected life in Brazil?
4. What is inflation? How has inflation affected life in Brazil?

---

* Politics of Development refers to government decisions and policies which affect the development of a country's natural resources and industries.

Economic development—growth of industry and business

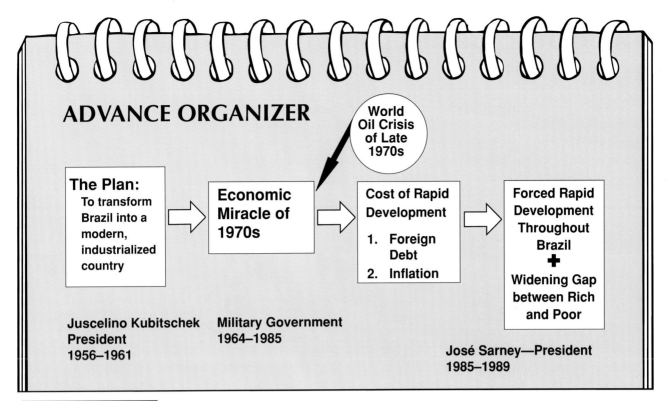

ADVANCE ORGANIZER

World Oil Crisis of Late 1970s

The Plan:
To transform Brazil into a modern, industrialized country

➡️

Economic Miracle of 1970s

➡️

Cost of Rapid Development
1. Foreign Debt
2. Inflation

➡️

Forced Rapid Development Throughout Brazil
✚
Widening Gap between Rich and Poor

Juscelino Kubitschek President 1956–1961

Military Government 1964–1985

José Sarney—President 1985–1989

Problem Solving

1. Explore possible answers to the following.

   Consider economic development in Brazil in the last thirty years. What effect has economic development had on settlement patterns, the physical environment, and living conditions in Brazil?

2. Use what you have already learned about Brazil to develop a hypothesis for the problem. What might be the positive and negative effects of economic development on settlement patterns? On the natural environment? On living conditions in Brazil? Copy and use chart #1 to record this information.*

3. As you read through the chapter, list the economic development plans and activities since 1960. Copy and use chart #2 to record this information. Add the positive and negative effects of these development activities. Remember that you must examine the effect of economic development on settlement patterns, the natural environment, and living conditions.

4. At the end of the chapter you will be asked to develop a concluding statement on the effects of Brazil's economic development since 1960.

*Charts #1 and #2 available as black-line masters in the Teacher Resource Package.

Chart #1

Problem: _____
_____

Hypothesis:
  Settlement Patterns:
    Positive Effects _____

    Negative Effects _____

  Natural Environment:
    Positive Effects _____

    Negative Effects _____

  Living Conditions:
    Positive Effects _____

    Negative Effects _____

Sample

Chart #2

Economic Development in Brazil Since 1960		
Development Plans:		
Effect On:	+	−
Settlement Patterns		
Natural Environment		
Living Conditions		

Sample

The Government's Development Plan 1950–1989

Since the early 1950s, the Brazilian government has attempted to develop Brazil's natural resources. The government has tried to expand Brazil's industries. It wants to make Brazil into one of the world's wealthy industrialized nations. This section will examine the decisions made by the Brazilian government in an effort to achieve this goal.

Brazil in 1950

Rapidly Increasing Population:

By 1950 Brazil's population had substantially increased. There were now great demands for agricultural land, housing, jobs, health care, and education.

Lack of Capital:

There was little individual or government capital for investment in industries, resource development, or improved transportation.

Quality of Life:

Brazil had a low per capita income. Most people barely made enough money to supply their basic needs. Sanitation facilities, schooling, and medical services were not available. Life expectancy rates were low. Infant mortality rates were high.

One-Product Economy:

Brazil's economy was based on one or two agricultural exports. Coffee, for example, accounted for nearly 50% of Brazil's exports.

Few Industries:

The land and mineral resources in the interior regions of the country were not developed. Brazil's hydro-electric potential was not developed. There was no highway access to the interior regions.

Subsistence Agriculture:

Most of the population engaged in agriculture. The farmers could only grow enough to feed themselves. They did not grow enough to sell what they produced.

Juscelino Kubitschek, President 1956–1961

Juscelino Kubitschek was elected President of Brazil in 1956. Kubitschek believed that Brazil had tremendous economic potential. He believed that Brazil was destined to become one of the world's wealthy industrialized countries. He promised the Brazilian people that his government would give Brazil "fifty years of progress in five years."

Kubitschek had many plans to develop Brazil. The most ambitious of these plans was to build a new capital city, Brasília, in the interior wilderness. He also wanted to build a highway system across Brazil. He hoped that by opening up the interior regions of their country, Brazilians could begin to develop their vast wealth of natural resources. He wanted them to expand their industries. Kubitschek hoped Brazil would quickly become one of the world's modern industrialized nations.

Many things, however, would have to change before Brazil could be considered a modern, industrialized nation.

Kubitschek—pronounced koo-bi-check

Conditions that Must Exist before a Nation Can Become a Modern Industrialized Nation

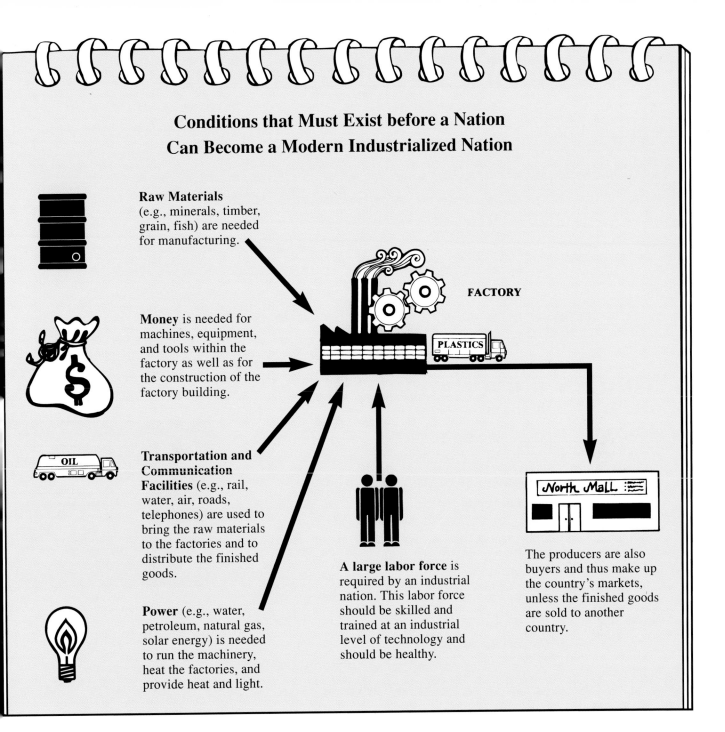

Raw Materials (e.g., minerals, timber, grain, fish) are needed for manufacturing.

Money is needed for machines, equipment, and tools within the factory as well as for the construction of the factory building.

Transportation and Communication Facilities (e.g., rail, water, air, roads, telephones) are used to bring the raw materials to the factories and to distribute the finished goods.

Power (e.g., water, petroleum, natural gas, solar energy) is needed to run the machinery, heat the factories, and provide heat and light.

A large labor force is required by an industrial nation. This labor force should be skilled and trained at an industrial level of technology and should be healthy.

The producers are also buyers and thus make up the country's markets, unless the finished goods are sold to another country.

FACTORY

PLASTICS

North Mall

For Your Notebook

1. Why did many Brazilians believe that their country would have a great future? Why did they believe that Brazil would one day be a leading power in the world?

2. In your notebook, make a chart similar to the one on the right. List all the conditions that economists believe are necessary for a country to become industrialized. Place a star beside each condition that Brazil already had in place when Juscelino Kubitschek became President in 1956. Under the remaining headings, list what Brazil might do to acquire the other conditions necessary for industrial development.

Conditions For an Industrialized Country	
Raw Materials	
Money	
Transportation	
Power	
Labor Force	
Consumers	

Sample

The "Economic Miracle" of the 1970s

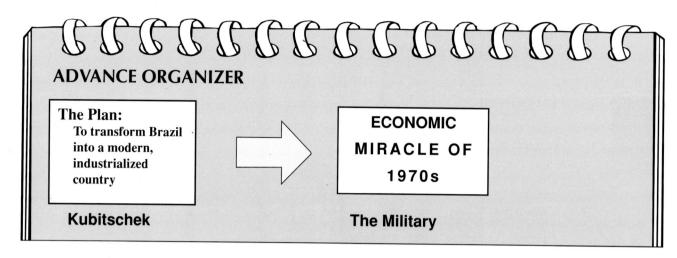

ADVANCE ORGANIZER

The Plan:
To transform Brazil into a modern, industrialized country

→ ECONOMIC MIRACLE OF 1970s

Kubitschek

The Military

Military Government 1964–1985

The military took over control of the Brazilian government in 1964. From 1964 until 1985 military generals controlled the Brazilian government. It installed a series of generals as presidents of Brazil.

The military government continued with the economic development plans that were started by President Kubitschek in the early 1960s. Like Kubitschek, the military generals based their economic development projects on the idea of a "Great Brazil." They believed that Brazil could one day be a powerful world leader. The government's development plans included opening up and settling the vast interior, developing more of Brazil's natural resources, expanding industries, increasing exports, constructing new hydro-electric dams, and building highways into the interior.

The military government also financed the construction of Brazil's first nuclear power generators. It also started Brazil's space program. In the 1970s Brazil was able to launch its own rockets and satellites.

Unfortunately, many of the military government's projects were designed to increase the image of Brazil in the eyes of the world. They did not actually improve the economy of Brazil.

Military Rule in Brazil
- President chosen by military leaders
- all political parties dissolved except the "official" government party and the "official" opposition party; both of these parties controlled by the military
- trade unions outlawed
- city mayors appointed by military government
- candidates for state governors chosen by the military
- censorship of television, radio, and newspaper articles criticizing the government
- people speaking out against the military government arrested and sent to prison without trial
- President given authority to make secret laws
- voting mandatory; people fined if they did not vote; candidates, however, all chosen by the military government

The Military's Development Plans

Expand Industries and Increase Exports

The military government encouraged **multinational corporations** from the United States, Canada, Germany, and Japan to open factories and invest in new industries in Brazil. Most of the new industries produced cars, appliances, clothing, and military weapons. They were built in the São Paulo area.

Foreign Loans

The military government arranged for millions of dollars worth of loans from other countries and the World Bank. These loans were to finance the building of highways, railways, hydro-electric dams, nuclear reactors, industries, mines, and military aircraft. These loans make up Brazil's **foreign debt**.

Develop More of Brazil's Natural Resources

The military government worked to find new markets for Brazilian manufactured goods, minerals, agricultural products, and "cash crops." Agricultural crops that can be sold to other countries for large sums of money are called CASH CROPS. The government encouraged the production of soybeans, corn, oranges, and cattle by offering large land development companies reduced taxes. They were also offered the opportunity to purchase land in the interior for very low prices.

Construct New Hydro-Electric Projects

The military government wanted to provide inexpensive electrical power to encourage industries. It began construction on several massive hydro-electric projects. The Itaipú Dam in southern Brazil, for example, is one of the largest hydro-electric projects in the world.

Build Highways into the Interior

Highways were built through the interior. They provide access to the land, timber, and mineral resources of the North and Center West regions. To provide year-round transportation, the highways had to be paved. The military government arranged millions of dollars in loans from the World Bank to pay for the paving of these new highways.

Open Up and Settle the Vast Interior

The military government encouraged the settlement of the interior regions of the Center West and North regions by paving the BR-364 Highway to Rondônia. It offered free land to settlers. It also offered reduced taxes and cheap land prices to cattle ranchers, timber companies, and large land development companies.

Multinational—a corporation (a company) that has headquarters in one country and branch plants in other countries
Foreign Debt—money owed to foreign countries and foreign banks

Brazil in 1979: Economic Miracle

Under the military government, Brazil had a period of exceptional economic growth and development. For a time it looked as if Kubitschek's plan of turning Brazil into a modern industrialized nation in five years might actually happen. Between 1968 and 1979 the increase in the **Gross National Product (GNP)** reached 10% a year. Few countries in the world have experienced such high annual economic growth rates. This period of outstanding economic growth is often called Brazil's "Economic Miracle."

PERCENTAGE INCREASE IN GNP

Period	Gross National Product (%)	Agriculture	Industry
1947-1955	6.8	4.8	9.0
1956-1961	7.3	5.2	10.4
1962-1967	3.5	4.1	3.5
1968-1974	10.0	3.7	12.2
1975	5.2	5.0	5.1
1977	5.4	11.8	3.9
1978	4.8	-2.6	7.4
1979	6.7	5.0	6.6
1980	7.9	6.3	7.9
1981	-3.5	6.8	-8.4

Source: Getulio Vargas Foundation

AUTOMOBILE PRODUCTION

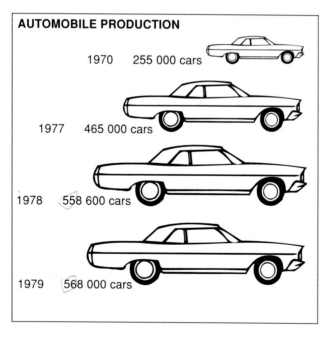

1970   255 000 cars

1977   465 000 cars

1978   558 600 cars

1979   568 000 cars

GROSS NATIONAL PRODUCT IN MILLIONS OF $

1960	$ 35 815 000
1974	$ 102 196 400
1978	$ 139 568 000
1985	$ 210 000 000
1986	$ 270 000 000

Gross National Product—the total money value of a country's goods and services produced in a certain time period

TOTAL EXPORTS (US$)

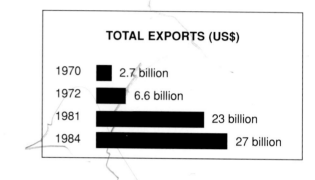

1970	2.7 billion
1972	6.6 billion
1981	23 billion
1984	27 billion

PERCENTAGE OF POPULATION ENGAGED IN AGRICULTURE/MINING/MANUFACTURING

Census Year	Agriculture and Mining	Manufacturing
1940	65.88	7.45
1950	59.90	9.40
1960	53.96	8.59
1970	44.28	10.97
1980	29.93	15.55

Source: Banco do Brasil

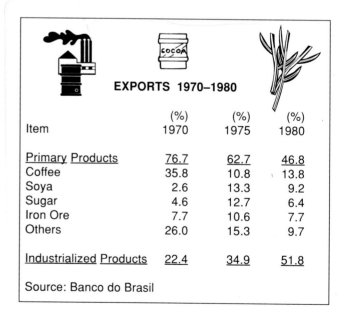

EXPORTS 1970–1980

Item	(%) 1970	(%) 1975	(%) 1980
Primary Products	76.7	62.7	46.8
Coffee	35.8	10.8	13.8
Soya	2.6	13.3	9.2
Sugar	4.6	12.7	6.4
Iron Ore	7.7	10.6	7.7
Others	26.0	15.3	9.7
Industrialized Products	22.4	34.9	51.8

Source: Banco do Brasil

A Chance For the "Good Life"

The 1970s in Brazil brought new prosperity to a great many people. The number of people employed nearly doubled. Over 14 million people in Brazil had jobs. Incomes for factory workers increased. For the first time, some prosperity began to trickle down to the millions of working families. Workers who could find a factory or construction job in the southern cities suddenly had a chance for a good life. Gloria and her family are typical examples. Her family, like many millions of families from the Northeast, moved to São Paulo during the 1970s. They came south in search of jobs and a better life. They wanted a chance to share in Brazil's "economic miracle." Gloria's story follows:

São Paulo
April 1978

(Factual Narrative)

My husband Claudio and his brother Sergio left Ceará (in the Northeast) in 1969. They went to São Paulo to find work. We had heard that there were many good paying jobs in São Paulo's new factories. They went to live with their uncle. He had a job in a car factory in São Bernardo outside São Paulo. Luckily, Claudio's uncle was able to help him get a job in the car factory. My husband is very good with his hands and quickly became a welder at the factory. As a skilled worker he earned a good salary. His wages were much more than we ever expected. Claudio earned more in three months at the car factory than he earned all year in Ceará. Sergio was a carpenter in Ceará. He had no difficulty finding a job in São Paulo. The city's increasing population and the many new factories caused a construction boom. If you were a skilled worker, there were plenty of good jobs.

Claudio lived with his uncle for the first year while he built us a small house. In a little less than two years, he had saved enough money to send for us. It was a long and difficult trip. However, Claudio had sent us money for the bus and food along the way.

We have lived in São Paulo now for nearly six years. The move has been very good for my family. We have the small house Claudio built in São Bernardo (a suburb of São Paulo). Every time there is a little extra cash, my husband gets help from his relatives and friends. Together, they build another room onto the house. Our house has electricity, piped water, and a septic system. In the last few years we have purchased many new things for our home. We could never have dreamed of owning these things in Ceará. We have furniture, a color television, a refrigerator, and a gas stove. My husband is saving money to buy a secondhand car. I would like a washing machine first. My relatives in Ceará find it hard to believe that we live in such a house and own so many things.

Since we moved to São Paulo, I have found a job in the nearby hospital. My earnings help buy things for my children and our house. We can go to the movies and shop at the new shopping malls. My children have good clothes. We can even take Sunday trips to the beach.

181

There is great **optimism** in Brazil today. Things are finally improving for the average people in Brazil. My husband and I are working hard and we can see some improvement in our lives. I have even greater hopes for my three children. My husband and I can now provide our children with an education. In Ceará we could not afford to send the children to high school. Here all my children have finished primary school and two are in high school. Now that things are improving in Brazil, we can hope for good careers for our children. My oldest son hopes to go to the *collegio* and study engineering. My second son would like to be an accountant for the government. My daughter wants to be a teacher. It would have been impossible to hope for these careers for my children a few years ago. Now, if my children study and get a good education, they can get good jobs. Our family will make progress.

People feel that Brazil is finally taking its place among the world's great industrial countries. We can be proud to be Brazilians. My husband and I read in the newspapers about the high cost of oil and gasoline. We know how much the government owes to foreign banks. There is even talk that some factories will have to close. Then there could be much unemployment. That seems impossible. I believe the future is very bright for Brazil. We have great resources and we have people who want to work hard for a better life. We cannot go backwards to the poverty we once knew. Things can only continue to get better for Brazil and the people. The last few years have brought great success for my country and my family. I have great hopes for the future of my country. I have great hopes for my family and the future of my children.

Optimism—looking on the bright side of life; believing that everything will turn out for the best

The End of the "Miracle"

In 1973 the world price for oil soared. Brazil relied heavily on the **import** of oil for cars and trucks. The regions in the interior opened up by the new highways relied on truck transportation for supplies. Many of Brazil's new industries used oil to power their machinery. Brazil was forced to use more and more of its money from **exports** to pay for oil imports. It was also forced to borrow more money from foreign banks to pay for oil imports.

As the cost of oil continued to rise, many countries in the world experienced economic difficulties. Other countries did not have the money to buy Brazil's export goods.

- The amount of exports to other countries dropped.
- Prices for goods rose.
- Car production dropped.
- Factories closed.
- Unemployment increased.
- Incomes dropped.
- Government revenues dropped.
- The Brazilian government was forced to borrow more money to pay earlier debts to foreign banks.
- The government was forced to cut spending on housing, health, education, and sanitation services.
- By 1981, Brazil's years of outstanding economic growth were over.

Sugar Cane Alcohol

The Brazilian government wanted to solve the oil shortage problem. It began a program to use alcohol made from sugar cane to run cars and trucks. The government encouraged the cultivation of sugar cane for alcohol. It gave land developers generous tax reductions. It also gave companies large grants of money to develop alcohol production plants. Large areas of the Northeast were taken over by government corporations or foreign companies. They grew sugar cane for the alcohol industry. At first, the alcohol was mixed with gasoline. That made a mixture called gasohol. Today, however, nearly all new Brazilian-made cars and trucks run on 100% alcohol.

The Price of Development

The development program of the military government left Brazil with many economic problems. There were difficulties with the "big project-development at any cost" projects of the military government. They used up much of Brazil's resources. There was little money left for the government to invest in improving housing, health care, education, wages, or food production.

The goal of the government's development projects had been to improve living conditions. It wanted to create jobs for Brazilian workers by making Brazil into a modern, industrialized nation. The government believed that living conditions in Brazil would improve if great amounts of wealth were created as quickly as possible. This new wealth would eventually "trickle down" to the Brazilian working population. This theory did not work. A small percentage of Brazil's population experienced improved living conditions during the years of the "economic miracle." For many Brazilians living conditions worsened each year.

Imports—goods brought into a country from other countries

Exports—goods sold to other countries

Regional Development Differences

During the 1970s the economic differences amongst the regions in Brazil increased. The Southeast region received most of the benefit from the government's economic development projects. Foreign companies and the Brazilian government invested a great deal of money in the industries of the Southeast. The areas between São Paulo, Belo Horizonte, and Rio de Janeiro became known as Brazil's "Industrial Triangle." More than 80% of the country's manufacturing plants were located in this area. Wages were higher and employment opportunities were greater in the South. The government also invested more money in transportation, housing, education, health care, and other services in the Southeast.

Regional differences were particularly noticeable when the Southeast was compared to the Northeast. The Southeast enjoyed economic growth and rising incomes. Poverty and poor living conditions continued in the Northeast. It is estimated that in 1970 less than half the residents of the Northeast countryside had running water, electricity, schools, and health care facilities.

Wages in the Northeast were substantially less than those offered in the industrialized Southeast. The conditions in the Southeast were better. This resulted in millions of people from the Northeast migrating to the cities of the Southeast.

Development and the Environment

The development of Brazil's natural resources has been uncontrolled. This has resulted in the destruction of much of Brazil's natural environment. Industries have expanded rapidly without any environmental controls. This has produced extensive pollution of the air, land, and water. In the last twenty years factories and smelters have released tonnes of dangerous chemicals and pollutants into the air and rivers.

Vast areas of the natural vegetation were cleared. Mines, hydro-electric dams, farms, cattle ranches, and timber operations were developed. Fertilizers, defoliants, and chemicals to control insects have contributed to the destruction of the natural environment. There was also a lack of adequate facilities to dispose of sewage and garbage in the over-crowded cities. This has also caused environmental problems.

José Sarney, President 1985–1989

Living conditions in Brazil worsened. The military government became increasingly unpopular. By 1985, Brazil had had 23 years of military generals as Presidents. That year the military government allowed **Congress** to choose a **civilian** President.* The military generals believed they could influence the outcome of the election. They were sure that a military-supported candidate would win. They were mistaken. Tancredo Neves, a candidate not supported by the military, was elected in January 1985. Unfortunately, Neves became critically ill. He died before taking office. Vice-President José Sarney, a military-supported candidate, took over. He became the first civilian president of Brazil since 1964.

President José Sarney has faced many difficulties since he became President in 1985. One of the most crucial problems has been the economy of Brazil. The next section will examine three significant economic problems in Brazil. They include Brazil's massive foreign debt, skyrocketing inflation, and the increasing poverty.

Congress—elected representatives from throughout Brazil. Congress serves the same function as the House of Representatives in the United States and the House of Commons in Canada.
Civilian—not connected to the military
*Neves was actually elected by the Electoral College made up of members of Congress and some representatives of State Legislatures.

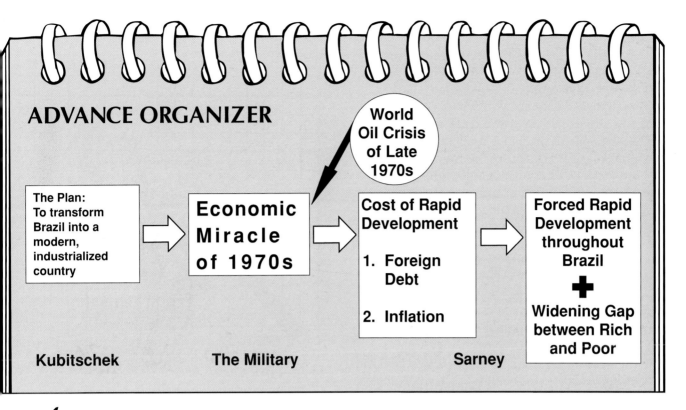

ADVANCE ORGANIZER

| The Plan: To transform Brazil into a modern, industrialized country | → | Economic Miracle of 1970s | → | World Oil Crisis of Late 1970s / Cost of Rapid Development 1. Foreign Debt 2. Inflation | → | Forced Rapid Development throughout Brazil + Widening Gap between Rich and Poor |

Kubitschek   The Military   Sarney

Foreign Debt

FOREIGN DEBT is the amount of money a country owes to foreign banks, to the World Bank, or to other development banks. These banks lend money to developing countries. The Brazilian government borrowed extensively from foreign banks and the World Bank. They needed money to finance economic development projects. This left Brazil in the 1980s with a staggering foreign debt. In 1989, Brazil owed foreign banks over $121 billion (US). Brazil's foreign debt is the largest in the developing world.

The Effect of the Foreign Debt

The foreign debt has influenced almost all the decisions made by the Brazilian government since 1985. The debt is a main cause of the sky-rocketing inflation. The foreign debt is the reason why the government has forged ahead with the development of the interior rain forests. The foreign debt has contributed to the massive cut in government spending on social needs. These include housing, education, and medical facilities. The government is struggling to meet debt payments. Living conditions for millions of Brazilians are getting worse. This can be directly tied to the government's attempts to use Brazil's resources to make debt payments.

Brazil has one of the best performing economies in the world. To date the Brazilian government has not been able to use the wealth generated by this industrial output. The money has not improved living conditions or financed further economic development. Most, if not all, of Brazil's GNP is used to pay the interest charges on its massive foreign debt.

Canadian Banks

Brazil owes nearly six billion dollars to Canadian banks as of 1989. While Brazil is trying to pay back this debt, it can often only manage to pay back some of the interest charges. As a result, Brazil's huge debt affects Canadians. To make up for huge Brazilian losses, Canadian banks increase their small fees and interest rates. These increases affect Canadian consumers and other world customers.

Inflation

INFLATION is the rate at which money loses its value over time. It is the rate at which prices for goods and services increase over time. High inflation means that money loses its value quickly. Prices rise rapidly. Exceedingly high inflation is one of the major problems of the government of President José Sarney.

Inflation, however, is not a new problem for Brazilians. High inflation started when President Kubitschek began developing the interior of the country. This was in the early 1960s. The government had to finance the building of Brasília and other development projects. It began printing more money. The result was that the money was worth less and less. As the money lost value, prices for goods and services increased. Inflation became an everyday part of life in Brazil.

The military government (1964–1985) also had to finance Brazil's rapid industrial development. They printed more and more money. They also borrowed large sums of money from foreign banks. Inflation rates during the military government reached 400%.

Today, the Brazilian government prints even more money. It wants to buy the US dollars needed to pay the interest on its 121-billion-dollar foreign debt. More and more money goes into circulation. Its value drops. Prices increase. Inflation soars higher and higher. Several times since 1985, the Brazilian government has tried freezing prices and wages. They want to control inflation. For a short time inflation was kept under control. As soon as the freeze was lifted, inflation soared to new highs.

Indexing

Inflation soared higher and higher after 1985. The government began indexing salaries. INDEXING means that salaries automatically increase at the same rate as inflation. If inflation for a month was 15%, then salaries would increase by 15%. The workers covered by indexing were most often government workers. They were also workers in industries covered by a union contract.

Many Brazilian workers were not included in the indexing scheme. As prices increased rapidly, their wages fell far behind. Life became very difficult for those caught in the soaring inflation. Even indexing could not keep up with the rising prices.

Hyperinflation

Inflation in Brazil is so high it is called hyperinflation. Inflation statistics for Brazil are usually given as monthly rates rather than annual rates. Through 1988, the inflation rate was averaging 30% a month. This works out to a yearly inflation rate of 1 000%! By comparison, North Americans live with inflation rates of 4 to 5% per year. Based on the monthly inflation rates for the first part of 1989, the annual inflation rate will likely exceed 1 500%.

It is hard to imagine price increases of 1 000%. Because Brazilian money today is worth so much less, the price of two glasses of soda pop would have bought a refrigerator four years ago. The price of filling up a car with alcohol in Brazil today would have bought a compact car five years ago.

Inflation is often easier to understand using North American examples. In the 1940s an admission for an afternoon movie ticket was 10¢. Today $6.00 is a common price to see a movie. In the 1950s a bottle of pop cost 12¢. Today, a can of pop is 95¢. For the price of a microwave oven today, a family could have purchased a car in the1920s. In the late 1960s you could purchase a new, small car for $1 800. Today that same car would cost $10 000. In North America the change in value of money and the rise in prices has been spread over twenty or forty years. In Brazil, prices show the same rapid increases during a single year.

What is it Like to Live With 1 000% Inflation?

Inflation has made the prices in Brazil unreal! Brazilian money that was once worth a great deal is now worth very little. The amount on my restaurant bill for a cold drink today would have been the same amount needed to buy a refrigerator four years ago. That is what inflation has done to life in Brazil!

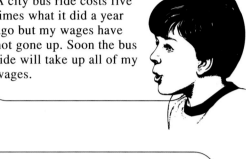

I work delivering *cafezina* to office workers. It costs me half my day's wages to take the bus into town from the suburbs. A city bus ride costs five times what it did a year ago but my wages have not gone up. Soon the bus ride will take up all of my wages.

Inflation has made grocery shopping quite an ordeal. Prices are often marked up 1% each day. I spent much of my day going from shop to shop comparing prices. Like most of my friends, I try to stock up on basic supplies. By the end of the month an item can be three times the price I paid at the beginning of the month. Our kitchen cupboards are filled with bags of beans, rice, flour, sugar, and coffee I bought several months ago when the prices were lower. Despite the high inflation we have always had money for food, fuel for the car, and clothing. My husband is a factory manager with a salary **indexed** to inflation. With the high interest rates we have also made money on the money invested in bonds and our bank savings accounts. We own our own home in the suburbs and don't face large rent increases.

Tomatoes have gone up 60 % in one week! The price of eggs has nearly doubled in the last month. Now the prices for beans and rice are going up. With these prices there are lots of hungry people in Brazil. I don't know how I am going to feed my family if prices keep going up. I work as a maid and my pay is not indexed. I have only had a small raise in the last year. I try to be paid by the day and I spend my money as soon as I get it. If I save any it will be worth less and I won't be able to buy as much food with it.

Inflation means that I must make decisions about the money I have in the bank every day. Brazilians with $2 000 can put their money in special "overnight" bank accounts. I make a little more than 1% interest a day, which keeps me up with inflation. Each day I have to decide where to put my money to get the best rate. Sometimes I put my money in gold or in special savings accounts that can earn up to 17% a month. In this kind of inflation there is a lot of money to be made because interest rates are so high and prices go up so fast. Most stocks listed on the stock exchange in Rio de Janeiro doubled in value last year. If you have money to put into bonds, savings accounts, or stocks, you can make a great deal of money with this high inflation.

I am a nurse in a hospital and my husband is a bank employee. Last year we were arranging to buy a ten year old car, furnishing our apartment, eating out, and taking small holidays. This year is very different. Now we never eat out. We never know how much groceries will cost for the week. The interest payments on the car loan are so high we have to sell the car. The apartment rent has increased 350% in the last year. We may have to sell our furniture and move in with my husband's parents. My husband and I both have good jobs with wages that are supposed to be indexed to the inflation rate. In the last year inflation has been so high that the raises never seem to keep up. I have taken another job and work over 80 hours a week. Even with the extra job, we cannot keep up with the rising costs.

Indexed—salary adjusted to rise with the cost of living
Cafezina—strong, sweet Brazilian coffee

CHAPTER SUMMARY

Before the 1960s, Brazil's economy was largely agricultural. Today, Brazil is ranked among the world's top industrialized countries. Brazil's economic development was started by President Kubitschek. His plan was to industrialize Brazil and open up and settle the interior regions of the country. The military governments that ruled Brazil between 1964 and 1985 continued those development plans. They borrowed large amounts of money from foreign banks to expand industries, increase exports, and finance development projects. Highways were built into the interior. Settlers were encouraged to clear and develop the rain forests. Huge mining projects and some of the world's largest hydro-electric dams were built. For many, Brazil's "economic miracle" brought new prosperity.

The soaring price of oil marked the end of Brazil's economic growth. Brazil has faced severe economic difficulties since 1981. Inflation is more than 1 000% a year. Brazil has the largest foreign debt of any country in the world. The gap between rich and poor is wider than in the past. Resource development, inflation, preservation of the environment, and repayment of the foreign debt are important issues in Brazil. They will strongly influence government decisions in the next decade.

CHAPTER REVIEW

For Your Notebook

1. How did the military governments continue to develop Brazil into an industrialized economy?
2. Why are the years 1968–79 often called Brazil's "economic miracle"?
3. What factors caused the slowdown in Brazil's economic growth?
4. In your own words, describe how inflation affects life in Brazil.
5. Why is it so difficult for many working Brazilians to improve their living conditions?
6. To what extent does Brazil's huge foreign debt affect Brazil's natural environment?

7.  Use the information you have gathered to develop a concluding statement for this problem: What effect has economic development had on settlement patterns, the physical environment, and living conditions in Brazil? In your opinion, were Brazil's years of rapid economic development a benefit to the country?

Exploring Further

1. Imagine you are doing a TV special on life in Brazil today. Make a list of questions you would ask Brazilians.
2. Find examples of inflation in operation in your country.

3.

(Continued from Chapter Review on page 173)

To what extent do you think Brazil considers its physical environment as it develops its natural resources? Use the information on your Decision Making Chart. Evaluate the alternatives, as well as the negative and the positive conseqences of each alternative. Make a decision on the issue. Be prepared to justify your decision with data from your chart. Now that you have made a decision, consider what action plans would best support your decision.

? Problem Solving

This case study looks at lifestyles in Brazil's large cities. As you read through the case study consider these two problems:

1. **How is life in Brazilian cities similar to or different from life in North American cities?**

2. **In your opinion, who has benefited from Brazil's economic development?**

Using the problem solving model introduced on page 3, develop two charts to record your findings. After reading through the case study, prepare concluding statements to answer the problems.

Life in the Cities

"Brazil is rich but the people are poor."

Brazilian cities are places of startling contrasts. For the rich, the MATERIAL BENEFITS of economic development have been very real. In Brazil the wealthy live comfortable lives. They have good housing, hospitals, and schools for their children. They can afford luxuries such as restaurants, shopping malls, automobiles, microwave ovens, VCRs, and color TVs. The poor have very different lives.

Many economists believe that Brazil's "economic miracle" of the 1970s did not provide long lasting benefits for the majority of the population. During the economic prosperity of the 1970s, the MIDDLE CLASS (those who earn middle incomes) appeared to be increasing in numbers. In recent years, however, unemployment and high inflation have reduced the numbers of middle class Brazilians. Since the early 1980s the number of middle class Brazilians has decreased and the number of poor Brazilians has increased. Many economists believe that narrowing the gap between the rich and poor will be one of the government's major challenges in the next decade.

Studying life in a typical Brazilian city offers you a chance to imagine what it might be like to live and work in Brazil. It also allows you to compare the lifestyles of the wealthy, the middle class, and the poor.

1989:   Upper Class   5% of population own 80% of the wealth

1989   Middle Class   21% of population

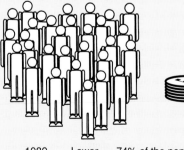

1989   Lower Class   74% of the population

Living and Working in Brazil

Wages in Brazil

In Brazil the government has established a MINIMUM MONTHLY SALARY. This minimum income is used to compare people's wages. However, employers are not required to pay workers this minimum salary. It is only used as a reference point. In 1988 the government minimum monthly salary was $58.80 US.* As the chart on the right indicates, in 1988 nearly 45% of the workers in the official work force earned this wage or less. The government statistics, however, only include workers holding official, registered jobs. A large percentage of the Brazilian population works at temporary or unregistered jobs. These jobs are not included in the official workforce statistics. Most of these workers earn less than half the minimum monthly salary. For example, a maid working for a household in Rio de Janeiro may earn only $30.00 a month and not be included in the government statistics.

Employment by Sectors

Much of Brazil's official work force is employed in low-paying jobs. Agricultural workers usually earn less than one minimum salary. Jobs in the service sector generally pay one minimum salary. The service sector includes teachers, nurses, firemen, police officers, and people who work in hotels and distribution. Many doctors in public hospitals earn two minimum salaries. Jobs in manufacturing, transportation, and communications pay higher wages, but only to skilled workers. Skilled factory workers can generally earn two minimum salaries. Unskilled factory workers earn one minimum salary. Government jobs tend to be among the better paying jobs. Government workers may earn two to five minimum salaries.

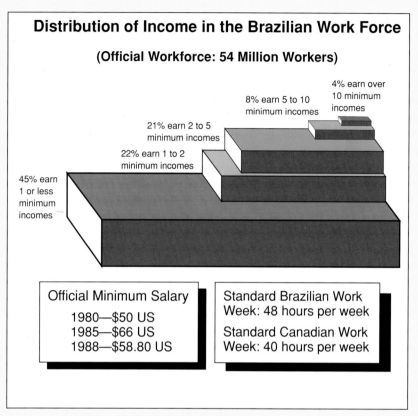

Distribution of Income in the Brazilian Work Force

(Official Workforce: 54 Million Workers)

- 45% earn 1 or less minimum incomes
- 22% earn 1 to 2 minimum incomes
- 21% earn 2 to 5 minimum incomes
- 8% earn 5 to 10 minimum incomes
- 4% earn over 10 minimum incomes

Official Minimum Salary
1980—$50 US
1985—$66 US
1988—$58.80 US

Standard Brazilian Work Week: 48 hours per week
Standard Canadian Work Week: 40 hours per week

How the Brazilian Work Force Stacks Up

The chart on the right shows the percentages of the official Brazilian workforce employed in different sectors in 1986. The millions of children, teenagers, and adults who work at unofficial temporary or part-time jobs are not included in these government statistics. Unemployment in Brazil is also much higher than the official figures. Millions of unregistered adult and teenage workers are unemployed.

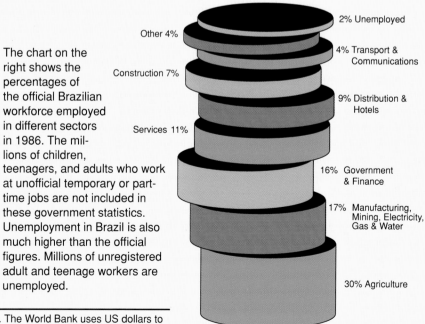

- 2% Unemployed
- 4% Transport & Communications
- Other 4%
- Construction 7%
- 9% Distribution & Hotels
- Services 11%
- 16% Government & Finance
- 17% Manufacturing, Mining, Electricity, Gas & Water
- 30% Agriculture

* Minimum monthly salary is given in US dollars. The World Bank uses US dollars to express international wages so they can be compared easily.

Urban Household Services and Consumer Goods 1980

The illustration shows the percentage of urban households in Brazil that have selected consumer goods and services. These percentages represent only those households living in homes and apartments in cities. *Favelas* are usually not included in official statistics. Most homes in *favelas* do not have running water, sewers, or refrigerators. Some *favela* homes may share electricity. Fewer households in the rural areas have running water, sewers, or electricity. Rural families also own less refrigerators, telephones, televisions, and automobiles. Rural statistics are shown in brackets for comparison.

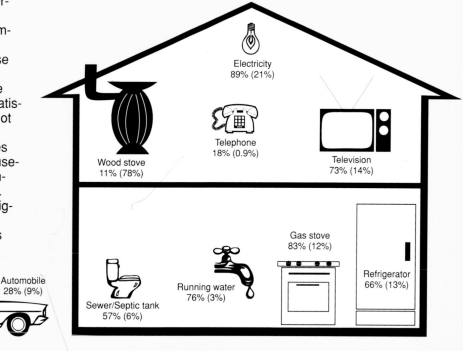

Electricity
89% (21%)

Telephone
18% (0.9%)

Television
73% (14%)

Wood stove
11% (78%)

Gas stove
83% (12%)

Refrigerator
66% (13%)

Sewer/Septic tank
57% (6%)

Running water
76% (3%)

Automobile
28% (9%)

Cost of Living

Many Brazilians' lives can be seen in terms of what it costs in hours of work to buy food and selected consumer items. Most of the working population in Brazil earns one minimum salary or less. These workers have a difficult time providing their families with shelter, food, clothing, transportation, health care, and entertainment.

The chart below on the left shows the amount of work time required to feed a family of four for one month in 1984. These figures apply to workers who earn one minimum salary or less. Many of these families live in poverty because they cannot earn enough money to fulfill their needs.

The chart below on the right shows how long Brazilians must work at minimum salary to purchase specific food and consumer goods. A North American reference is included for comparison. The North American statistics are based on the average weekly take-home pay of $430 in 1986.*

Average work hours per month	156 hrs
Hours required to feed a family of four for one month (basic nutrition only)	154 hrs, 34 mins
Time remaining to provide for other needs (health, clothing, housing, transportation, entertainment)	1 hr, 26 minutes

COST OF LIVING—DECEMBER 1984		
ITEM	BRAZIL 1984	NORTH AMERICA 1986
2 litres milk	3.5 hours	20 minutes
1 kg meat	16.0 hours	30 minutes
movie ticket	7 hours	30 minutes
bus fare	1 hour	15 minutes
shoes	70 hours	4 hours
compact car	10 years	7 months

* Based on a 40 hour work week, Statistics Canada

CASE STUDY: Life in the Cities

Sociologists often group societies into three general CLASSES: lower, middle, and upper. These groupings are determined by similarities in income, housing, education, and **aspirations**. However, as the following studies show, there are variations in the classes themselves.

What Is It Like to Be Part of the Lower Class in Brazil?

In Brazil the poor make up a large percentage of the population. Increased unemployment, rising inflation, droughts in the Northeast, and the cutback in government spending since 1981 has increased the number of poor Brazilians. The poor in Brazil usually earn less than one minimum salary a month.

In the cities, the poor usually live in crowded *favelas* on the hillsides or on the outskirts. *Favela* homes are often made from pieces of wood and bricks collected from the city streets. The roofs are often sheets of corrugated iron or plastic held down by stones or bricks. A poor family may own a few pieces of furniture such as a kitchen table, wooden chair and bench, and a mattress. Most homes in *favelas* are without running water, electricity, or sewage systems. Many homes do share a cold water tap and an electrical line with several other *favela* homes.

The poor own few electrical appliances. A poor family may have a small black and white television set.

Meals for poorer Brazilians usually consist of rice, beans, and manioc. Meat is eaten only occasionally. Coffee and a bun eaten at breakfast may be the only meal of the day for adults and children.

Everyone in a poor family tries to work. Even the very youngest try to find jobs to help add to the family's income. Many children start

74%

Sociologist—someone who studies human society and its problems
Aspirations—people's ambitions or goals; what people believe they can achieve

192

working when they are seven or eight. Young girls may do laundry or cleaning for well-off families. Boys might sell papers, juices, fruits, and other items on the city streets, wash cars, shine shoes, or deliver goods for a shop or office. Many youngsters earn money by begging. Others try scavenging paper, metal, and glass at the city dump to sell to scrap dealers.

Children of poor families often do not have an opportunity to attend school. There are few schools in the *favelas*. Classrooms are often crowded with more than 40 students. Books, papers, and pencils are too expensive for many poor families. Many of the poor cannot read or write.

There are very few health services in the *favela*. Many young children die from influenza, measles, and pneumonia. Poor families do not have the money to spend on doctors or medicines. Even aspirins, bandages, and cough syrups are luxuries. Most poor families cannot afford to go to dentists or purchase glasses for family members.

Many children from poor families eventually leave the *favelas* and live on their own. They sleep under the highway underpasses or in back lanes. They beg on the streets and work at odd jobs to support themselves. Sometimes these street children are as young as eight years old. Some recent estimates indicate there many be three million children living on the streets in Rio de Janeiro and São Paulo.

For most poor Brazilians there is little time or money for leisure activities. Street dancing, singing, and watching television are popular leisure activities. Those families that can afford tickets like to go to soccer games and movies. Carnival is an important leisure activity for the poor. A great deal of effort and money is put into producing elaborate costumes, floats, and dances for Carnival. For an entire week the people in the cities sing and dance 24 hours a day at free street dances and parades.

For the poor in Brazil it is a daily struggle to provide food, shelter, and clothing for their families.

Lower Class Lifestyles

What Is It Like to Be Part of the Middle Class in Brazil?

The middle class in Brazil includes a very wide range of income levels. Some middle class families have very high incomes. Others earn only slightly more than the poor. The middle class includes the owners of small businesses, managers, administrators, and highly skilled workers. Government employees, doctors working in public hospitals, highly skilled factory workers, and office workers would be included in the middle class.

Since 1981, the number of middle class Brazilians has slowly decreased. High unemployment rates and high inflation rates have caused problems for the middle class. Many members of the lower middle class have been pushed into the ranks of the poor.

Middle class families usually live in apartments. The apartments are often in older buildings. They are farther away from the beaches and closer to the city's business areas. These apartments have smaller living spaces but many have balconies that add to the living area. Only a few of the richer middle class can afford houses in the city. Many of the middle class live in houses in the suburbs outside the large cities. Refrigerators, color TVs, and other electrical appliances are common in homes of many well off Brazilians. A lower middle class family usually owns a television but few other electrical appliances. Reasonably well off households usually employ at least one maid for cleaning and shopping. Laundry is generally sent out to women from the *favelas*.

Middle class families that earn higher incomes may be able to afford a small Brazilian-made car. For lower-income families, purchasing a car and fuel would be well beyond their incomes.

Middle class Brazilians shop at the small stores in their neighborhoods. The higher income families can also afford to shop at the large shopping malls. These malls have a wide variety of electrical appliances, furniture, clothing, shoes, jewellery, and foods.

Middle class families buy food at the market stalls and smaller grocery stores. The better off also shop at the large supermarkets. These stores have greater variety of meats and food products. Many of the food products are imported and very expensive. Most of the middle class can afford meat as part of their daily meals.

Children of middle class families can attend public or private schools. Most middle class families hope their children will finish high school and attend a technical school or public university. Many children in middle class families with lower incomes must leave school to find work and help support the family.

Many of the middle class travel throughout Brazil but only a few can afford international travel. Holidays for the better off are often spent at nearby beach and mountain resorts. Visiting friends and relatives is also popular.

For those families who can afford it, eating out is popular. Middle class families frequently eat at restaurants and sidewalk cafés that serve Brazilian specialties. They also go to Brazilian barbecue restaurants called *churrascos*. Chinese and Italian food is popular, as is North American "fast food"— hamburgers and pizzas.

Leisure time after work and on the weekends is spent at the beaches or city parks. Soccer and movies are popular leisure time activities. Many of the lower income members of the middle class work long hours six days a week. There is often very little leisure time for these families.

Life in a middle class family in Brazil varies according to the family's income. Some middle class families live very comfortably, while others struggle to make ends meet.

Middle Class Lifestyles

What Is It Like to Be Part of the Upper Class in Brazil?

In Brazil the wealthy make up a small percentage of the population. However, they control a great deal of the country's wealth. A World Bank report in 1989 indicated that the wealthiest 5% of Brazil's population received over 80% of the country's income.* The lifestyles of the wealthy in Brazil are comparable to the lifestyles of the very wealthy in North America.

Very well off Brazilians live in spacious, air-conditioned apartments or private homes. They live in the best parts of the cities. Their apartments are on quiet, tree-lined streets that often border the cities' beaches. Their apartment buildings and private homes are well-guarded with 24-hour security guards. Some exclusive housing estates outside the cities are protected by private police services. Many wealthy Brazilians own houses on country estates as well as luxurious apartments in the city.

Wealthy households employ several maids to do the cooking, cleaning, and washing. A live-in nanny may be employed to look after the children.

Rich Brazilians usually own one or more automobiles. Many employ a driver. Family members are driven to work and shopping. Youngsters are often transported to and from school by the chauffeur.

Wealthy families can afford to send their children to the best private schools. The children of wealthy families often attend university in Brazil. They may then study at prestigious universities in North America or Europe.

Leisure time for wealthy Brazilians is often spent on the beaches, at exclusive beach resorts, or in the many mountain resorts in Brazil. They often belong to private clubs that provide golfing, swimming, sailing, and tennis.

*For comparison, in Canada and the United States the top 10% have 23% of the income.

200

Horse racing and motor car racing are also popular pastimes for the well off.

The wealthy travel widely in Brazil and outside the country. They often travel to Argentina for shopping and winter ski vacations. They also go to vacation spots in North America or Europe.

Wealthy Brazilians can afford to enjoy the many art galleries, theaters, nightclubs, and restaurants in the cities. Brazil's better restaurants offer them the finest in international foods.

The wealthy do not make up a large percentage of the population in Brazil. However, they often hold powerful positions in the government and have a great deal of influence.

Upper Class Lifestyles

202

? Problem Solving

1. Evaluate the information gathered from this chapter. Prepare a concluding statement that answers these two questions:

   How is life in Brazilian cities similar to or different from life in North American cities?

   In your opinion, who has benefited from Brazil's economic development?

3. Use the information you have gained from studying this book to answer the following question:

   How does life in Brazil differ from life in North America?

THE FUTURE

In the coming decade, several issues will influence the relationship between the Brazilian people and their physical environment.

The Government

One issue centers on whether Brazil will continue with a democratic government or return to a military dictatorship. The armed forces still play an important part in Brazilian politics. Military generals hold important government positions. They exert a powerful influence on government policies. President Sarney has been backed by the military and followed the military's advice on many issues. The military is strongly committed to developing Brazil's natural resources and settling the frontier areas. A pro-military president could be elected in the November 1989 election.* This concerns environmentalists and Indian leaders. They are unsure about a military government's response to their efforts to preserve large areas of Brazil's natural environment from development.

Resource Development versus Environmental Concerns

In the next decade the Brazilian government will be faced with the issue of resource development. They will have to examine the effect of that development on Brazil's natural environment. There are no easy answers to the questions that arise. Does Brazil really need the proposed hydro-electric dams in the Amazon rain forest? Are there other ways to provide land for the millions of landless farmers without clearing the rain forest? What is the overall cost to Brazil and the rest of the world if the rain forest is destroyed?

Indian Land Claims

Like Canada and the United States, Brazil will be struggling to find solutions to Indian land claims. The government has recognized Indian rights to large areas of the rain forest. However the demands for access to that land are strong and varied. Different groups want to use it for resource development, hydro-electric projects, cattle ranches, and farmland. Settling the Indian land claims issue will be one factor in determining the amount of the rain forest that will be cleared and developed during the next decade.

Foreign Debt

An economic issue facing the Brazilian government will be the repayment of Brazil's enormous foreign debt. It will be very difficult to do this while still improving living conditions for the millions of poor families. In order to pay the foreign debt, the Brazilian government has cut back on spending. These cuts have been social services such as housing, education, health care, piped water, and sewer systems. The government has also reduced the minimum wage. Many Brazilians believe that this is not the way for Brazil to begin paying a debt. They believe that the government should not cut spending. Instead, they want the government to continue to develop mineral, hydro-electric, and timber resources, expand agricultural exports, and increase industrial output. All of these development activities have a substantial impact on the natural environment.

---

* Brazilians will vote for a new President in November, 1989. In 1993, they will vote on whether they want a monarch, a prime minister, or a president to head the government.

Gap between Rich and Poor

Reducing the widening gap between the few rich Brazilians and the millions of poor Brazilians is another issue facing the Brazilian government. Improving the living conditions of the growing numbers of poor Brazilians will not be easy. The government needs to provide them with employment, good salaries, housing, health and education services. These needs could directly affect what use is made of Brazil's natural environment. Many Brazilians believe one way to improve living conditions is to speed up development of Brazil's natural resources.

Land Reform

Land reform will continue to be an issue in the next decade. Landless farmers and squatters in Brazil will continue to demand access to farmlands. They may continue to invade large estates and occupy undeveloped land. Opening and clearing new areas of the Amazon rain forest does provide farmland. Consequently, it may continue to be used as a solution to the land reform issue. Unless there is a large scale redistribution of existing farmland, the rain forest will likely continue to be cleared to provide farmland.

Population Growth

Brazil's population increases will continue to be an issue in the coming decade. At least another four million people are added to Brazil's population each year. Brazil's economy will need to find ways to support a growing population. It must provide enough jobs, housing, food, health, education, transportation, and water and sewer facilities. The government will be pressured to continue developing Brazil's mineral, timber, hydro-electric, and agricultural resources. Development could provide jobs, and land for an increasing population.

Credits

Additional Illustration: Linda Jenson, Shelah Ruth, Marjorie Westera
Additional Photography: Jeff Gibbs, Mary Beth Smith, Richard Deposki, Trudie BonBernard, World Wide Photos, Inc.
Maps of Brasília-page 114: Ministry of External Relations, Government of Brazil
Narrative "Poison Fishing," page 48, adapted from Heart of the Forest, Adrian Cowell, Alfred A. Knopf, New York, 1961
Material for interviews, points-of-view, and narratives taken from interviews with Brazilians and from the following publications and documentaries:
Abel, Alan. "Dreams of Amazonia." The Journal, CBC, 1988.
Allard, William Albert & Lorne McIntyre. "Rondônia: Brazil's Imperiled Rain Forest." Washington DC: National Geographic, December 1988.
Brdiges, Tyler. "Trees fall, protests rise over the Amazon." Christian Science Monitor, September 1988.
"Finding ways to farm the Amazon and save it." Christian Science Monitor, September 1988.
Cowell, Adrian. "Murder in the Amazon." Frontline, WGBH, Boston.
Cowell, Adrian. "Decade of Destruction." (series), Central Independent Television, 1985.
"Brazil." (series) Peter Riding producer, BBC, London, 1985.
Ehrlich, Paul R. & Anne H. "Brazil: Flight to the Cities." Washington DC: National Geographic, December 1988.
Hurley, Judith and Danaher, Kevin. Brazil: A Paradise Lost? Judith Hurley and Kevin Danaher, Institute for Food and Development Policy, San Francisco, 1987.
"Hyperinflation makes Brazilians financial wizards," Ottawa Citizen, Ottawa, 1988.
McIntyre, Lorne."Rondônia: Last Days of Eden." Washington DC: National Geographic, December 1988.
Steckles, Gary. "Brazil is back on brink of economic ruin," Montreal Gazette, Montreal, 1987.
Turner, Steve. "Pain Forest: Brazil's clash between development and preservation." In These Times, May 1989.
"Update: Latin America." Washington DC: Washington Office on Latin America, 1987-1989.
Vesilind, Priit J. "Brazil: Moment of Promise and Pain." Washington DC: National Geographic, March 1987.
"1000% Inflation." produced by Larry Lando, 60 Minutes, CBS, New York 1988.
Statistics used in this text taken from the following:
Anuario Estatico do Brasil 1980, Fundacao Institutio Brasileiro de Geografia e Estatistica, 41, Rio de Janeiro, 1980.
Background on Brazil. Toronto: Brazil-Canada Chamber of Commerce, 1986.
Banco do Brasil, Rio de Janeiro
Brazil: Human Resources Special Report. Peter T. Knight. Washington DC: World Bank Country Study, 1979.
Brazil: A Handbook of Historical Statistics. Armin K. Ludwig. Boston: G.K. Hall, 1985.
Brazil's Economy in the Eighties. Edited by Jorge Salazar-Carilo and Roberto Fendt, Jr. New York: Pergamon Press, 1985.
Canada A Portrait, 52nd Edition. Ottawa: Statistics Canada, 1989.
Canada World Almanac & Book of Facts. Toronto: Global Press, 1989.
Getulio Vargas Foundation, Sao Paulo
Handbook of International Trade and Development. New York: United Nations, 1988.
Information Please 1989 Almanac, 42nd Edition. Boston: Houghton Mifflin Co., 1989.
Instituto Brasileiro de Geografia e Estatistica (IBGE), Rio de Janeiro.
Newsletter Brazil. São Paulo: Banco de Boston, First National Bank of Boston, 1988-89.
Perspectives on Poverty and Income in Brazil. David Denslow, Jr. and William G. Tyler. World Bank Staff Working Paper, Number 601, Washington DC: World Bank, 1983.
Tabulacoes Avancadas do Censo Demogafico, 1980, Volume - Tomo 2 (Rio de Janeiro: IBGE 1981).
World Development Report 1988. New York: World Bank, 1988.
World in Figures. Boston: G.K. Hall & Co., 1988.
Problem solving and thinking skills based on material from the following:
Developing Minds: A Resource Book for Teaching Thinking. Edited by Arthur L. Costa. Virginia: Association for Supervision and Curriculum Development, 1985.
Catch Them Thinking: A Handbook of Classroom Strategies. Jim Bellanca and Robin Fogarty. Illinois: Imperial International Learning Corp., 1986.

Bibliography

Bierman, John with Richard House. "Murder in the Amazon." Macleans, January, 1989.
Birchall, Gary. South America Lands of the Southern Cross. Ontario: Fitzhenry & Whiteside Ltd, 1978.
Blakemore, Harold & Smith, Clifford (editor). Latin America: Geographic Perspectives. London: Methuen Books, 1971.
Botting, Douglas. Rio. Amsterdam: Time-Life Books, 1977.
Brazil. Amsterdam: Time-Life Books Inc., 1986.
Brazil: A Country Study. United States Government. Washington DC: Department of the Army, 1983
Brazil Today: Dams Threaten Xingu. London: Survival International, 1987.
Bridges, Tyler. "Will new road in Amazon pave way for wealth or devastation?" Christian Science Monitor, September 1988.
Burns, E. Bradford. A History of Brazil. (2d ed.) New York: Columbia University Press, 1980.
Dostert, Pierre Etienne. Latin America 1988: World Today Series, 22nd Edition. Washington DC: Stryker-Post Publications, 1988.
"Contato." Washington DC: Brazil Network, 1987-1989.
Elder, Norman. The Thing of Darkness. Toronto: New Canada Press, 1979.
Europa Year Book 1988. London: Europa Publications Limited, 1988.
House, Richard. "Defending the Amazon." Macleans, September 1988.
Info Brazil. Washington DC: Center of Brazilian Studies, The Johns Hopkins University, 1988-1989.
Keen, Benjamin and Wasserman, Mark. A Short History of Latin America, Second Edition. Boston: Houghton Mifflin Co, 1984
Lee, John and Taylor, Ronald A. "Ravage in the rain forests." US News & World Review, March 1986.
Lockhard, James and Schwartz, Stuart B. Early Latin America: A History of Colonial Spanish America and Brazil. Cambridge: Cambridge University Press, 1983.
Margolis, Mac. "Fire season endangers the Amazon." The Washington Post, September 1988.
Malkus, Alida. The Amazon River of Promise. New York: McGraw-Hill Book Company, 1970
Mahar, Dennis J. Government Policies and Deforestation in Brazil's Amazon Region. Washington DC: World Bank, 1989.
McIntrye, Lorne. "The Amazon." Washington DC: National Geographic, October 1972.
Moyer, Larry. Brazil Primer. Philadelphia: American Friends Service Committee, 1985.
One Earth: Why Care? Red Cross International Development Resource Package. Toronto: Canadian Red Cross Society, 1979
Onley, David C. "The Greenhouse Effect." Bridges, Feb-March, 1989.
Poppino, Rollie E. Brazil: the Land and People, Second Edition. New York: Oxford University Press, 1973
Robock, Stefan H. Brazil: A Study in Development Progress. Lexington, Massachusetts: Lexington Books, 1975.
Schreider, Helen & Frank. Amazon. Washington DC: National Geographic Society, 1970.
Simons, Marlise. "Brazil Acts to slow destruction of Amazon forest." New York Times, October 1988.
Starkell, Don. Paddle to the Amazon. Edited by Charles Wilkins. Toronto: McClelland and Stewart, 1987.
Sting and Dutilleus, Jean-Pierre. Jungle Stories: The Fight for the Amazon. London: Barrie & Jenkins, 1989.
Stone, Roger D. Dreams of Amazonia. New York: Penguin Books, 1985.
Switkes, Glenn. "World Bank Backs the Drowning of Amazonia." World Rivers Review, September/October 1988.
Teaching Geography: A Model for Action. Washington DC. National Geographic Society, 1988.
Todd, Dave. "Tears fall in the Rainforest." Southam News: The Vancouver Sun, February, 1989.
Tyler, W.G. The Brazilian Industrial Economy. Lexington: Lexington Books, 1981.
Wagley, Charles. An Introduction to to Brazil (rev. ed.) New York: Columbia University Press, 1971.

Glossary

Absolute Location—finding the exact location of any place using a grid system of parallels of latitude and meridians of longitude

Acre—far western state in Brazil, pronounced **awk**-ray

Agricultural potential—how suitable the land is for agricultural purposes

Agronomist—someone who studies soils and crop management

Amerindians—native groups who live throughout North and South America

Anthropologist—someone who studies the origin, development, and customs of people and their societies

Antibiotics—substances that kill harmful microorganisms

Architect—designer of buildings

Armadillo—an armored, burrowing animal

Aspirations—people's ambitions or goals; what people believe they can achieve

Bahia—a state in the Northeast; pronounced beye-**ay**-yah

Bauxite—mineral containing aluminum

Bias—opinions stated as facts to influence another person

Birth Rate—the number of babies born for every thousand people in a country

Caatinga—vegetation of the Northeast region of Brazil; combination of small bushes, grasses, cacti, and thornbushes

Cacão—plant whose seed pods produce chocolate

Cafezina—strong, sweet Brazilian coffee

Captaincy—the name given to the long thin plots of land by the Portuguese government when they divided Brazil between the rich Portuguese families

Carajás—city in the northern state of Pará; pronounced cair-a-**jazz**

Caribbean—Cuba, Haiti, Dominican Republic, Puerto Rico, Trinidad and Tobago, and the Lesser Antilles nations

Cash crops—Agricultural crops which are sold to other countries for large amounts of money

Central America—Belize, Costa Rica, El Salvador, Guatemala, Honduras, Nicaragua, Panama

Cerrado—vegetation of the Center West region of Brazil; combination of trees and grasslands; also called savanna

Chicle nuts—nuts used to produce chewing gum

Civilian—not connected to the military

Class (Social Class)— groups of people (lower, middle and upper) determined by similarities in income, housing, education, and aspirations

Clear-cut logging—the destruction of a large amount of unneeded trees for the gain of a few desired trees

Clergy—people trained to do religious work; priests, ministers, rabbis

Climate—typical weather conditions of an area over a long period of time

Cloverleaf—a highway structure which allows traffic to curve upward or downward to join traffic on other highways without having to stop for traffic lights

Compromise Plan—a plan whereby each side gives up part of what they demand in order to settle the dispute

Congress—elected representatives from throughout Brazil. Congress serves the same function as the House of Representatives in the United States and the House of Commons in Canada.

Contaminate—pollute

Cruzados—Brazilian money; pronounced kroo-zah-dohs

Culture Shock—the sudden introduction of a new way of life

Culture—a way of life

Curare—a poisonous extract from certain tropical American plants which causes paralysis of the muscles; pronounced kyu-ra-reh

Customs—something done by habit; tradition

Death Rate—the number of deaths for every thousand people in a country

Decade—a 10 year period

Defoliant—chemical that causes leaves to fall from plants and trees -

Deforestation—the clearing of forests

Dehydration—the excessive removal of water

Deport—send out of the country

Desertification—making or becoming a desert

Detrimental—negative, harmful or causing loss

Diversified economy—economy based upon many agricultural products, raw materials and manufactured goods to trade

Donatory system—the granting of large areas of Brazil to individuals

Drought—a long period with no rain

Economic boom—a time period when resources are in high demand

Economic development—growth of industry and business

Economics—the development and regulation of resources

Economist—a person who is trained in the science of economics, who studies the way wealth is produced, distributed, and used

Ecosystem—the system formed by the interaction between living things and their environment

Emerald—a bright green precious stone

Emigration—when people leave their home country to move permanently to another country; emigrate from ...

Environmentalists—people who are concerned about protecting and preserving life on the planet

Environment—one's surroundings, including plants, animals, geography, and human construction

Equator—imaginary line of latitude that divides the earth into two halves

Evict—expel or put out by a legal process from land or a building

Export—goods sold to other countries

Extinct—no longer existing

Factual Narrative—a fictional story that is based on true facts

Farinha—flour made from ground manioc roots

Favela—an area of very poor housing; pronounced fah-**vehl**-ah

Fictionalized—a fictionalized newspaper report or story is one that tells a story that didn't really happen. However, the background information in a fictionalized report is based on real situations. In this book, they are called Factual Narratives.

Foreign debt—money owed to foreign countries and foreign or international banks. Between 1960 and 1989, the Brazilian government borrowed large sums of money to build Brasília, to build the new highways, and to finance hydro-electric projects.

Garimpeiros—independent prospectors; pronounced gar-im-**pear**-eeos

Greenhouse Effect—gases in the earth's atmosphere act like the glass roof of a greenhouse to warm the earth's surface

Gross National Product—the total money value of a country's goods and services produced in a certain time period

Growth Rate—the overall increase in population each year

Hardwoods—the terms "hard" and "soft" do not necessarily refer to the physical properties of the timber. The terms are derived from the ways in which the trees reproduce.

Immigrant—a person from another country who has come to a new country to live

Immigration—people from a foreign country coming to a new country as permanent residents; immigrate to ...

Imports—goods brought into a country from other countries

Inaccessible—difficult or impossible to reach

Incentive—encouragement or payment

Indexed—salary adjusted to rise with the cost of living

Infant Mortality Rate—a way of showing how many babies under one year of age die each year

Inflation—The rate at which money loses its value over time; the rate at which prices for goods and services increase over time

Interior—land some distance from the coast; in the inner part of the country; away from the coastal areas. In Brazil, interior is a term that usually refers to the North and Center West regions. In the 1960's, the term interior meant the Center West region: Brasília, Mato Grosso, and Mato Grosso do Sul. By the 1970's, the term interior included Rondônia, Acre, Amazonas, Roraima, and Pará.

Internal migration—moving from place of birth to live in another area of the same country

International Environmentalists—people from all over the world who are concerned about protecting and preserving life on the planet

Jacaré—a Brazilian alligator; pronounced ja-car-**ay**

Jesuits—an order of the Roman Catholic religion

Kayapó—group of people living in the rain forest at the very center of Brazil; pronounced k-eye-a-poh

Kubitschek—President of Brazil from 1956 to 1961; pronounced **koo**-bi-check

Land distribution—the way that land ownership is shared among the people

Land reform—taking some land away from the rich and dividing it among the poor, landless farmers; a government policy

Land speculators—own large amounts of land and sell when the price is high. They do not develop the land.

Land use—what land is chosen for development and how it is developed

Latex—the raw rubber that drips from the rubber tree when the tree is cut

Leach—dissolve out by running water through slowly

League—measure of distance, approximately 3 miles or 4.8 kilometres

Life Expectancy—the average age to which most people in a country can expect to live

Lobby—a person or group that tries to influence decision-makers

Malaria—a disease with chills and fevers; spread by a parasite through mosquito bites

Malnutrition—lack of nourishment, physical problems caused by not eating enough good food

Manioc—a plant with a root like a sweet potato, also called cassava

Material benefits—housing, hospitals, schools, luxuries

Meridians of Longitude—vertical lines of the grid system used by maps and globes

Migrant—someone who moves from one area or country to another

Migration—people moving from one place to settle in another

Minimum monthly salary—the lowest average salary as described by the government. Many people earn less than this wage.

Multinational—a corporation (a company) that has headquarters in one country and branch plants in other countries

Natural environment—See Physical environment.

Natural resources—materials from nature such as natural gas, water, trees, and furs from animals

Natural vegetation—mixture of trees, shrubs, and grasses that grow without interference from humans

Nomadic—moving from place to place

Nordestino—a person from the Northeast

Northern hemisphere—the part of the earth's surface north of the Equator on a globe

Nutrients—food for plants or animals; minerals in the soil that provide food and nourishment for plants

Nutrition—food that supplies necessary nutrients for good health

One product economy—an economy that depends on exporting only one or two agricultural or raw material products

Optimism—looking on the bright side of life; believing that everything will turn out for the best

Papayas—dark, sweet orange fruit, eaten raw or as a sauce

Parallels of latitude—horizontal lines of the grid system used by maps and globes

Parasites—animals or plants that take their food from another living body without having to kill them

Peccary—a pig-like animal of Central and South America, related to some North American species

Photosynthesis—process in which the energy from sunlight is used by green plants to produce food substances from carbon dioxide and water

Physical environment—one's surroundings including plants, animals and geography. Also called Natural environment.

Piranha—a Brazilian river fish; pronounced peer-**ah**-nyah

Pistoleiros—hired gunmen; pronounced pistol-**ehy**-ros

Plains—flat land

Plantains—an edible fruit similar to a banana

Plantations—large estates where crops are grown

Plateau—high, level land

Political—pertains to government policy

Population density—the average number of people per square kilometre in a country

Population—the total number of people in a county, region, city, or specific area

Posseiros—squatters, landless homesteaders who illegally occupy land owned by other people; pronounced poh-**sare**-ohs

Poverty-stricken—very poor

Precipitation—moisture that falls to the ground as rain, snow, or hail

Primary economic activity—harvesting or extraction of natural resources (raw materials)

Prime meridian—an imaginary line that divides the earth into two halves, the Western and Eastern Hemispheres

Prince Regent—a prince who reigns while the real king or queen is unable to do so

Prosperity—success, financial well-being

Quaternary economic activity—includes activities which involve planning, research, advising industries, or high level management

Relative location—where a place is located in relation to other places in the world

Reserves—large areas of land that are for the exclusive use of the Indians

Residents—people who live in a particular area

Rites—ceremonies, especially religious

Royal Court—all the government officials and advisors to the king

Rubber Barons—individuals who became extremely wealthy from the rubber trade

Sanitation services—disposal of sewage and refuse from homes

Satellite cities—towns or small cities on the outskirts of a large city

Savanna—vegetation of the Center West region of Brazil; combination of trees and grasslands; also called cerrado

Scrub—a mixture of woody bushes and shrubs

Secondary economic activity—often called manufacturing, the process of turning raw materials into a product

Seringueiro—Brazilian word for rubber tapper or someone who gathers rubber from the rubber trees; pronounced sair-in-**gair**-ohs

Sertão—the interior of the Northeast region of Brazil; pronounced sair-tow to rhyme with now

Settlement and settlement pattern—shows where people live and what use they make of the natural (or physical) environment

Silt—earth washed down by a river

Slash-and-Burn agriculture—also called Shifting Agriculture, involves the cutting and burning of trees

Smelter—a plant where minerals are extracted from the ore dug from the ground

Social—characterized by friendliness, association with others, communication

Sociologist—someone who studies human society and its problems

Soil fertility—the capability of soil to support plant life

Soil—a natural surface of the land capable of supporting plants

Solar radiation—the heat from the sun

Southern hemisphere—the part of the earth's surface south of the Equator on a globe

Soya beans—beans rich in protein

Subsistence agriculture—able to grow only enough food to keep alive

Sugar cane—a tall grass whose stalks contain a large amount of sweet juice

Taguatinga—one of Brasília's seven satellite cities; pronounced ta-wa-ching-uh

Thermal radiation—the heat of the sun that the earth returns to the atmosphere

Timbo—a green vine that twists and climbs up the trunks of trees. It is used by natives to poison fish making them easier to catch.

Toninas—river dolphin; pronounced tone-**een**-ahs

Tordesillas—Treaty of Tordesillas (1494); prepared by the Pope to divide newly discovered lands between Spain and Portugal; pronounced tor-day-see-yahs

Topography—also called landforms or landscape. Includes the surface features of the land such as mountains, hills, plateaus, and valleys.

Toucan—a bird of Central and tropical parts of South America, known for its large beak and bright coloring

Toxic—harmful, dangerous

Traditional—based on the beliefs, customs, and stories that are passed on from one generation to another

Tributaries—rivers that flow into the larger river

Tuyuyú—a stork that is nearly two metres tall. It builds nests large enough to hold a human; pronounced two-you-**you**

Urbanization—large numbers of people moving from rural areas to the cities

Viscous—thick like syrup or glue

Vulcanization—a process which makes natural rubber more stable over a larger range of temperatures

World Bank—Officially called the International Bank for Reconstruction and Development, it is loosely attached to the United Nations. The World Bank provides loans and technical assistance for economic development projects in developing countries.

Yanomami—tribe in North Brazil; pronounced yan-oh-mam-ee

Zebu—a mixed breed of Brazilian and Indian cattle

INDEX

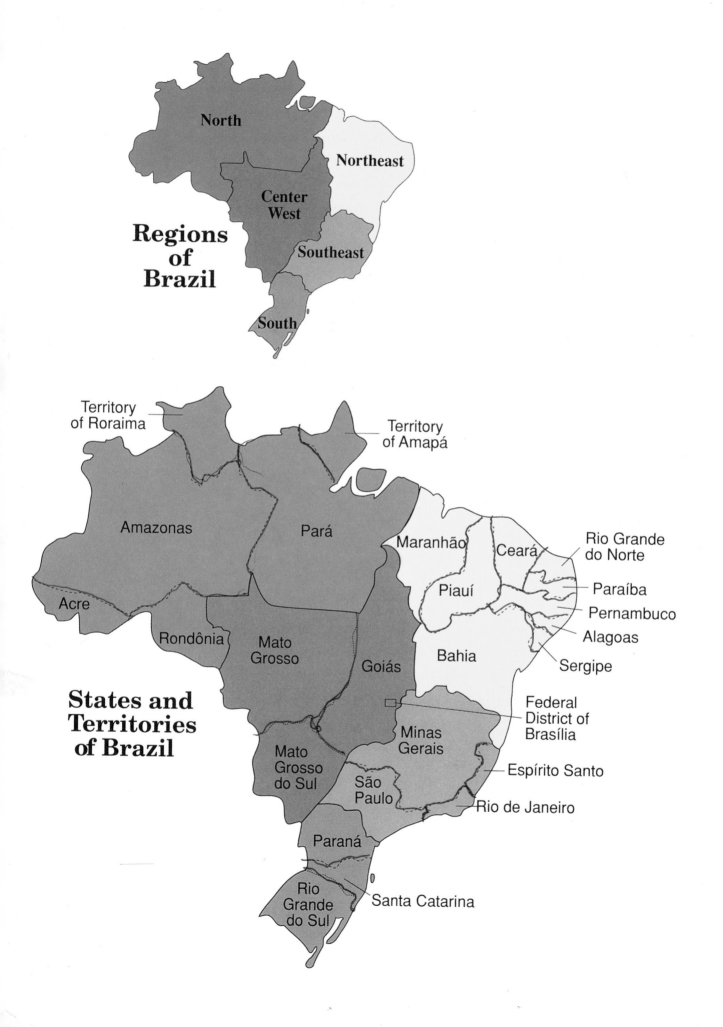

Regions of Brazil

North

Northeast

Center West

Southeast

South

States and Territories of Brazil

Territory of Roraima

Territory of Amapá

Amazonas

Pará

Maranhão

Ceará

Rio Grande do Norte

Piauí

Paraíba

Pernambuco

Acre

Alagoas

Rondônia

Mato Grosso

Goiás

Bahia

Sergipe

Federal District of Brasília

Minas Gerais

Espírito Santo

Mato Grosso do Sul

São Paulo

Rio de Janeiro

Paraná

Rio Grande do Sul

Santa Catarina